Personal Style Blogs
Appearances that Fascinate

Rosie Findlay

intellect Bristol, UK / Chicago, USA

First published in the UK in 2017 by
Intellect, The Mill, Parnall Road, Fishponds, Bristol, BS16 3JG, UK

First published in the USA in 2017 by
Intellect, The University of Chicago Press, 1427 E. 60th Street,
Chicago, IL 60637, USA

A catalogue record for this book is available from the
British Library.

Copy-editor: MPS Technologies
Cover designer: Alex Szalbot
Production manager: Katie Evans
Typesetting: Contentra Technologies
Indexer: Silvia Benvenuto

Print ISBN: 978-1-78320-834-0
ePDF ISBN: 978-1-78320-835-7
ePUB ISBN: 978-1-78320-836-4

Printed and bound by Page Bros, UK

Contents

Acknowledgements

I am deeply grateful for the many colleagues and friends who have offered their support, friendship, insight and guidance as I developed this work. Much of my research was conducted during my candidature as a doctoral student in the Department of Theatre and Performance Studies at the University of Sydney, a department singular in its collegiality and warmth. I am especially grateful to Ian Maxwell and Amanda Card, my supervisors for this project, whose feedback on my research was invaluable and whose encouragement was utterly indispensible.

A myriad of deepest thanks also go to Chris Hay, Kath Bicknell, Kyra Clarke and Zak Millar, Lindy Ma, Bel Clough, Meg Mason, Mark Coleman, Ash Sheehan, Nick DeNeff, Jamie Davidson, Stella North, Karen De Perthuis, Prudence Black, Agnès Rocamora, Johannes Reponen, Nik Mijovic and Daniel Caulfield-Sriklad. My thanks to each of you run the gamut: from encouraging my ideas and sharing yours with me; for your friendship (and sympathy) when my writing hit a wall and for reading when my words found their feet again; for recommending books, thinkers and bloggers; for kindred conversations; and for helping me realize the look and feel of *Fashademic* and this book. Thank you all so very much.

I also wish to thank all the bloggers who shared their stories with me for this project – Julie Fredrickson, Rosalind Jana, Danielle Meder, Jessica Quirk, Isabel Slone, Kayla Telford-Brock and Jamie Wdziekonski – and to those who graciously gave me their permission to reproduce screenshots and images from their blog: Jane Aldridge, Laia Garcia, Brooke Kao, Ragini Nag Rao, Arabelle Sicardi, *Vogue Australia* and Leandra Medine and the team at *Man Repeller*. I am grateful, too, for the funding offered by the London College of Fashion to support the production of this book.

Finally, and most importantly, I wish to thank my parents Stuart and Sarah, and Granny Charlotte, for their constant and unconditional love and support. I couldn't have done this work – and can't imagine valuing reading, thinking and writing as deeply as I do – without your influence and encouragement.

Introduction

[...] where street and interior are one, historical time is broken up into kaleidoscopic distractions and momentary come-ons, myriad displays of ephemera, thresholds for the passage for [...] 'the ghosts of material things'.
  – Howard Eiland and Kevin McLaughlin in 'Translator's foreword' to
  The Arcades Project (Benjamin 2002)

The unfinished 'major project of Benjamin's mature years' (Buck-Morss 1989: iv), *The Arcades Project* (*Passagen-Werk*) consists of a vast collection of cultural philosopher Walter Benjamin's notes on nineteenth-century Paris. It was a project in which he sought to trace the origins of modernism – namely Paris, the archetypal modern city – in the materials of the nineteenth-century, the 'debris of mass culture' that, for Benjamin, contained the 'source of philosophical truth' (1989: iv).

Benjamin's notes were collected (and published) in *convolutes*, a term which Eiland and McLaughlin trace to the German *Konvolut*. It refers to 'a larger or smaller assemblage [...] of manuscripts or printed materials that belong together', in English also carrying the connotation of 'being in a convoluted form' (Eiland and McLaughlin in Benjamin 2002: xiv). So it is with Benjamin's work, as his expansive, itinerant ideas are compiled into dossiers around a theme – 'Fashion', 'Boredom, Eternal Return', and 'The Seine, The Oldest Paris', for example – in which readers find historical source material arranged next to Benjamin's oblique notes to self, before stumbling onto excerpts of poetry by Baudelaire.

In the act of reading this work we partake in a kind of sedentary *flânerie* as we move through the phantasmagorical city, Benjamin's nineteenth-century Paris growing around us through his collated notes and fragments. When I first encountered *The Arcades Project*, I was struck by the similarity between reading the *convolutes* and reading personal style blogs, for reading style blogs is an uncannily similar experience. They too are comprised of fragments of text and images arranged around a theme – *blogposts* – that together constitute an image, albeit of a *style blogger* rather than an epoch, as in the case of Benjamin's work.

Here, too, the stationary reader travels through a peopled landscape; what they encounter, however, is not the reimagined Paris of burgeoning modernism, but bloggers' styled performances of self in a different liminal terrain, the spaces of their blogs. Here, too, as Jouhandeau observed of Benjamin's work, the effect is to render the blogger as 'everyone's contemporary' (Jouhandeau in Benjamin 2002: 66), in relation to whom the reader is positioned, by the conversational mode of address characteristic of personal blogs, as a curious, engaged passer-by.

This ambulatory mode of reading is aided by the hyperlinks that pervade such blogs: coded texts functioning as portals to other webpages that populate in a new window. On style blogs these often link to a previous post, a friend's blog or an online store, possibilities with tangential relevance to the original post, holding it in balance with a teeming network of websites, blogs, images and ideas. In fact, until recently, it was customary for style bloggers to keep a *blogroll*, or a list of hyperlinked titles of blogs that they liked, in the sidebar of their own. These titles often ran together like blank verse:

july stars
white lightning
sea of ghosts
fashiontoast
hard liquor, soft holes
geometric sleep
fashion pirate
what is reality anyway?

– legends that, with a single click, would spirit the reader onto another blog written in a different voice, peopled with images of another blogger performing their personal style through outfit posts that ran down the page, back through time. For, once published, a blogpost remains anchored in its position in the reverse chronological order of a blog, while simultaneously existing in itself as a distinct cultural artefact of a blogger's opinions and outfit, as experienced in the day in which it was composed. And so the reader is peripatetic, conducted 'into vanished time' (Benjamin 2002: 416), or the a-temporal continuous present of blogs, as well as intangible place, an imagined and fantastical world inhabited by a style blogger's digitally performed self.

The style blogosphere is comprised of innumerable blogs. It thrives with informality, tangential connections, and the passions, ideas and enigmatic co-presence of bloggers and their readers. Style blogs are fantastical and everyday, public and domestic, personal and professional, each distinct and steeped in the individual aesthetic and performed selfhood of the blogger who created it. Both individually and collectively, they give rise to a new narrative about fashion and style, about the interplay between dressed self and the eye of the beholder.

Here is a beginning, then, as told through the courses charted by three early style bloggers – Susanna 'Susie Bubble' Lau, who started *Style Bubble* in March 2006, Rumi Neely, whose blog *fashiontoast* was first published in January 2008, and Tavi Gevinson, who created *Style Rookie* in March 2008. Three young women created three blogs upon which they could publish materials circulating their interest in fashion and personal style with the vaguely sensed, unqualifiable and desired 'you' brought into proximity by the Internet. They did this primarily by staging amateur photo shoots featuring their daily outfits, enlisting the help of willing relatives and friends to take their photographs, posing in front of a camera on self-timer or, like Susie in the beginning, contorting themselves so that the lens captured their whole reflection in the full-length mirror in their bedroom.

They wore clothes that helped them realize the look they wanted for themselves, whether that be pinning a plastic basket to a hip after being inspired by a designer's anti-organic, structural aesthetic, or shopping eBay to find the heavy designer boots, micro-shorts and floaty tops that would become their signature. The photographs they took of these outfits slowly grew more sophisticated, as they experimented with outdoor locations, posing on a sun-drenched street, or in a wheat field, locations that had increasingly little to do with their outfit but that presented a picturesque backdrop.

These posts, flecked as they are with personal anecdotes, descriptions of 'delicious' clothes and opinions declaring that '[eBay] is truly the land where dreams come true' (Neely, *fashiontoast*, 16 January 2009), demonstrate the specificity of discourse that circulates on the style blogosphere. Style bloggers don't adopt the fashionable person's urbane, 'blasé-cool' demeanour, which as Elizabeth Wilson describes, 'mask[s] all emotions, save triumph' (1984: 9); rather, Susie, Rumi and Tavi blogged as enthusiastic consumers, 'everywoman's style icons' (Bourne 2010) who shaped their personal style according to their taste, and furthermore, who invited their readers to engage with them at the interface of that style.

That this enthusiasm was intrinsically tied to the fashion product gradually led to fashion labels and their PR extending opportunities to certain style bloggers: mailing clothes to them as gifts, inviting bloggers to their studios or workshops so they could see how the goods they admired were made, and eventually inviting some to attend their fashion shows. Within a year of starting her blog, Tavi received hand-knitted Rodarte tights and a cardigan as a gift from the label's designers. Susie was one of fifteen bloggers invited by Chanel to visit a series of locations important to the house: their *parfumerie* in Neuilly; the route that Coco Chanel used to walk between the Ritz hotel and her shop on Rue Cambon; and, holy of holies, a tour of Chanel's apartment, famously closed to the public. Rumi was signed as a model by the Next Model Management agency and was shot as the 'face' of high street label Forever 21 as part of the launch of their flagship store in Times Square, later blogging about how weird it was to hail a cab with her face on it.

Opportunities such as these, as well as the novelty of style blogging, led to widespread media interest in bloggers. With their increased visibility came the expansion and rapid transformation of the style blogosphere, as more people created blogs of their own and in ever-increasing number adopted conventions that had proven successful for the blogs that preceded them. The rapid shift is evident in the content of their blogs: for example, Tavi joked about the unlikelihood of meeting 'the big Mama Vogue herself' on *Style Rookie* in 2008, and blogged a photograph of herself with Anna Wintour less than two years later.

These experiences, although not shared by all bloggers, illustrate the main aspects of style blogging with which this book engages: its history and development as a sub-genre of fashion blogging; the styled selves bloggers publicly perform on the spaces of their blogs; the distanced sociality between bloggers and readers; and the response of the fashion industry to style bloggers' amateur and independent fashion reportage. In so doing, it provides a comprehensive overview of what personal style blogging is and what it means for those who do it. Each chapter addresses a different aspect of the practice, offering detailed analysis that develops central themes that cumulatively build into a cohesive map of style blogging. Some of these themes are explored more explicitly than others, which thread through the fabric of my argument, yet all have arisen from my close study of the style blogosphere, both in the eighteen months before commencing this research and during the four years of my doctoral candidature, when the majority of this work was originally developed.

This book asks what style bloggers think they are doing, what the practice means for them and what it means for their readers. It intertwines the lived experience of those who constitute the style blogosphere with broader discussions, such as the significance of the practice for fashion communication and for private individuals – who are mostly female and young – writing publicly about their opinions, interests and lives. The dominant themes explored in this work are the performance of self that occurs through clothing on a digital platform for an audience, and the tension between the 'old' and the 'young' (to borrow from Bourdieu 1993a: 57), be it teenaged girl bloggers and their disapproving adult critics, or the professional fashion media opposing the challenge posed by style bloggers' unauthorized fashion communication.

This work also makes definitional arguments about style blogging by providing a language with which we can speak about style blogs, one that can be advanced as the blogosphere continues to develop. I here establish how we can construe the spaces of style blogs, how the style blogger-reader relationship can be conceptualized and how outfit posts can be understood as complex and reflexive performances of self through style.

My first chapter outlines the history of personal style blogging as a sub-genre of the fashion blogosphere, tracing its origins through fashion-based websites and forums as well as early fashion blogs. What emerged as I researched this project was a distinction between two phases of style blogging, both of which were predicated on a different ethos and comprised of a distinct mode of blogging. I map these two phases, and in doing so, demonstrate that style blogging was shaped not only by the practice of early style bloggers but also by the digital media that informed how they blogged. The characteristics that still demarcate style blogging as a specific kind of fashion-based blogging were developed by early bloggers, whose contributions were implicitly challenged and built upon by the style bloggers who came after, themselves influenced by the media coverage and commercial opportunities that had become part of what style blogging offered.

The theme of style blogging 'offering' something is taken up in the next chapter as I examine the gendered criticism that style bloggers have attracted by writing publicly about their personal interest in fashion. Rather than being understood as risky or narcissistic, style blogging can be situated within the lineage of feminine sociality and writing about personal experience, both of which are antecedents to this mode of expression. A significant concern here is what kind of communication and forms of sociality style blogs engender between bloggers and their readers. I argue that style blogs are intimate spaces of identity play and social engagement between peers, albeit at a remove of time and place, drawing on the work of Angela McRobbie and Jenny Garber (2000) and Siân Lincoln (2004) to read style blogs as the digital equivalent of girls' bedrooms. Style bloggers demonstrate a number of competencies to negotiate their public presence, as evident in the interviews and analyses of blogposts presented in this chapter, which reveal the capability of many girl bloggers to navigate the challenges and potential risks of being visible and, in some ways accessible, online.

The question of communication is further considered in Chapter Three, as I extend my analysis into a re-reading of style blogs as *intimate publics*, adapting Lauren Berlant's work on publics. Surprisingly, little has been written about the reciprocal and affective relationship between personal style bloggers and their readers, a gap that this chapter seeks to address. I describe the intimacy at a remove that characterizes the blogger-reader relationship, drawing on my own experiences as a blogger and a reader, as well as the survey responses I gathered from readers of style blogs to formulate an overview of the dynamics of this relationship. The term I adopt here, intimate publics, accounts for the affective quality inherent in relationality on style blogs, as well as the ways that style blogs address an unknown but felt and in some ways familiar audience.

I turn in Chapter Four to consider the ways that style bloggers employ the capacities of blogs to perform stylish selves, selves that are performatively enacted through blogged text and images. This position encourages a re-consideration of the digital identities of style bloggers, moving away from the notion of blogs facilitating an unmediated expression of self to a more nuanced analysis of the interplay between digitally writing/presenting the self and identity.

This discussion has two main points, both of which are predicated on concepts of performance and performativity. In the first, I look at outfit post photography as a development of fashion photography, one in which the style blogger positions herself within *fashion's imaginary*, an imaginary that circulates through the fantastical and fictional world of professional fashion photography. Markedly different here is that style bloggers are assuming the role of 'fashion's ideal', a figure that inhabits the imagined world of fashion imagery but which is subverted on style blogs by the knowledge that these bloggers are not characters but people depicting their lives. There is a slippage between what is revealed and what is concealed in these posts, as is contiguous with the ambiguous world of fashion photography where the visual currency is aspiration and desire.

Yet outfit posts also function as performance in another way – or, rather, I argue that they are performative, as style bloggers bring their digital selves into being by creating and publishing them. I look here at the ways that personal style feeds into this becoming self by conducting a case study of Rosalind Jana, a British blogger who concealed and then revealed her severe scoliosis from her readers as a means of reconciling herself with her condition.

The final chapter of this book situates personal style blogs within the field of fashion media, arguing that the practice has developed from a position of exclusion, countering the discourse and values of the fashion industry, to holding a contested yet increasingly consolidated position within the field. This shift is examined through a Bourdieusian analysis of the struggle for legitimacy, both between style bloggers and the professional fashion media as well as between opposing groups of style bloggers. I here examine the manner in which certain bloggers have been consecrated by dominant agents in the field, and for what reasons, and detail the rupture this has caused within the style blogosphere. In these ways, this book charts the development of the style blogosphere in relation to the fashion media, arguing that the practice of style blogging challenges the established hierarchy of the field while its organizing ethos and characteristics are themselves developed by the fashion media, resulting in the consecration of some style bloggers over others.

Style blogs as online performances of self

The multitude of different disciplinary approaches already applied to the study of personal style blogs speaks to the range of possible lines of enquiry that might illuminate this phenomenon. Indeed, by sitting at the nexus of a number of conceptual intersections, style blogging requires a range of theoretical perspectives to address its multiple facets.

The insights and perspectives garnered in my work have been shaped by my situation as a scholar within performance studies, a hybrid discipline that invites us to consider the diversity of human performance with a range of theoretical approaches. As performance studies scholar Richard Schechner has noted, 'there is no finality to performance studies, either theoretically or operationally. There are many voices, opinions, methods, and subjects' (2002: 1).

In that spirit, the development and research focus of this study was guided by my situation as a scholar in the Department of Theatre and Performance Studies at the University of Sydney, which builds its theoretical focus on what Maxwell defines as 'four pillars': historiography, anthropology, embodiment and analysis (2006: 37). A central underlying aim, influenced by the work of anthropologist Clifford Geertz, is to approach an understanding of what the subjects of a study think they are doing. This approach directs our attention away from reading texts towards engaging with process – or the 'performance' – which Schechner calls the 'between': the 'actions, interactions, and relationships' that constitute human sociality (2002: 24).

Understood in this way, the concept of performance itself comes to encompass everyday performances as well as live, aesthetic performances – or 'performance (p)' and 'Performance (P)' (Lewis 2013: 9) – two modes that constitute two ends of a continuum rather than operating in binary opposition. This distinction allows for slippages between 'P/p' performances, a fluid conception of human behaviour within which style blogs are situated, comprised as they are of both everyday performances of self (as activity enacted out of a blogger's everyday life) and aesthetic Performances of a kind, as bloggers style and display a performative self for their readers on their blogs.

This identifying feature of style blogging – the performance of a styled self for readers – is accounted for by Goffman's definition of performance as:

> [...] all the activity of an individual which occurs during a period marked by his [sic] continuous presence before a particular set of observers and which has some influence on the observers.
>
> (1973: 22)

The key aspects of this definition – an individual, their activity, before a set of observers, with influence on the observers – are developed by Fitzpatrick's work on performance, in which he draws out the complexities between performer and audience. He writes that performance involves a performer displaying 'personal resources' or 'performative skill' to an audience in a situation in which their behaviour is 'framed' as particular and therefore marked as a performance (1995: 51). Fitzpatrick argues that this transaction is more complex than an interaction, specifically because of the performer's responsibility to display their skill – what anthropologist and folklorist Richard Bauman calls 'communicative competence' (quoted in Fitzpatrick 1995: 51).

In these terms, we can understand bloggers as assuming the role of performer, their behaviour framed as performance by its location on the site of their blog. Readers constitute the audience, who respond to the display of a blogger's personal resources – their style, their physical appearance, their skill at writing blogposts and so on – and whose engagement with a blogger's performed self is facilitated by their blog being accessible online. This latter point marks a 'continuous presence' (as identified as an aspect of performance by Goffman), if not in a temporal sense, then in a sense of being continuously publicly available. The influence that style bloggers wield on their observers is evident in a number of ways, not least as implied by the proliferation of commercial agreements between bloggers and fashion labels, but also through their influence on their readers as authorities on style, and evident in the circulation of fashion trends particular to the style blogosphere.

In conceptualizing bloggers as performers, the notion of their behaviour as performance becomes a central concept. What this perspective contests is the notion of the self as a stable, fixed entity that can then be represented on a blog. I will argue that *aspects* of self can be expressed through blogging, but that these actions are not indicative of a prior, offline selfhood; rather, following the lead of de Beauvoir and Butler, I take a phenomenologically inflected position, arguing that the self is a self *becoming*. This is not to suggest that the body pre-exists as some kind of *tabula rasa* but rather that identity is flexible, enacted and 'tenuously constituted in time' (Butler 1988: 519), informed by an individual's corporeal body, their subjectivity and their position within their own sociocultural life-world. As 'one does one's body', one 'does' one's identity, the performance of which is contingent on context; or, in Butler's own words, which 'must be understood as the taking up and rendering specific of a set of historical possibilities' (1988: 521).

Of course, when we approach people-in-their-clothes online, people made visible through careful representation of their selves and accounts of their lived experience, we are also approaching texts. By reading style blogs as sites at which bloggers perform their style for their readers, my work seeks to reconcile theories of the embodied nature of intersectional identity formation through clothing with the distance and virtuality that characterizes digital technologies. In this spirit, this book examines the kinds of selves brought into being on style blogs, and questions the relationship between those blogged selves and the style displayed on them, both in the imagery of outfit posts and through the language employed by bloggers to perform themselves for their readers.

Performance studies also inflected my implementation of a practice-led methodology, as it is a discipline that favours observation and participant-observation as modes of gathering knowledge about a subject. Schechner goes as far as to argue that 'the relationship between studying performance and doing performance is integral', advocating anthropological fieldwork even in studying one's own culture to assume a 'Brechtian distance, allowing for criticism […] and personal commentary as well as sympathetic participation' (2002: 2).

This approach becomes fundamental when considering style blogs, which are predominantly composed by girls and young women. In developing an overview of what style blogging is, I am attempting to understand the writing and performances of self of thousands of individuals who are more than capable of speaking for themselves. In fact, part of what makes style blogs such an exciting development in the history of women's writing is just that: young women and girls now have recourse to speak publicly about their own lived experience and creatively display aspects of their selfhood. In light of this, it is essential to me as a researcher to understand what these bloggers and their readers think they are doing so as not to claim to speak for them without acknowledging that they themselves are able to speak – and do, often daily – on their blogs.

Researching style blogs

My sentiments in conducting research on personal style blogs have often echoed those of Etienne Gilson who, reflecting on researching the work of Dante, observed:

> [a]s for the vast literature […] I cannot think of it without experiencing a kind of dizziness. One cannot open an Italian review without saying to oneself: 'Another book, another article that I ought to have read before expressing my opinion on this question!'
> (1963: x)

Dizzying, too, is the prospect of attempting to survey the entire style blogosphere and come to a comprehensive conclusion that encompasses it for the reader. Such an attempt would be quixotic if not ridiculous: the style blogosphere is ever expanding, the blogs that constitute it constantly being updated, abandoned or created. As Viviane Serfaty observed in her own study on American online diaries, an author's claim to an exhaustive study of digital cultures is 'precluded by the sheer infiniteness of Internet contents' (2004: 16).

Rather than attempt to cover all aspects of the style blogosphere, then, my methodological approach was developed to address my own specific research concerns: an interest in what blogging means for the bloggers and readers who do it and what the emergence of this sub-genre of fashion blogging has meant for the concept of the individual in the public sphere and for the communication of fashion knowledge. Each method educes different elements of style blogging in an attempt to engage with it in the midst of its complexity and dynamism.

I have here separated the three main approaches I took in gathering research, although in practice they were being simultaneously enacted. Each method led to the other two in a kind of hermeneutic circle, if the text being studied could be substituted for the style blogosphere – by which I designate bloggers, their readers and the blogs upon which these two parties converge. My first methodological approach was participant-observation: I conducted an auto-ethnography by starting a blog, *Fashademic*, to engage at an interpersonal level with other bloggers and readers and so to understand blogging from the inside out. I also conducted interviews with a range of bloggers, and linked an anonymous survey to my blog to be completed by my readers, to gain insight into how these people conceived of what they were doing and what it meant to them. Finally, I sought to balance these approaches by engaging in textual analysis, in which I critically engaged with a range of style blogs. To echo performance studies scholar Ian Maxwell, I 'do not wish to privilege one mode of knowing over another' but to suggest through the employment of three epistemological approaches that 'different modes of knowing will produce different kinds of knowledge' (2002: 44), and that these kinds of knowledge together constitute a more thorough theoretical perspective.

I first encountered style blogs in late 2008, whilst living in Toronto. Already an avid reader of street style blogs, I came upon a number of early style blogs in the casual way germane to the Internet: one click, and I was in a new country peopled by strangers who – excitingly – spoke my language. They were like me and I was like them: fashion fans. We weren't fashion fans the way people are now, following the fashion famous on Instagram or trying to break into the 'scene' in our respective locations. Rather, we were the types who grew up poring over images in treasured magazines, who remembered collections once seen on Style.com and never forgotten and who tried to recreate the looks we loved – wherever they were encountered, be they on the street, in an editorial or conjured by our own imaginations – whether or not we had access to the desired fashion product.

Following these bloggers – shoe-mad Jane Aldridge in Texas who mixed vertiginous designer heels with 1980s vintage; Californian Rumi Neely who shifted from wearing floral minidresses from Urban Outfitters to an aesthetic of floaty mixed with bodycon that would become her trademark; Susie Bubble in London who never met a print she didn't like; Camille Rushnaedy who always posed for her outfit posts between the edge of the fireplace in her living room and a rather large ceramic urn; Tavi Gevinson who lived in suburban Illinois and crafted looks inspired by fictional characters and runway looks; fashion student Brooke Kao who bemoaned 'the fashion void that is D.C.' (also the name of her blog) and snapped her outfit posts in her empty design studio between classes, and so many others – became part of my everyday. I was excited to discover these people and, inspired by them, started my own fashion blog, called *Anywhere Anywear*. My favourite post should illustrate the kind of fashion interest that was being enacted then on the style blogosphere: being mutually inspired by the all-white aesthetic of the Chanel 2009 couture show and my first winter in the Northern Hemisphere, I crafted a Chanel 2.55 bag out of snow for the express purpose of blogging it. I used a ruler to carve the quilting and shaped the clasp made of interlocking C's with fingers that gradually turned numb. Of course I then took photographs of my masterpiece in a kind of Chanel-esque monochrome flat-lay with carefully arranged black leather gloves. This snowy homage would seem kind of odd to most people in my life, but I felt that online, people would get it.

I call this way of engaging with fashion a *fashion interest* after the Latin inflection of the word meaning to differ or be important, having an interest denoting a possession of something. The first style bloggers and their readers had an interest in fashion in the truest sense, possessing fashion conceptually, performing style through their posts and creatively inhabiting the possibilities and aesthetics of clothing. Tavi created outfits out of hand-me-downs, Etsy finds and glister from her childhood dress up box. Laia (*Geometric Sleep*) eulogized the Marc Jacobs heels from 2001 that got away. Queen Michelle (*Kingdom of Style*) rhapsodized about her new Black Milk leggings and modelled them to us from her backyard in Glasgow. Perhaps these longings and creative impulses were fostered by their distance from the professional fashion industry, not experienced so much as an exclusion (as it is often termed) than as something that was located entirely elsewhere. These bloggers had their own ways of communing with fashion, and to articulate and celebrate these on the early style blogosphere was sufficient.

Besides a mutual fashion interest, I shared other similarities with these early style bloggers: despite our differences in nationality, ethnic identity, age and geographic location, like them, I was also a middle-class English-speaking young woman with regular access to a computer and an Internet connection. As I moved back to Sydney to pursue my doctorate, I discarded *Anywhere Anywear*, deleting its archives and starting afresh with *Fashademic* in 2010 when I commenced my candidature. Although I had dabbled in fashion blogging, *Anywhere Anywear* was not a style blog, and although reading other blogs taught me the conventions of the genre, I did not know how it felt to do it myself. I started *Fashademic* for this reason, yet I also wished to contrast my own experiences of reading and blogging against those of others, which led me to conduct interviews. The answers given in interviews prompted me to go back and re-read blogposts, to contrast what bloggers said in conversation with what they had blogged, which also gave rise to new questions. The three methodological approaches I employed were thus enmeshed, each always drawing my enquiries into a more complex engagement with style blogging while also prompting me towards the other approaches to balance the limitations of each. In this next section I will outline these limitations and also the strengths of the three aspects of my methodology, justifying my approach and demonstrating how the inherent biases of these approaches are somewhat addressed by their simultaneous implementation.

Researcher as personal style blogger

Creating *Fashademic* involved selecting a blog-hosting platform upon which to create my blog (I chose Blogger), choosing a blog title and selecting which template to use, which I tweaked by selectively recoding its HTML.[1] Most of this was relatively simple: the Blogger template is deliberately designed to be easy for first-time users to navigate. I also created a statistics tracking account on a free website and embedded the tracking code into my HTML so that I could observe the traffic on my blog. During the course of my candidature, I also linked a dedicated Facebook page and Twitter account to *Fashademic*, using these social media platforms to reach new readers and to publish different content that complemented the content of my blogposts.[2] I usually blogged multiple times a week, but the regularity of my posting fluctuated throughout my candidature, sometimes resulting in multiple posts a day, sometimes only once per week.

I posted about a range of subjects related to my studies and experiences as a post-graduate student and also on my interest in fashion, with a particular focus on creating posts that fulfilled the conventions of style blogging. That is, I wrote in a conversational tone about my personal style and taste in fashion, and blogged outfit posts as well as fashion-based content that I reblogged from other websites. Moreover, I accepted opportunities as they arose to do what other style bloggers did: I attended fashion shows at Rosemount Australia Fashion Week in 2011; I styled and shot product couriered to my house as negotiated with a label's PR agency; I attended 'blogger events'; and was directly approached numerous times by small fashion labels for coverage or to advertise on my blog.[3] At the same time, I read other style blogs on a daily basis, occasionally making contact with bloggers about their posts, or products or articles that I thought might be of interest to them. In all of these ways, I immersed myself as much as possible in the practice of style blogging, although I never pursued this as a commercial enterprise nor a full-time occupation. My blog was therefore more akin to early style blogs, an activity pursued for pleasure as an amateur, although my participation was also inflected by my position as a researcher and observer.

There are a number of reasons that this methodological approach was important for my research. As previously discussed, mediating performance practice and theoretical study produces an anthropologically inflected mode of embodied knowing, making visible to the researcher aspects of a practice that would otherwise elude them. The knowledge at stake here is that which an individual has about their everyday activities, which is opaque and difficult to access without participation in those very activities that make it available. A blogger might, for example, say in an interview that they do not really know who is reading their blog but that they have a sense for the kinds of people that might constitute their readership. In blogging myself, I felt first-hand what this sensed knowing is like: an affinity with a largely anonymous presence, a kind of familiarity that influenced the way that I wrote 'to them' and that flared into pleased surprise when someone new wrote me an e-mail or left a comment saying they liked my blog.

This example illustrates the intimate knowing that arises from doing something, a knowing that casts a new understanding on the significance of an activity for those who engage in it. The embodied self of the auto-ethnographer becomes a locus of knowledge, in that, as Luvaas writes, 'paying particular attention to one's thoughts, feelings, and physical sensations [constitutes] a form of ethnographic "data"' (2016: 12). At the same time, the automatic knowing that arises from immersing oneself in doing must be balanced against periods of reflexivity, as the researcher moves between proximity and critical distance in order to make sense of what they have experienced or continue to experience. This combination of personal perspective and distanced analysis – or what anthropologist Clifford Geertz would call 'experience-near' and 'experience-distant' concepts – works to create a thorough epistemological understanding of an activity by getting at it through the understanding of its constituents and then analysing the way that they account for what it is that they are doing (1983: 57). In being a blogger myself, then, I was not only seeking to 'make the familiar strange' (see Geertz 1975), but also to make the strange familiar by incorporating blogging into my everyday life.

Of course, participant observation is not without its significant biases. Digital theorist Viviane Serfaty argues that it 'entails a number of specific distortions' due to the direct contact with subjects and immersion in their activities (2004: 11). Furthermore, as Maxwell argues, it is important to acknowledge 'the very active role of the ethnographer in constructing the object they might have, at one time, claimed to be simply describing' (2002: 111). In that spirit, then, I follow Maxwell's lead in being reflexive according to the practice (as advocated by Bourdieu) of paying heed to, and acknowledging the epistemological effects of, the specific biases that my position in relation to – indeed, within – the field of style blogging will have engendered in my research.

In order to extend a *sens pratique* (or 'practical sense') of a field, which he likens to a sportsman's 'feel for the game', Bourdieu advocates that an agent – here, myself as researcher-blogger – is reflexive about their relation to and practices within cultural fields (Webb et al. 2002: 49). This reflexivity works against a researcher's naturalization of a field – that is, the way that we inherently know, embody and understand the logics and imperatives of the field – which perpetuates the pre-existing frameworks by which the field is internally organized rather than to expose and challenge them. In order to do this, Bourdieu advises paying particular attention to three aspects of one's practice: our social and cultural origins; our position in the field in which we are located; and to be aware of our 'intellectual bias' (Bourdieu was talking specifically about academics conducting research), by which he meant to avoid abstracting practices and 'to see them as ideas to be contemplated, rather than problems to be solved' (2002: 50–51).

To briefly apply Bourdieu's method to myself, then, I acknowledge that the way I approach style blogs is mediated by my own interest in the phenomenon, as well as my process of knowing as a research student. As well as sharing a sociocultural background similar to that of many other style bloggers, I also share a proximal age and gender with the principal demographic of style bloggers: girls and young women. As previously described, like all style bloggers, I too had a prior interest in and enjoyment of fashion, and furthermore, I have enjoyed the socio-economic ability to accrue a wardrobe of clothes that were not purchased primarily for function or necessity. Whilst the socio-economic status of bloggers greatly varies from the affluent who frequently buy designer items to those who only 'thrift' or wear second-hand clothes (which admittedly is sometimes also for ethical and environmental rather than financial reasons), style bloggers for the most part enjoy the means, at least in some capacity, to consume clothes and accessories according to desire rather than need, a situation that I shared.

These similarities alone demonstrate my proximity to the field of style blogging, and yet overarching these is that, like many style bloggers, I am part of the generation first claimed as 'digital natives' (Prensky 2001), having grown up during a time in which the use of digital technologies in everyday life in the West was burgeoning. Digital nativity encompasses anyone who is a so-called 'native speaker' of digital technologies (2001: 1) by way of being born into a world where such technologies are commonplace. Coded into the concept is the situation of such people within a socio-economic bracket where it is financially possible for digital technologies to be integrated into daily practices and accessible in sites at which they live: their homes, schools, universities and so on. Such a bracket is one in which most style bloggers (including myself) are situated, as attested by the regularity of their posting from their home, phone or personal computer, and visually supported with images taken on personal digital cameras. The technologies that have been gradual additions to my life have come to feel natural to me, to the extent that even though I remember a time when technologies like mobile phones or Internet connectivity were novel, they now feel like integral and irreplaceable components of my everyday life.

Marc Prensky makes this very argument, stating that so ubiquitous and comprehensive is this immersion in technologies for my generation (and those subsequent) that we 'think and process information fundamentally differently from [our] predecessors' (2001: 2). Without wishing to engage with the physiological aspect of Prensky's argument – that this different processing of information is attributable to the structure of our brains being physically changed as a result of prolonged immersion in technological activities – the distinction he makes between those who grew up with technologies such as the Internet and those who did not, and how we think about these technologies as well as how we use them, is useful here.

The insider-ness that I experience as a '"native speaker" of the digital language of computers, video games and the Internet' positions me differently within the field of style blogging than someone who is what Prensky would call a 'digital immigrant', or who has adopted technologies but was not 'born into' them (2001: 1–2). Certain behaviours that might appear as natural to me may seem problematic to other theorists, a point illustrated by new media professor Clay Shirky who commented that 'it is a constant surprise to those of us over a certain age [...] that large parts of our life can end up online. But that's not a behavior anyone under 30 has had to unlearn' (quoted in Nussbaum 2007: 3).

Thus, some of my sociocultural origins and my position in relation to the field are revealed: a middle-class young woman who grew up during the time of the widespread adoption of technologies into the daily leisure and work lives of civilians. These factors obviously affected my process of knowing style blogging, not only in that they made certain aspects of the practice seem unremarkable to me through my shared familiarity with the technologies style bloggers employ as well as the factors that make such an activity possible in the first place, but also in that these similarities may have made it easier for me to engage with the field as a blogger: I wrote and looked and seemed like 'one of them' as in many senses, I was.

Yet my position was also constituted in and through distance. I started a style blog as part of my research methodology, after all, not primarily because I had a desire to start one. Thus, my participation in the style blogosphere was also inflected by my role as a researcher, as I blogged to gather material with which I could unpack the practice. Indeed, my position as a researcher/blogger marked me as different within the style blogosphere by virtue of my academic motivation for blogging. I wrote about my research in my posts and identified myself as a Ph.D. candidate researching personal style blogs on my 'About Me' page and in my 'Bio' on the right-hand side of my blog (see Figure 1). As such, I felt myself to be in the minority on the style blogosphere, feeling my involvement to be partial as I was always shifting between being immersed in the doing and analysing myself doing the doing.

In this way, my participation was mediated by my reflexivity, perhaps limiting the involvement that I was having by drawing me back and leading me to consider what I – and those around me – was doing. It is difficult not to be reminded of Bourdieu here, and the third aspect he cites as important for overcoming the limitations under which we labour in the field of research, which is 'intellectual bias', or the tendency of academics to 'abstract'

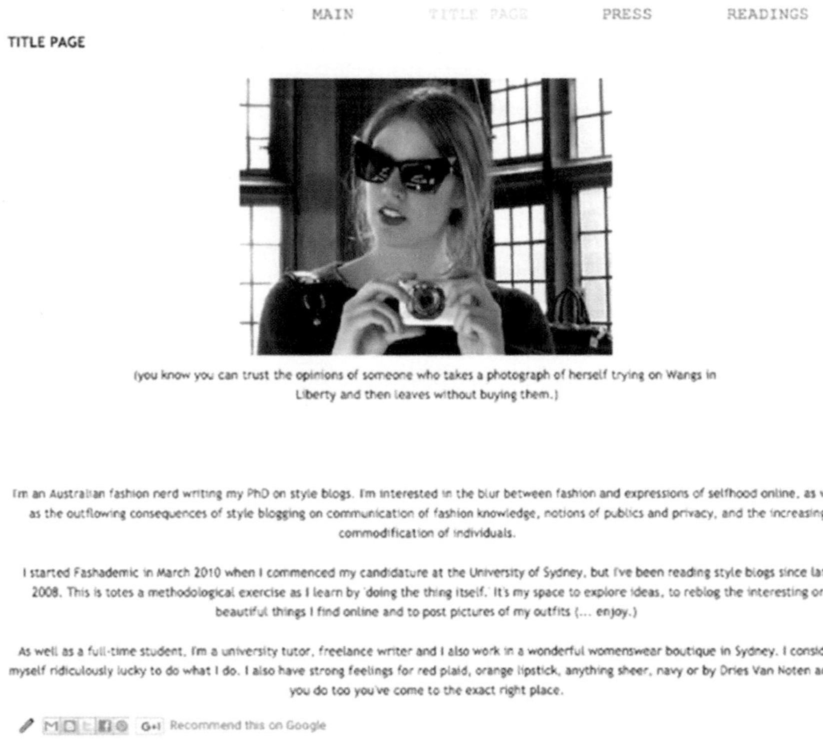

MAIN   TITLE PAGE   PRESS   READINGS

TITLE PAGE

(you know you can trust the opinions of someone who takes a photograph of herself trying on Wangs in Liberty and then leaves without buying them.)

I'm an Australian fashion nerd writing my PhD on style blogs. I'm interested in the blur between fashion and expressions of selfhood online, as well as the outflowing consequences of style blogging on communication of fashion knowledge, notions of publics and privacy, and the increasing commodification of individuals.

I started Fashademic in March 2010 when I commenced my candidature at the University of Sydney, but I've been reading style blogs since late 2008. This is totes a methodological exercise as I learn by 'doing the thing itself'. It's my space to explore ideas, to reblog the interesting or beautiful things I find online and to post pictures of my outfits (... enjoy.)

As well as a full-time student, I'm a university tutor, freelance writer and I also work in a wonderful womenswear boutique in Sydney. I consider myself ridiculously lucky to do what I do. I also have strong feelings for red plaid, orange lipstick, anything sheer, navy or by Dries Van Noten and if you do too you've come to the exact right place.

G+1 Recommend this on Google

Figure 1: This screenshot of the About Me section ('Title Page') of *Fashademic* demonstrates the tone in which I wrote to my readers and how I flagged that I was conducting research through my blogging practice.

practices and see them as 'ideas to be contemplated' (Webb et al. 2002: 50–51). Yet despite my tendency to engage in the blogosphere while bearing my research interests in mind, my very engagement in its practices – taking and uploading outfit photos, interacting with companies that wished to work with me to monetize my readership and writing about my personal style – prevented me from abstracting it. My sustained readership of certain style blogs led me to feel an affectionate familiarity with their bloggers, and my own blogging revealed to me affective aspects of blogging that I had otherwise not experienced, aspects I will describe more fully as they arise throughout this work.

For these reasons, I would not characterize my experiences of style blogging as typical. Furthermore, *Fashademic* was not a typical style blog. As such, while this experience usefully draws out aspects of the experience of style blogging, it is not necessarily representative of the experiences of style bloggers who primarily blog about their personal style. However, the value of this ethnographic research should not be discounted because of this specificity, as the similarities of situation between myself and other style bloggers, the content of my blog as mostly characteristic of a style blog (as I will later demonstrate) and my extended participation on the style blogosphere made available a wealth of knowledge that would otherwise be difficult to access.

As a corollary, I had a somewhat self-selecting readership, as I assume that those reading *Fashademic* were readers interested in my scholarly pursuits as well as the rest of the blog's content, which would usually be the sole focus of a style blog. My readership, then, was not necessarily representative of style blog readers. Yet at the same time, as their responses to my anonymous survey indicated, many read a range of style blogs, and so their responses in regards to why they read style blogs and their perceived connection to style bloggers offer a valuable insight.

I deliberately sought to include a wide range of experiences of style blogging from other bloggers and readers so that my work would not overly represent my own experience. What was striking were the similarities between my own experiences and those of others despite the specificities of *Fashademic* and my own intermediate position on the blogosphere as researcher/blogger. My experiences of style blogging, then, while particular, were consistent with a range of other bloggers' experiences. I will draw out these similarities throughout this work, making clear the context of my own experience and nuancing it with the lived experience of other bloggers. This is a significant aspect of ethnographic practice, as what is at stake is 'specifically, the lived, embodied experience of others' (Maxwell 2002: 110): ethnographic research does not seek to privilege the experiences of the researcher but rather to bring the researcher closer to the lived experience of others.

In conversation with others

I usually approached bloggers for interview on the basis of their posts: if a style blogger had written a post reflecting on their blogging experiences, I would e-mail them explaining my project and asking them to speak with me. On one occasion, I approached an Australian blogger (Kayla Telford-Brock) who I knew as a friend before we both started blogging, and our interview grew out of a prior conversation we had about the influence of other blogs on our own. The rest of the interviewees were people I had never met before contacting them in regards to this project.

I sought a diverse range of bloggers, interviewing seven in total: six female and one male ranging between the ages of 16 years old to in their early 30s. Two were Australian, two Canadian, two were American and one was British. I also approached a number of other bloggers who made no reply to my advances – two Australian, two American and one British. Most of my interviews were conducted over Skype due to my location in Sydney, Australia, which made conducting interviews in person difficult.

I also wrote a short survey comprising of multiple choice and short answer questions for readers of style blogs to reflect anonymously on their own experiences. I did this in order to counter and contrast my own observations of being a reader with those of others. I created the survey using a free website (Survey Monkey), a link to which I embedded in a post introducing the survey to my readers (see Findlay, *Fashademic*, 10 January 2012a), which I also pasted into my blog's HTML so that a pop-up window would populate in my reader's browsers when they came to my blog. I also posted a link to this survey on my profile on the Independent Fashion Bloggers website, with a short text inviting any interested blog readers to participate. The survey was active from January 2012 to July 2013 and during this time 84 people responded.

Reading what they blogged

My third methodological approach was to approach style blogs as published literary and visual works that can be analysed as such to be further understood. This is an approach defended by Viviane Serfaty, who wrote an excellent discussion on the ethical challenges facing a researcher of online personal writing (2004). Serfaty defends the use of the online diaries she studied as primary sources, and the identificatory, copyright and privacy issues this entailed, on the grounds that they 'were certainly personal, often intimate but not private' (2004:12), and that they could therefore be analysed as literary works designed for public consumption. This is a perspective easily applied to personal style blogs, as although they are private texts in the sense that they are written from an individual's point of view, they are also public in the sense that they are published on a freely accessible platform: a blog on the Internet. Moreover, bloggers often actively seek to build their readership by interacting with others in the comments section underneath their posts and creating a presence on various social media sites that are linked to their blogs in an attempt to expose their work to a bigger potential audience. During my candidature these included Facebook Groups (which became 'Pages' in mid-2012), Twitter and Instagram accounts, and Pinterest boards.

Studying blogs as texts balanced the subjectivity of my participant-observation data in a similar way to interviews, by incorporating material from a range of authors, thereby producing a more cohesive and comprehensive picture of this kind of blogging. At the same time, unlike interviews, the content of blogs is written for a wide audience, not directed at a researcher, and so also addresses the potential bias of interviews. That is, an interviewee may frame their responses to reflect what they think the researcher wants to hear: as anthropologist Michael Jackson suggests, 'the knowledge whereby one lives is not necessarily identical with the knowledge whereby one explains life' (1996: 2).

In a broader sense, as my work is focused on style blogging as a practice it was important for me to examine what bloggers do when they blog: how are they performing themselves through the technological, visual and linguistic devices employed in their posts? How can we conceive of their contribution to fashion communication? What kinds of selves are made visible and what is obscured in such posts? These questions arose through the course of this research and were not sufficiently addressed by my other two methodological approaches.

I read as wide a cross section of blogs as I could, often clicking through the blogroll of blogs I already read to discover new ones. I made a habit of looking at every personal style blog I found mentioned in mainstream media news articles and profiles in fashion magazines as well as general readership photo-books on style blogs, so that I would discover as many as possible. I read blogs written from within cities and blogs kept from suburban bedrooms. I read blogs written by college graduates that seemed to find overnight success thanks to coverage in mastheads like the *New York Times* – as was the case for Leandra Medine of *Man Repeller* (Aleksander 2010) – as well as blogs that seemed to only be read by a cluster of a blogger's close friends and 'blogfriends' (Meder 2012).

However, I did limit the blogs I closely studied in two significant ways: I chose to focus primarily on blogs written in English by girls and young women, given that they constitute the majority of the style blogosphere. Interestingly, while there are a number of style blogs written by men, the tone of much of the criticism style blogs attract is historically consistent with critiques made more generally of women's contributions to public discourse: too personal, irrelevant, immature and unseemly. This parallel guided my focus, as did my interest in the significance of this widespread and influential emergence of public texts written by girls and young women.

The sheer number of style blogs from around the world that are written in English, as well as the influence many early English-speaking bloggers had on the development of the practice, led me to the conclusion that such a focus would be representative of the overall shape and dynamics of the style blogosphere. In fact, studies that have been conducted thus far on blogs written in languages other than English and those blogging from outside the West (such as Palmgren 2010 on Scandinavian style blogs and Luvaas 2013 on Indonesian style blogs) have demonstrated that the characteristics of style blogs are remarkably consistent throughout the blogosphere regardless of the cultural specificities of these blogs. Nevertheless, I read as widely as I could, following blogs from the United States, Canada, the United Kingdom, France, Japan, Sweden, Australia, India and the Philippines, written by women and girls writing from vastly different subject positions.

At the time of writing, Luvaas's article is the only theoretical work on fashion blogging outside of the developed world to have been published. It is important to acknowledge the work of style bloggers writing from the margins of an already marginalized sub-genre of the blogosphere, and yet unfortunately it is beyond the capacities of this study to contribute in a substantive way to such a discussion. In writing an overview of the practice with a focus on its implications on communications and the performativity of fashion and identity, I have focused on the similarities between different sub-genres and localities of blogging rather than the specificities and cultural implications of localized practices. Nonetheless, further studies on style blogs written in languages other than English are needed to more fully interrogate this practice and to consider the work of style bloggers in areas such as mainland China, who are prolific and whose practice has not yet been approached by researchers. Such studies would usefully broaden our understanding of this phenomenon, and I hope that my work will elucidate aspects of style blogging that can be challenged, nuanced or extended by subsequent studies.

The problem of subjectivity

Even with my varied and prolonged reading, I was drawn to some blogs more than others based on my personal preferences, as is consistent with readership in general of this sub-genre (see Chapter Three). Being founded as they are on the personalities and perspectives of individuals, the reasons for readers to follow the blogs they do are often subjective and informed by personal taste and interests. In the course of my research I found, as did Viviane Serfaty before me, that 'some [texts] acquired more presence and character than others', and that the subjective aspect of reading could not be extracted from my choice of material to focus on (2004: 16). However, like Serfaty, I always looked to the characteristics that were shared between blogs, using particular case studies to demonstrate wider patterns at work in the style blogosphere.

Of course, as Serfaty acknowledges, there is no such thing as objective observation (2004: 18): that my work is influenced by my own subjectivity does not entail that it lacks rigour. The object of study here is an entity with permeable boundaries, one that has required a careful consideration of how to make meaning while allowing for its inherent complexities and the many voices that constitute it. If, as Serfaty argues, 'distortion is the very condition any researcher has to labor under' (2004: 18) then perhaps all that can be done is acknowledge one's personal relation to the subject and attempt to counteract this through the employment of multiple methodological approaches. Having outlined my approach and the work of other researchers that has informed and spurred my own, I will now delve into the social and textual origins of the style blogosphere. Many of the characteristics and developments of style blogging have emerged and consolidated based upon media that preceded such blogs and the work of early fashion bloggers who paved the way for those who followed them onto the blogosphere. It is this historical precedent that shaped the contemporary style blogosphere, and to which I now turn.

Notes

1 'HTML', or Hypertext Markup Language, is the main language used to create web pages, blogs and other information that can be displayed in a Web browser. It is written using specific codes that determine the appearance of a blog including layout, colour schemes, fonts and so on.
2 The *Fashademic* Facebook page is no longer active, deleted in mid-2013 when I deleted my personal Facebook account.
3 The event was rebranded and retitled 'Mercedes-Benz Fashion Week Australia' (MBAFW) in 2012.

Chapter 1

A Succession of Quick Leaps

For the casual reader of fashion magazines, it must have seemed that style blogs came out of nowhere. There had been some scattered reports on this growing phenomenon between 2006 and 2008, but nothing to rival the widespread media coverage prompted by the front row placement of a few select bloggers during the Spring/ Summer Ready-to-Wear (RTW) season in September 2009.[1] That season, during which the fashion industry migrates, over four consecutive weeks, from New York to London to Milan to Paris to view the new collections, marked the moment when style blogging as a genre first moved from its position on the fringes of the fashion media to being literally invited into the industry.

Within the global fashion industry, it is widely acknowledged that the four fashion weeks of the annual Spring/Summer RTW season, in addition to the Fall/Winter RTW collections shown each February, are of paramount importance. It is during these periods that the new collections of both established and emergent fashion labels are shown to a largely invite-only audience. These collections designate – and indeed, set the agenda for – the trends for the upcoming season, and to be invited is a mark of prestige, an indication of having a place within the competitive and hierarchical fashion industry. Indeed, Entwistle and Rocamora suggest that the primary function of such fashion presentations is for the audience to see and to be seen, the importance of physically being in attendance surpassing the importance of viewing what is displayed on the catwalk (2006: 743).[2]

Guests are issued with either seated or standing tickets for a show and for many, proximity to the catwalk is of crucial importance. As a general rule, the front row is reserved for celebrity VIPs, the corporate owners of the showing label, and fashion critics and editors from the most prestigious fashion and news media publications. From this vantage point, these audience members enjoy an unobstructed view of the catwalk and are also in the best position from which to be viewed by the other guests in attendance (see Entwistle and Rocamora 2006).

Considering these factors, it is little wonder that the news media responded with a furore when a cluster of independent style bloggers began to appear on the front row in 2009. One *New York Times* article, headlined 'Bloggers crash fashion's front row' read:

[F]ashion bloggers have ascended from the nosebleed seats to the front row with such alacrity that a long-held social code among editors, one that prizes position and experience above outward displays of ambition or enjoyment, has practically been obliterated.

(Wilson 2009)

Other prominent news and fashion media outlets ran similar stories with titles such as 'Style bloggers take centre stage' (*Financial Times*), 'Bloggers take over the front row' (US *InStyle* magazine) and 'Fashion bloggers, where they belong: In the front row' (*Mediaite*), all reporting that bloggers were now being recognized as fashion authorities in their own right despite their unorthodox style of reportage (in the case of some, their age) and their relative lack of experience within the industry (see Copping 2009; King 2009; Wilson 2009; Zucker 2009).

That Spring/Summer RTW 2010 fashion season can be seen as style blogging's coming-of-age. The front row placement of bloggers at prestigious shows such as Marc Jacobs, Yohji Yamamoto and Dolce and Gabbana indicated a welcome of sorts from the kinds of designers whose work such bloggers had traditionally admired from the remove of their blogs. It was, however, a figurative coming-of-age, as style bloggers were not unequivocally welcomed by the fashion industry, and most will never receive invites to attend such events. What the Spring/Summer RTW 2009 season represented, both to the fashion industry and to bloggers, was that blogs had 'arrived': bloggers' influence and reach as communicators had been recognized by those who had the power to invite them in. This episode can also be conceived of as a savvy PR move on the part of the labels who invited bloggers to sit front row. It aligned these brands with the perceived alternative cool of bloggers whilst engendering lots of news coverage of their shows. So much is evident in a critique of the seating at Dolce and Gabbana made by Scott Schuman, who described the arrangement of front row seats accessorized with laptops as making him (and the other bloggers) look like dancing monkeys while generating 'a humongous amount of press' for the Italian label (Pappademas 2012).

Since that highly publicized moment, style blogging as a practice has grown exponentially, in number, reach and visibility. The total number of fashion-related blogs on the blogosphere numbered two million in 2006 (Corcoran 2006), whereas by 2010, there were two million fashion-related blogs on blogging platform Blogger alone (Rocamora 2011). It is rare to find a contemporary, mainstream fashion magazine for sale that does not feature at least one style blogger somewhere within its pages, either as a guest columnist, an interviewee or someone whose self-shot outfit photographs are printed as a source of visual inspiration for readers. Of course, for every style blogger enjoying widespread recognition, there are countless others who blog in relative obscurity. They too post photographs of their daily outfits, write about the items they covet and reblog images from fashion campaigns and editorials. Collectively, all of these personal style blogs constitute the style blogosphere, a vast and networked conglomerate of blogs with the shared focus on the personal style and fashion interest of individual bloggers.

This chapter provides a comprehensive overview of style blogs and their development and diversification as a distinct sub-genre of the fashion blogosphere. I define style blogs and outline their distinct generic characteristics, distinguishing them from the other sub-genres that comprise the fashion blogosphere, before mapping the origins of personal style blogging through the archive, tracing the earliest fashion blogs and drawing on the oral histories of two of the first fashion bloggers to sketch a portrait of what the early days of fashion blogging were like. I also trace the multitude of websites and forums that precipitated the emergence of personal style blogging as a distinct sub-genre in order to demonstrate that it did not spring from the ether but has tangible connections to prior digital practices.

In the final part of this chapter, I identify two distinct periods of personal style blogging, which I name *first wave* and *second wave style blogging*, to demonstrate its mutable composition, ever-shaped as it is by the contributions of the people who blog it into being as well as the digital environment within which it originally flourished. The way that people 'do' style blogging is not fixed but has and will continue to change. This is only to be expected from a medium, which like both the Internet that made its existence possible and fashion itself, 'lives on the principle of permanent change' (Lovink 2008: xi).

What is a style blog?

To commence a discussion about style blogs, we first need to understand what they are. The word 'blog' stems from 'weblog' (a contraction of the words 'web' and 'log'), a term that dates back to the late 1990s (Rocamora and Bartlett 2009: 105). It derives from the form the first blogs took: logs of links to other blogs and websites (see Blood 2000). A blog, then, can be defined as an online platform for the regular publication (or 'posting') of short texts, images and videos, created and maintained by an individual. Posts are arranged in reverse chronological order, and are either archived by month or categorized according to keywords, or both. They are often comprised of a blend of original content produced by a blogger, be it images, text or video, and content that is reblogged from other websites and publications, selected and organized according to that blogger's personal taste. On most blogs, readers are able to comment on posts, their response displayed in a stream of comments from other users, which subsequent readers are able to view by clicking the 'comments' link under each post.

Personal blogs are often written from the first-person perspective, 'a platform for the exchange of anecdotes and personal reflections' that, in style, are 'rarely polished', likened by Rocamora and Bartlett to 'a genre of "chatter"' (2009: 106). Indeed, blogging is characterized by its informal, conversational tone and its highly individualized, publicly shared content. Most blogs have a central identifying theme around which the majority of the content is organized, be it politics, food, motherhood, music, the daily life of the blogger or, in the case of style blogs, fashion and personal style. Style blogs, then, are a particular kind of fashion-based weblog in which the content is particularly focused on fashion and style as it pertains to and is practised in the life of the blogger.

Style bloggers make no claim to objectivity; unlike industry-based fashion blogs (such as those run by magazines, labels or fashion critics), their blogs represent an individual's opinion, rather than a corporate position. This is evident in the words of self-professed 'fashion geek' Susie Lau, who said of starting her own blog, that she wanted:

[…] to keep it quite personal. By personal, I don't mean that in a 'Dear Diary' kind of way but I mean *Style Bubble* is about blogging my own observations, thoughts and experiences in fashion, making use of my daily fashion life, in the shops that I encounter, the trends that I try, the ups and downs of my style, the designers that I come across.

(Jacob 2008)

As is the case with traditional media, including publicity material generated in the wider fashion industry, a style blog must have a 'point of view': a distinct perspective that sets one apart from one's peers, attracting their attention and, perhaps, their admiration. This emphasis on individuality and the importance of individual perspective is demonstrated in the kind of content that is central to style blogs, most of which is an iteration, whether literal or not, of a blogger's personal taste in clothing, what will here be called their 'style'. On this blogosphere, style is primarily demonstrated by the publication of a series of photographs of a blogger posing in an outfit of their own styling, known as *outfit posts*. They are the defining feature of this sub-genre, differentiating personal style blogs from other types of fashion-based weblogs.

Outfit posts have been a key feature of style blogs since they began to appear on the blogosphere (see George 2009; Palmgren 2010; Rocamora 2011). The conventions of outfit posts include a blogger styling a range of garments and accessories from their own wardrobe (and, increasingly, clothing that is sent to them by labels and PR companies) and assuming a series of poses for multiple photographs, which they then edit and upload. Bloggers often cite the designer or provenance of the garments they are wearing in their images and usually write some brief accompanying text about their clothing or their recent activities. While originally a catalogue of the blogger's daily outfits, over time these posts have largely transformed into the display of outfits styled for the purposes of being blogged. I will discuss this development in more detail in Chapter Four.

The content of personal style blogs is not limited to outfit posts, of course. While some blogs are more or less exclusively comprised of these types of posts, many also post an array of other fashion-related information. The catch-all 'other information' covers a vast and ever-adapting array of content, as style blogging is a genre that is formed and re-formed as bloggers contribute to it. The content of style blogs, then, as with many other genres of blogs, usually comprises of a mix of reblogged and original content. Content that is commonly reblogged includes (but is not limited to) scans of editorial (the industry term for the fashion photographic spreads particular to fashion magazines), advertising campaigns, lookbooks (a collection of photographs styled and collated to display a label's new fashion collection) and fashion films released by fashion labels and houses, stills from the catwalks of fashion weeks and street style photographs taken from other blogs.

It is more common for externally produced fashion imagery to be reblogged than fashion criticism or written content, which is in keeping with fashion's character as a primarily visual medium. An example of this can be found on Australian style blog *Oracle Fox*. Its blogger,

Amanda 'Mandy' Shadforth, explained that she started her blog 'because I felt like I needed somewhere to put all of the images that I loved' (Revlon Australia 2013). In April 2011 alone, Mandy posted lookbooks from labels Lucette, Wildfox, Young Huntings, Shakuhachi, Opening Ceremony and others, as well as editorial imagery from magazines such as *West End*, *Harper's Bazaar Australia* and *Oyster*, street style blogs and photo-sharing website Flickr (see *Oracle Fox*, April 2011). That said, reblogging is less common on the contemporary style blogosphere as producing original content has become a point of pride for bloggers, a way of asserting legitimacy and a unique point of view. Where content is reblogged now is usually due to a blogger publishing externally produced content that they were featured in: Susie Bubble publishing a selection of street style shots taken of her during fashion month, say, or Rhea Gupte reblogging an editorial she shot with *Cosmopolitan India* (see Gupte, *Fuss*, 2014).

Mixed with this externally produced content is material created by bloggers. As well as outfit post imagery, this content may include independent coverage of the happenings of the fashion industry; reviews or reports on the shows of the fashion weeks of leading fashion cities (New York, London, Milan, Paris) or those of their blogger's respective countries of residence; a blogger's personal reflections on fashion and style; recounts of the events of their daily lives (though these usually refer back to fashion and style in some way); advice to readers about how to recreate items designed by fashion labels on a budget, or guides on how to do things, such as apply make-up looks or tell if an alleged luxury good is genuine or fake; and reviews and recommendations on brands that they like or are promoting through their blog.

Laia Garcia's blog *Geometric Sleep* illustrates this kind of content. Since the blog's inception in 2006, Laia has published reviews of New York Fashion Week shows alongside reposted imagery from the catwalk and posted photographs of products that she wanted or regretted not buying as well as outfit posts. Figures 2 and 3 show some of the variety of this content.

In 'Short and studded', Laia discusses the benefits of the pictured Pour La Victoire boots in the kind of personalized vernacular inherent to the blogosphere: they remind her of Alexander Wang booties 'without the crazy price tag or (the obviously intentional/ironic) street-girl vibe' (Garcia 2009c). In the post overleaf (Figure 2), titled 'Let's get real fashion-y for a minute', Laia critiques the choice of models American *Vogue* published on a billfold cover for their May 2009 issue. She allocates or deducts points for the choice of each model against whether or not she is truly (according to Laia) a 'model of the moment' (as the magazine claims), and then suggests four replacement models who, for her, better fit the moniker (see Garcia 2009b). Figure 3 also displays a screenshot of one of Laia's outfit posts, in which she blogs about a t-shirt designed by then-fellow blogger Tavi and photographs it as part of two different outfits (Garcia 2009a).

Indeed, style bloggers can, and do, write and post pictures on anything they find interesting from the world of fashion, be it the fashion industry itself, fashion as a concept, or fashion as it is realized in their own lives. Ultimately, regardless of the form it takes, the two central themes of all of the content on a style blog are fashion and personal

Figure 2: A screenshot of two posts published on *Geometric Sleep* on 13 April and 14 April respectively.

Figure 3: A screenshot of one of Laia's outfit posts, published on *Geometric Sleep* on 6 April 2009.

style. These are often virtually inextricably linked, as the fashion imagery on a blog – whether comprised of photographs of products they wish to buy or reblogged editorial content – is usually posted because it appeals to the blogger's own taste, thus functioning as another iteration of their style. By the same token, a blogger's personal style is visually represented both by this kind of imagery and their self-produced outfit posts, the accompanying text of which often describes why they are wearing these particular clothes and accessories.

Here, fashion and personal style feed into one another, working to both literally and figuratively clad the online self of a style blogger. I will take this concept up more fully in Chapter Four where I unpack the notion of style and argue that it is an ongoing embodied process of becoming rather than a visual articulation of a prior, stable identity. For now, it is simply worth noting that the tastes and interests of the blogger are the organizing theme of a style blog.

The sub-genres of the fashion blogosphere

In 2003, Clay Shirky predicted that a point would come where 'the term "blog" would be stretched beyond its original concrete meaning by users, as has been the case with the examples of "home page" and "portal"' (Shirky, quoted in Bruns and Jacobs 2006: 2). Digital theorists Axel Bruns and Joanne Jacobs argued that this point had already been passed in 2006, as blogs by then were appearing in many different guises – 'as community discussion boards, as news bulletins, or as creative outlets' – arguing that 'in the future, we will have to speak of specific sub-genres of blogging' (2).

Writing in 2016 I can attest that this future has been realized, resulting in the necessity to differentiate between the different sub-genres of fashion blogging, which is itself a sub-genre of the blogosphere. As Susie Lau notes in her foreword to *Style Feed*, 'as the platform [of blogging] began to grow in popularity, sub-categories emerged under the umbrella term "fashion blogs"' (Oliver 2012: 9). All of these blogs can loosely be categorized either as independent or corporate. This is a distinction made by Agnès Rocamora who explains that independent blogs are those created by private individuals in distinction to corporate blogs that represent the interest and perspective of a fashion institution such as a magazine, a brand, a label or a store (2011: 409).

Personal style blogs are independent blogs, as are street style blogs and many other fashion-based personal blogs that are loosely defined by Lau as 'blogs that can be recognized as fully fledged websites or media outlets' (Oliver 2012: 10). The two sub-categories that are most proliferous on the fashion blogosphere are personal style and street style blogs, two sub-genres of the fashion blogosphere that are distinct from one another despite having many similarities. This often leads them to be confused with each other, which seems to occur because they both represent an individual and often 'outsider' perspective on fashion (see Allen 2009; Rocamora 2009; Khamis and Munt 2010), and because both types of blogs rose in visibility within the fashion industry at the same time. In the example of the bloggers attending fashion week described at the beginning of this chapter, Scott Schuman (*The Sartorialist*), Tommy Ton (*Jak & Jil*, now defunct) and Garance Doré (*Garance Doré*) are street style photography bloggers; Susie Lau (*Style Bubble*), Bryan Grey-Yambao (*Bryanboy*) and Tavi Gevinson (*Style Rookie*) are all examples of personal style bloggers. The two sub-genres run in an almost-parallel trajectory: the first street style blog was *The Sartorialist*, started in 2005, closely followed by the *Facehunter* blog, started by Yvan Rodic in January 2006, and the earliest personal style blogs appeared online from mid-2006.

Distinct to personal style blogs, however, street style blogs emerged out of the tradition of street style photography, and are comprised of often-untrained photographers taking images of stylish individuals who they encounter on the street. Of course, whereas street style photographers publish their images in print media, street style bloggers upload theirs onto their blog, often with minimal, if any, commentary. Susie Lau writes that for these bloggers, 'blogging is a vehicle to showcase their photography and their ability to capture a particular zeitgeist on the streets' (Oliver 2012: 10). However, as with the work of notable street style photographers Shoichi Aoki (*FRUiTS*) and the late Bill Cunningham, street style bloggers focus on stylish individuals encountered on the street rather than forming a portfolio of images on street life in all of its guises, as was the function of street style photography in the nineteenth century when the genre first developed (see Scott 2007; Luvaas 2016).

As is consistent with most creative forms in the postmodern era, there is overlap between the two sub-genres of personal style and street style blogging. Personal style bloggers sometimes reblog imagery from street style blogs, and may also blog their admiration of the style of certain figures who appear regularly on street style blogs and street style galleries on fashion websites. Conversely, street style photographers often take photographs of style bloggers and upload them on their own blogs. Moreover, there is an increasing blurring of the distinction between these two kinds of blogs as some street style photographers fold accounts of their own lives and photographs of themselves amongst the images of their friends and people they encounter, creating a kind of hybrid between the two sub-genres (see *Hanneli* and *Garance Doré*).

Despite these similarities, the focus of street style blogs is on the person being photographed, rather than on the photographers themselves. These blogs are organized by the eye of the photographer and it is their sense of style that is being demonstrated as much as that of the subjects in the photographs; yet, the intimacy of personal revelation and representation that is evident on style blogs is not present on those exhibiting street style. This different focus is evident in Scott Schuman's reflection that:

> [...] when I'm taking a picture of someone, I don't really put their names down [...] because it's just not that important. You know, I'm taking a picture of someone, it's my perception of who they are. I'm taking it the way I'm taking it because [...] I want to enjoy the picture.
>
> (Schuman in BigThink 2011)

If the content of a street style blog is focused through a street style photographer's eye – and, accordingly, their taste and skill behind the camera – then the content of a personal style blog is focused through the performative selfhood of a style blogger. This is an ongoing, reflexive communication that simultaneously expresses a blogger's interests to their audience whilst reflecting who they feel they are back to themselves. In this way, the content of a style blog metaphorically dresses the online selfhood of a blogger even as they upload photographs of their dressed selves for their followers to see. Fashion on a style blog is reframed within the blogger's personal sphere and acts as an indicator of what they appreciate and who they feel themselves to be.

Sub-genres within personal style blogging

While this creative public display of one's personal style is the hallmark of personal style blogging, there is also increasing diversification within the sub-genre as different bloggers tailor their blog's focus to reflect their own ethos on or experience of fashion. As is to be expected with a mode of communication predicated on individual perspective, there are a number of emergent sub-genres within style blogging that are worth mentioning to indicate the scope and diversity of this kind of fashion blogging. If we take the definition and description I have so far provided to be the norm, the characteristics of other kinds of style blogs that constitute an alternative space within the style blogosphere come into focus.

Of these minority sub-genres, the most distinct are *fatshion style blogs*.[3] These are personal style blogs maintained by girls and young women with an interest in style who also identify as 'curvy', 'plus-size' or 'fat', words these bloggers employ about themselves on their blogs (see Kinsman 2012). While fatshion bloggers employ the conventions of personal style blogging on their blogs – publishing outfit posts and writing in a conversational tone about fashion – they have traditionally written their blogs as alternative spaces, a response to their exclusion from the mainstream fashion industry.[4] Sociologist Catherine Connell reads these blogs as sites of political resistance being enacted through the dressed self, as fatshion bloggers produce a counter-discourse in opposition to the hegemonic thin, Caucasian 'fashionable' body. Not only do these blogs display fat girls proudly blogging their style, the very notion of a desirable body is entirely reframed. As Connell writes, the bloggers she studied

[…] rarely used the language of 'flattering' to describe their fashion, which would imply that fat fashion should disguise or minimize fatness. Rather, users complement each other on how their outfits *highlighted* fatness; comments regularly included direct references to visible fatness as cute, sexy, and enviable.

(2013: 213)

'Fat' is here recoded as non-shameful, claimed as part of the identity of fatshion bloggers and often referred to in the titles of their blogs, such as *Thicker Than Your Average Girl*, *Curves to Kill*, *Fat Girls Like Fashion Too*, *Manolo for the Big Girl* and *Diary of a Fatshionista*. As a corollary, it is common for fatshion bloggers to write about their bodies and experiences of dressing, weaving their personal narratives with other content focusing on fashion and their everyday lives. This may be as throwaway as including the size of the clothes they're wearing in their outfit posts or more in-depth, such as posts discussing their pride in their size and shape. In providing a space for the discussion of a personal relationship to dress, fatshion blogs also function as sites at which bloggers share ambivalence about their appearance or their frustration at finding clothes in 'straight' stores, which may not sell in the sizes they require. As such, the re-claiming of fat and the display of 'unruly bodies' (Connell 2013: 212) also entails a blogged navigation of the affective experience of these bodies in relationship to an industry that reinforces hegemonic ideals of gender and size as well as the possible censure of a society that demands non-normative bodies to be concealed from view.

We see this complexity in a post Lauren Darling published on her blog *Pocket Rocket Fashion* (tag line: 'Fun. Fashionable. *Fat*') in 2012. In this post, Lauren described the first time she wore a new dress from Primark that showed her 'VBO', or Visible Belly Outline. The photos included in the post show Lauren posing in the sleeveless white shift with black polka dots, which she paired with black opaque tights and a red-lipped smile, and are accompanied by text that explains that she bought the dress

> [...] knowing it probably wouldn't disguise my belly. I just wanted to try. But even though it was ridiculously tight, I kinda ... liked it? I showed a few people, and they liked it too.
>
> The thing is, as much as I'm a cheerleader for people who break fashion rules [...] I think I've never been confident enough to do so myself. Even now I find myself apologising for people's view before even realising what I've said. It's just automatic.
>
> (Darling, *Pocket Rocket Fashion,* 19 November 2012)

She describes putting the dress on in the loos at an East End pub before going dancing, her writing bringing us briefly closer to her inner world as she negotiates her desire to wear the fitted dress with the social censure she anticipates receiving as fat young woman showing her body through her clothes.

These narratives do not have a parallel on most style blogs that are not fatshion; yet, these are mixed with the kind of chatty, personal writing about fashion common to style blogs in general. In this way, fatshion blogs present stories alternative to the mainstream, their bloggers tacitly defiant and proud in their visibility, thereby making an implicit claim to fashionability by their very presence on the style blogosphere.

Fatshion blogs also function as a space at which bloggers can discuss their exclusion from mainstream fashion, an exclusion perpetuated by fashion labels not producing clothes in their size and by the absence of women of similar shape in advertisements or fashion editorial unless in a special 'curvy issue' (see Caruso 2011; Styles 2013). So much is evident in the words of Bethany Rutter of fatshion blog *Arched Eyebrow*, who believes that fatshion blogging has become popular

> [...] simply because we don't have a face or a voice anywhere else. All UK fashion journalism is written by slim people for slim people, so there's almost no point reading magazines if you're fat. That's why the Internet's become such an important place for plus-size fashion.
>
> (Rutter, quoted in Styles 2013)

This exclusion acting as an impetus for bloggers to create alternative spaces to circulate their fashion interest has also seen the emergence of the modest blogosphere, comprised of style bloggers mediating their religious faith with their desire to dress in ways they find exciting and stylish. Cultural studies theorist Reina Lewis argues that the Internet

[...] created opportunities for women not (or not directly) involved in commerce to publicise their ideas about modest dressing, producing new modes of fashion mediation that become a form of religious interpretation fostering women's voices and perspectives.

(2015: 240)

This online participation and exchange occurred simultaneously to the rise of e-commerce sites that addressed a demand for fashionable modest clothing that was not being met by mainstream fashion retailers who 'appear[ed] to have no interest in meeting [the] consumer needs' of this group (Lewis 2015: 240). These narratives parallel the emergence of style blogging as a genre in interesting ways: individuals writing from a desire to read and write the kinds of stories and representations of self that they were not seeing in other fashion media, rendering themselves – and their style – visible. Yet the particularities of these sub-genres should not be overlooked: where the commercial logics of the fashion industry have increasingly shaped how people blog, there is still a politics of representation and resistance being enacted on the style blogosphere, which takes shape through the consumption of clothing – buying and proudly wearing a fitted dress, say, or showing readers how to wear a 'camiband' for extra coverage over jeans or a bathing suit (see *JenMagazine* in Lewis 2015: 246). The constant throughout these blogs is that their central focus is the personal style of the blogger. The fact that the purpose to which this style is employed varies from blog to blog does not destabilize this definition of personal style blogs as a discrete sub-genre within fashion blogging. Rather, it offers a tool by which the vast, fluctuating and uncentred style blogosphere can be understood.

The emergence of fashion blogging

The first blogs were created between 1994 and 1998, and Jorn Barger coined the term 'weblog' in reference to his online journal, *Robot Wisdom* (Gurak et al. 2004). They emerged in the wake of other communicative digital technologies such as personal web pages, forums and e-mail lists (Blood 2000). Geert Lovink argues that blogs initially remained 'off the radar because they had no e-commerce component' (2008: x), a status that was challenged by the increasing internationalization and massive uptake of Internet use that took place in subsequent years. There were reportedly 50 blogs in existence in 1999 before the launch of ready-made blogging platforms, a number that escalated to 8 million by 2005 (Kaye 2005: 128). By 2008, according to online blog index Technorati, the entire blogosphere comprised of 184 million blogs and 346 million readers (White and Winn 2009).

There are a number of causes that led to the widespread proliferation of blogs in the early to mid-2000s. The 9/11 terrorist attack on the World Trade Centre complex and the Pentagon, and the subsequent war between the United States and Iraq have been identified as the major catalysts that accelerated the proliferation of blogging as a mode of communication (see Gauntlett 2004; Gurak et al. 2004; Brady 2005; Bruns 2006). The impulse behind this expansion has been theorized as a response to the social desires for community and dialogue that arise during a time of crisis, desires met by blogging due to blogs' capacity for instantaneous updating (allowing for new information to be easily disseminated) and their accessibility, enabling wide audiences to congregate, read and discuss events (Rocamora 2011: 408).

The spread of blogging was also facilitated by the development and launch of blogging content management platforms such as Blogger (launched in August 1999), WordPress (May 2003) and Typepad (October 2003). Although users with technological expertise were able to code and self-publish blogs before the early 2000s, these ready-made platforms made it possible for users to blog by using one of a number of pre-existing templates and, if they so chose, to customize their blog free or (as is the case with Typepad) for minimal charge.[5] The service offered by these platforms marked the moment when people without specialized skills in web design, HTML coding and JavaScript could enter the blogosphere, making blogging, in the words of Gurak et al., 'no more difficult than sending an e-mail' (2004).

The proliferation of blogs seemed to be centralized in the United States at first (Pederson and Macafee 2007: 1472) and the early coverage of blogs by mainstream media outlets focused on those written within North America. Much of the early press about blogs focuses on those concerned with politics and current affairs, which offered alternative opinion pieces and commentary on politics and current affairs rather than publishing content primarily based on the events of bloggers' personal lives (see Levy 2002; Manjoo 2002; Shachtman 2002; Rojas 2003). Many of the blogs that were the subject of news coverage were written by men, even though studies of North American bloggers at the time indicated that over half of all bloggers were women (Perseus UK 2003).

This imbalance in the representation of who was blogging led to the misconception that there were few women bloggers, and that women's blogs were 'less noteworthy than men's by virtue of their often domestic and personal sphere of reference' (Gregg 2006: 151). Such a misconception is compounded by the focus of many of the early studies on blogging, which concentrated on political blogs despite the fact that they 'comprise only about 11 percent of the blogosphere' (Pham 2011: 5). As Pham observes, 'this literature suggests that the blogosphere is dominated by men' even though by 2011, more women and girls created blogs than men and boys, and 'females under the age of twenty-nine are the most prolific bloggers and maintain their blogs for longer periods of time' (5).

The lack of mainstream media coverage of early non-pundit blogs might suggest that there were few blogs at this time engaging with other topics or that the contribution of women was limited to keeping online diaries on platforms such as LiveJournal. Yet as the aforementioned Perseus survey indicates, women accounted for over half of the blogging population, and as Gregg's research demonstrates, women were blogging about a range of interests ranging from feminist analyses of daily news to family life (see Gregg 2006). These included blogs on fashion; indeed, the first fashion-based blogs were on the blogosphere as early as 2001. Although both men and women kept these blogs, even in these early days of fashion blogging the majority of fashion bloggers were female.

Among these initial blogs were *She She Me*, which dates back to January 2001, *Primp* created in November 2001, and *DFR: Daily Fashion Report*, the only blog of these three created by a male blogger, started in February 2002. These early blogs do not cohere with one another in terms of style and content, and they bear little resemblance to personal style blogs, despite being their generic precursors. The writers of these blogs are partially visible at best, more present in the direct address and informal tone of their writing rather than any visual representation (save for an 'About Me' thumbnail image of Ernest Schmatolla, the creator of *DFR: Daily Fashion Report*).

She She Me reads as a series of diary entries penned by the fictional She She Me girls who lead lives reminiscent of those of the characters from the HBO series *Sex and the City*, and fashion comprises only one aspect of the blog's girl-about-town content rather than constituting its central focus. The content of *Primp* mainly consists of brief sentences recommending fashion products and accessories, accompanied by links to sites where they are available for view or purchase, which is congruent with the 'log' style of many early blogs. *DFR: Daily Fashion Report* reads as a series of opinions on the happenings of the fashion industry, written in a critical, gossipy tone by Schmatolla who writes in his Blogger. com 'About Me' profile that before launching the site he 'was for many years a New York fashion photographer' (2002). He alone amongst these early bloggers appears to have had a professional link to the fashion industry prior to establishing his blog.

'I wasn't the only one out there'

Although fashion blogging has had a 'relatively short lifespan' (Oliver 2012: 14), it has rapidly developed and expanded since it first appeared on the Internet. As such, it is difficult to appreciate what it must have been like to blog into the abyss, so to speak, and so I interviewed two of the first fashion bloggers to find out: Danielle Meder of *Final Fashion* and Julie Fredrickson of *Almost Girl*.[6] I will refer to the responses of both women in this section to weave an oral history of sorts of fashion blogging in the mid-2000s.

Danielle started her first blog on Blogger in February 2005, around the same time that she moved into a new apartment with an Internet connection. In her own words, she had found 'this brand new area I had time to explore!' and, in the process of so doing, found that there were other people who, like her, were

> […] interested in fashion from more of a philosophical, theoretical perspective, and for the first time in my life I experienced the kind of affinity you get when you find people who are interested in the same things that you are […] it was amazing to me that I wasn't the only one out there.
>
> (Meder 2012)

The two aspects of this experience – the opportunity to discuss fashion from a particular perspective not accounted for by other media, and the affinity with other like-minded bloggers – were also central to Julie's experience of early fashion blogging. She too started her blog to have a conversation about fashion online, interested as she was in

> […] starting a dialogue with people who had similar interests around fashion, as I found that the fashion media rarely spoke about the issues of interest to me and that the existing blog community that was publishing at the time tended to focus on other topics.
>
> (Fredrickson 2013)

The focus was more theoretical than sartorial, then – that is to say, 'no one was outfit blogging or talking about must haves in the blogosphere […] fashion bloggers were] mainly people interested in wider issues around fashion as opposed to being strictly about consumptive experiences' (Fredrickson 2013).

Unsurprisingly, the fashion blogosphere at this time was characterized by long-form written posts, only rarely punctuated by images. Such a blogosphere is hard to imagine for a contemporary fashion blogger, as original, high-resolution images are a cornerstone of the two most popular fashion blogging sub-genres, street style and personal style blogging. Yet according to Meder, early fashion blogs 'were much more about writing than about images' (Meder 2012). In fact, if images were posted at all, they were often single photographs taken by bloggers themselves to illustrate the post's written content, a visual support rather than a focal point (see Figures 4 and 5). This is partly attributable to the dominantly text-based user-generated modes of digital communication that preceded and influenced blogging – chat rooms, forums, MUDs and so on – yet, at the same time, 'images were harder to [get]: it used to be that on Google Images you'd hardly find anything' (Meder 2012).

In the 'small community [that] began to galvanize around fashion blogging' (Meder 2012), bloggers would engage in lengthy discussions through the comment threads and participate in 'carousels', in which a number of bloggers write about a subject – here, a specific aspect of fashion – and link to the posts of all the other participating bloggers. For the community in which Danielle and Julie took part, this was called 'Black Friday Blogging' and it began in November 2005, as

> […] kind of an experiment to see if fashion writing could focus on something that was a little different because obviously back then the fashion media landscape was a lot less various than it is now […] without the financial obligations of the mainstream media we could sort of take on topics and write about things that were still about fashion but didn't have anything to do with the type of media that we were familiar with seeing. It was an experimental time.
>
> (Meder 2012)

As well as sharing posts and having discussions in the comments, bloggers would occasionally meet up with one another. Danielle spoke of taking a trip to New York in 2006 to meet some

Figure 4: Screenshot of 'patternmaking', *Final Fashion*, 9 December 2005.

Figure 5: Screenshot of 'Proving I was there Oscar de la Renta pre-Fall 2007', *Almost Girl*, 5 December 2006.

of her 'blogfriends'. Likewise, Julie described how she became friends with both bloggers and readers 'many of whom remain friends to this day', characterizing the then-blogosphere as 'a small community of connected women that focused mostly on commentary' (Fredrickson 2013). The fashion blogosphere, then, was akin to a small community of bloggers who knew each other if not in person then through their blogs.

Final Fashion and *Almost Girl* were only two of the first fashion blogs to bring the fashion blogosphere into being. Written out of Canada and the United States, respectively, these were published alongside *The Budget Fashionista,* a blog about looking fashionable on a budget that was started by Kathryn Finney in 2003; *Spirit Fingers,* a chatty personal fashion blog written out of Hong Kong, created in July 2004; *Manolo the Shoe Blogger*, by an anonymous New Yorker who writes posts on celebrities and shoes, which has been active since its creation in October 2004; and many others blogging on niche aspects of fashion for readers 'from Hobart to Helsinki' (Zamiatin 2006).

Early influences on personal style blogs

Such was the landscape of the early fashion blogosphere. The development of personal style blogging as a distinct genre, however, was shaped by a number of enmeshed and concurrent influences, not simply its blogging forebears. This is perhaps appropriate for a genre based on fashion, itself an industry that draws inspiration from a number of sources to create original images and designs. As such, there were a number of forums, social media networks and fashion-based websites frequented by user communities interested in fashion and shopping that influenced the development of style blogs. This is evident both in the similarities between style blogs and these predecessors, and that bloggers would credit these sites and communities as influential in the creation of their own blogs.

A number of online forums were operational in the early 2000s within which registered users were able to discuss their interest in fashion and upload editorial images for the appreciation of others. One of the first such forums was the Fashion Spot (or tFS), created circa 2001. Until a few years ago, tFS was strictly a forum at which registered users could write about fashion on shared discussion boards. The site's content was thus user-generated and its members contributed voluntarily, presumably out of a common interest in fashion and a desire to participate in the virtual community.

Some early style bloggers have noted the influence of tFS and its community in the development personal style blogging. In her foreword to *Style Feed: The World's Top Fashion Blogs*, Susie Lau wrote that:

[t]he Fashion Spot was [...] where I first discovered the act of sharing your personal style, something that would rapidly spiral into today's phenomenon of fashion blogging. I'd take a picture of my outfit in the mirror, palms sweating, because it seemed such a preposterous act of narcissism at the time. A quick upload [...] and my self-image would be out there for members to bestow virtual karma points and encouraging comments on. The Fashion Spot was in effect the gestating cocoon for the beginnings of my own fashion blog and arguably the start of fashion blogging's explosion.

(Lau in Oliver 2012: 7)

Another early and popular fashion-based forum was foto decadent, created in 2004 as 'a community dedicated to avant-garde fashion photography' (according to the site's 'about' page) and hosted on blogging platform LiveJournal. Users would upload complete scans of fashion imagery – usually comprised of editorial spreads and advertising campaigns from past and current issues of fashion magazines – resulting in a user-generated online database for public viewing, downloading and sharing.

The influence of these early fashion-based forums on style blogs is evident both in their shared subjective mode of discussing fashion and practice of presenting a stream of externally produced fashion imagery down a page. Style bloggers often upload whole photo shoots that reflect their personal taste in fashion or feature models whose personal style inspires them. However, whilst personal sharing was central to communication on these early forums, when participating in them, users would engage in discussion with one another rather than present their own unmediated perspective in a continuous stream, as is the custom on style blogs. Neither were these forums sites at which users catalogued the daily events of their lives. However, there were already other sites on the World Wide Web at which users could – and were – doing just this.

One such site was MySpace (now 'Myspace'), which was launched in August 2003 and was the top-ranking social networking site in the United States in 2006 (Olsen 2006). Still an active site, MySpace offers users a basic page that they can modify to reflect their aesthetic preferences, decorating it with images and information about themselves and interests. At the time of its launch, MySpace also had a function allowing members to include blogs on their pages (Olsen 2006). Users would interact with one another by leaving comments on one another's 'walls', a precursor to other social networking sites such as Facebook.

This social interactivity based on sharing personal interests is a commonality between the practices of networking on MySpace and blogging. As Boyd Thomas, Peters and Tolson outline in their analysis of the communication of fashion knowledge on the site, online communities such as MySpace 'provide a free public forum where users can connect with friends and share information' (2007: 588), a function mirrored by personal blogs.

Significantly, MySpace also offered a number of content categories, which organized the interests of its members. One of these was called 'Fashion and Style', which by 2006 contained 34,127 public groups, all displaying 'some level of interest in fashion' (Thomas et al. 2007: 590). Indeed, Thomas and colleagues concluded their study by observing that 'the most common topic of discussion within the FashionLOVERS subgroup is personal style [… in which] many members of the community are anxious to share their own sense of fashion' (2007: 601).

Users' desire to engage with others by sharing their fashion interest online was also met through websites that facilitated outfit sharing. One of the earliest examples of this was a group on photo-sharing website Flickr called wardrobe_remix, created by Tricia Royal in September 2005. Initially described on the 'about' page as a 'DIY street fashion community', Royal thus directly addressed potential members of the group:

[I] believe the best stylists walk the streets, not the photo sets, nor the backstage of the runways. [T]he real style innovators are you and me: real, fashionable people, men and women alike. [H]ow do *you* put it together? [...] [W]hatever you wear, wherever it's [*sic*] source (designer, mass-market/high street, thrift/charity, handmade – it's ALL good): show us how you CREATIVELY put your everyday duds together! [P]ost your photograph in wardrobe_remix, and tell us about what you are wearing and why.

(Royal 2005)

Royal's words encapsulate the ethos of groups such as wardrobe_remix and others that peopled the Internet in subsequent years, such as ilikemystyle.net and LOOKBOOK.nu, both of which went live in 2008. That is, a celebration of the style of everyday people, with an emphasis on creativity, originality and individuality.

Whether membership was open or by invite-only, these sites published the self-taken photographs of users' daily outfits. Users could comment on the outfits of others, a practice that was, as with the contemporary style blogosphere, uniformly positive and affirming in tone. So much is apparent in an article on LOOKBOOK.nu published in 2009, in which one user was quoted as saying 'looks rarely attract negative commentary' and the kinds of comments 'top-rated pictures' received were gushing and uncritical ('"you're beautiful!" "gorgeous", "amazing!"') (Gardner 2009).

It is worth noting here that even though people were using the Internet in increasing number to connect with one another and write publicly about their similar interests (including fashion), traditional fashion media outlets scarcely had an online presence. One exception was the website Style.com, launched in September 2000 in partnership with fashion magazines American *Vogue* and *W* (Style.com 2012). At that time, Style.com reported on the events, shows and news of the fashion industry from an insider's perspective. It published almost-instantaneous reviews of the major fashion weeks as well as photographs of each look sent down the runway and offered a catalogue of images of top models, coverage of fashion parties and reportage on current trends and happenings in the fashion industry. In the words of former editor-in-chief Dirk Standen,

> [...] it opened up a fairly closed system to the world [...] it used to be only a few editors who went to those shows and they'd report on it three months later. Style.com wasn't alone here but it was first in that it did it in a very big way. It made everyone feel like a fashion insider [...] it opened it up in a way that makes everyone else feel like that they're kind of part of that world and have access to that world.
>
> (Grede 2011: 32)

The notion of 'insider-ness' is particularly important to a consideration of style blogs. Before the World Wide Web, information about fashion was largely – if not exclusively – reported by fashion magazines and critics writing for respected newspapers. The speed at which information was made available on Style.com was unprecedented, as was the visual catalogue of each look on the runway, not to mention the site's reach, accessible as it was to anyone with an Internet connection and a computer. This meant that not only could 'fashion obsessives' (Standen's characterization of the website's readership, Grede 2011: 32) read and see what was happening in the fashion industry that season, they could also gather information about what had been shown in past seasons.

In this way, a hitherto inaccessible stream of information became available for people with no prior access to fashion shows or studios: they could chart a designer's development from season to season on Style.com, and call to hand editorials from foreign *Vogues* at no cost on foto decadent. Moreover, they could then write about what they thought, liked and wanted to buy on tFS, and upload photographs of themselves interpreting fashion for themselves on wardrobe_remix. It was from this fertile ground that style blogs began to spring.

The short, passionate and close-knit history of personal style blogs

Although the development of personal style blogs was incremental, the moment at which they first crystallized as a distinct sub-genre was 2004–06. This was the moment when a number of blogs were created upon which bloggers not only wrote about fashion but also visually documented their personal style, and when the practice of 'what I wore' was taken from external sites and was embedded into a blogger's own site.

A number of these early personal style blogs have been very influential on the development of the genre and are recognized even beyond the style blogosphere. These include *Bryanboy*, which Filipino Bryan Grey-Yambao started in October 2004; the aforementioned *Style Bubble*, created by Susanna 'Susie Bubble' Lau in March 2006; and *Kingdom of Style*, the blog of Scottish 'Queens' Michelle Haswell and Marie Thomson, begun in August 2006. All of these blogs feature their bloggers displaying their dressed selves through outfit posts and writing about fashion and their style in the expressive, subjective manner particular to personal blogs. Of paramount importance on these early blogs, as well as those that followed them, were their blogger's personal style and their individual perspective on fashion as constituted in their own life; or at least that life as represented on the blogosphere.

While the focus of personal style blogs has remained constant throughout their short history, most can be categorized as being situated within one of the two distinct periods that have shaped the practice. I have termed these *first wave styling blogging* and *second wave style blogging*. The first wave began with the emergence of the first style blogs, an era that was succeeded towards the end of 2009 as widespread fashion and news media coverage saw a second wave of blogs emerge. These second wave blogs employed the same characteristics as first wave but with a significantly different aesthetic and a different underlying ethos. However, second wave did not entirely supersede first wave style blogging; rather, it came to be the dominant mode of style blogging. I developed this language of 'waves' after the four waves of feminism: both first and second wave style blogging saw a new ethos, new participants and, ultimately, a different manner of blogging sweeping through the blogosphere. Second wave style blogging, so widespread in its proliferation, with an aesthetic that has come to dominate the style blogosphere, also seemed to supersede what had come before and emphatically push it to the margins. Yet there are still first wave bloggers blogging now, and as such, the contemporary style blogosphere is composed of blogs from both waves. I will tease out dynamics of this in the remainder of this book. In the next section, I will outline the primary characteristics of these two waves to demonstrate that this is a medium whose make-up is contingent on the people doing the blogging and the opportunities and media coverage that are made available to them (and a particular 'them' at that).

First wave style blogging

Whilst there were certainly never any rules laid out by an organization or collection of bloggers about what they were seeking to do, or what style bloggers *should* be doing, in each wave there have been distinctive elements that have become characteristic of the practice. In first wave blogging, bloggers took the photographs for their outfit posts in the environs surrounding their homes, often in locations such as their living room, bedroom, backyard or even their workroom at fashion school, customarily using a tripod and their camera's timer to take their shots (see Figure 6). The outfits worn in these posts were assembled from an array of sources ranging from Etsy to thrift stores, high fashion labels (for some bloggers) and, more commonly, high street stores such as Forever 21 and American Apparel.[7] Style bloggers thus engaged in a kind of *bricolage*, to borrow from Lèvi-Strauss, making 'do with whatever [was] available whether perfect or imperfect, cheap or expensive, simple or elaborate' (quoted in Marion and Nairn 2011: 31) to craft creative performances of self. For Lèvi-Strauss, the process of assembling different components is dialogic, the meaning of the object depending on its role in the final combination, an aspect frequently evident in the dressed appearance of bloggers.

Here, as in second wave style blogging, style was a product of 'what they wore', and yet in first wave style blogging, the garment was not necessarily widely appreciated as stylish before a blogger wore it. The clothing worn in outfit posts was thus rendered stylish by being woven into a visually cohesive look by a blogger. So much is apparent in an outfit post by Tavi Gevinson, in which she poses in the backyard of her family home in Chicago wearing an outfit pieced together from a range of sources including Old Navy and Pamela Mann. Over the top, she tied a 'totally bonkerz blue basket cage thing' to her hip with twine, 'because last night I read an article about Gareth Pugh right before going to sleep and wanted to be all structured and reusing and stuff' (Gevinson, *Style Rookie,* 12 January 2009a).

This post exemplifies the qualities Lévi-Strauss identified as the characteristics of *bricolage*: a 'creative design process', shaped by a 'vaguely defined project determined by what is available and how it can be assembled', drawn from a finite array of materials redefined by their final combination (Marion and Nairn 2011: 32).

Of course, not all style bloggers of this period employed such a creative method of dressing, yet the principle of being inspired by a collection or editorial and interpreting it through clothes one could afford or already owned was characteristic of early style blogs. In first wave style blogging, having the means to acquire the luxury items that one desired was the exception rather than the rule. More common was to recreate a catwalk look, to make a DIY version of a desired item, or to explore the possibilities of combining various previously owned items with recently purchased ones. Moreover, outfit posts used to catalogue bloggers' daily outfits as opposed to displaying clothes specifically donned for the post's photo shoot, which has become the most common practice for second wave style bloggers, reflected in the other title by which these posts were known, 'what I wore'.

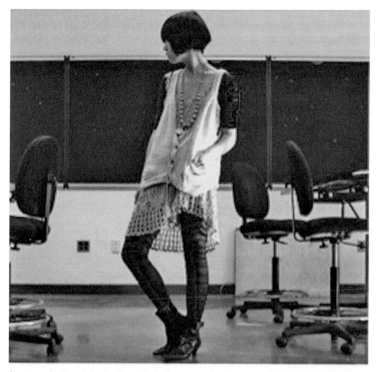

Figure 6: Art student Brooke Kao (*The Fashion Void That Is D.C.*) often posed for her outfit posts in her classroom studio, as seen in this post from 4 March 2009.

The cumulative effect of these characteristics – the *bricolage* outfits, the culture of adaptation, interpretation and DIY, and the photographs of outfits worn to school or work that day – imbued style blogs with an alternative aesthetic. They were the domain of creative, expressive (mostly) teenagers who photographed their mix 'n' match outfits as a means of expressing their interest in fashion and to perform their style from locations outside the traditional city centres of the fashion industry.

Style blogs at this time, then, were permeated by a sense of outsiders looking in – and not necessarily with the desire to be included. Rather, bloggers were having their own conversations about fashion and dressing their own style into view on a daily basis. The key concepts that the professional fashion media circulates each season – new trends, key pieces to invest in and so on – were absent from these sites, even as bloggers observed and commented upon the same collections upon which such seasonal mandates are based. Spiridakis likened these bloggers to the 'suburban girls with a craving for fashion [who] daydreamed via the pages of *Vogue*', language that underlines the distinction between this crop of fashion fans and those within the fashion media with traditional access to fashion (Spiridakis 2008).

Yet, first wave bloggers were not just positioned outside the fashion industry by virtue of their geographic location: they were also positioned as outsiders by the very activity of blogging itself. In the early days of fashion blogging, there was very little connection between the fashion industry and style bloggers. Blogs were widely perceived as an unknown entity, likened to the 'Wild West' by publicist Kelly Cutrone in 2008, and bloggers were more likely to be characterized by publicists as 'pesky' and 'lowly' than to be considered as legitimate communicators with a relevant point of view (see Ciarallo 2008). As such, bloggers were effectively writing from the side-lines. They were not people with journalism degrees or former industry professionals 'crossing over' onto a digital domain: they were amateurs, fans with a keen interest in fashion and a desire to share it, both visually and through their written content. Readers who enjoyed following blogs were inspired to start their own, the comments they left after the posts of others linking back to theirs. In this way, the style blogosphere gradually grew, seeming, like Bachelard's forest, to 'accumulate infinity within its own boundaries' (1994: 186).

Second wave style blogging

The period from late 2008 to mid–2010 can be understood as the threshold between first and second wave style blogging. The aforementioned news media coverage of style blogs from the Spring/Summer Ready-to-Wear season in 2009 had an ongoing ripple effect. Niche fashion publications such as *POP* and *LOVE* published features on style bloggers (see *POP* Issue 21, 2009 and *Love* Issue 2, 2009), and bloggers were increasingly offered opportunities from parties within the fashion industry. In 2009, Susie Lau was engaged to be the commissioning editor for Dazed Digital, the website of *Dazed* magazine, based on the quality of her blog's content, and Texan blogger Jane Aldridge was invited to the Crillon Ball at the recommendation of American *Vogue* and *Teen Vogue* (see Goto 2013; Aldridge 2009b). In 2010, Tavi Gevinson blogged about the Haute Couture shows in Paris for *POP* (Hintz-Zambrano 2010).

This time also marked the beginning of lucrative opportunities for bloggers to collaborate with established fashion brands: Jane Aldridge, whose style blog *Sea of Shoes* details her extensive shoe collection, designed a range of shoes for American retailer Urban Outfitters, and independent t-shirt company Borders and Frontiers invited a select number of fashion and style bloggers to design t-shirts, which were then advertised in the sidebar of their respective blogs (see Aldridge 2009a; O'Carroll 2009). These examples represent just some of the commercial opportunities being made available to certain bloggers as fashion publications and labels started to recognize style blogs as a platform for reaching potential customers.

Significantly, opportunities such as these changed the way that blogs were predominantly portrayed, at least by the mainstream media. The tone of the coverage evolved from surprise at the abilities, activity and age of bloggers to asserting their position and platform as tastemakers. The shift is perceptible in the language employed in the following two examples from the *New York Times*. In 2008 Elizabeth Spiridakis wrote that '[t]hey might not be able to drive yet, but their fashion sense is so incredible, it's actually intimidating [...] as an almost-30-year-old style blogger myself, I have to ask: Whom will I envy next? Kindergartners?' (Spiridakis 2008). By 2011, the newspaper announced that 'once considered fashion-obsessed amateurs, style bloggers have matured into tastemakers and savvy marketers who can command four- and five-figure fees from brands' (Kurutz 2011).

Of course, the terms first wave and second wave style blogging are not prescriptive: there is crossover between these phases. There are bloggers who started their blogs in the first wave whose work has gradually come to showcase more of a second wave ethos – Rumi Neely of *fashiontoast* and Jane Aldridge of *Sea of Shoes* are two such examples. Both now blog full-time, display advertisements on their blogs, have both collaborated with mainstream and niche fashion labels (including Forever 21, Urban Outfitters, RVCA and Gryphon between them) and, as evident in Figure 7, have developed a style of outfit posting that is less closely aligned with the 'when, where, how' of their outfits and more closely resembles the glamour of a fashion editorial spread.

By the same token, there are bloggers who started blogging during or after the transitional threshold of late 2008 to mid-2010 whose blogs embody many of the qualities inherent in first wave blogs. An example of this is *A Curious Fancy*, a style blog started in 2010 by Ragini Nag Rao, an Indian blogger who wrote in her first post that she's 'crap at following trends and just tend to follow my own script in my head' (2010). Ragini uploads outfit posts documenting what she wore that day, usually a mix of high street and vintage clothing that she styles into an outfit that speaks to her 'somewhat loli inspired and mostly theatrical' taste in clothes (Nag Rao 2010, see Figure 8).[8]

Marking the difference between these two movements, then, is not necessarily when they were started but the ethos underpinning the blog. The mentality of seeing a blog as an opportunity to generate income, as an online *curriculum vita* or to establish a professional platform as an authority on style (as well as a kind of celebrity status) is one that proliferated post-2009. It is a subtle distinction, and one best articulated by Danielle Meder when she blogged that rather than doing as she and her peers did, '[spending] years eking out small niches, figuring out the conventions of a new medium without a rule book, and investing time into things that seemed impossible to develop a living out of' (2011), these bloggers were able to log on to a field whose conventions had already been pioneered and to make a profit from it. The subtext to their emergence was an awareness of the commercial opportunities and fame blogging could afford. As Meder noted in that same post, Tavi Gevinson 'represents the end of an era when it was still possible to start a blog without ulterior motivations. Her guilelessness is un-calculated – her memedom is unintentional, and she is just as ambivalent, as she is ambitious' (2011).

Meder was here contrasting Gevinson to Bebe Zeva, a style blogger from Las Vegas, Nevada who started blogging in October 2010. In a profile by the *New York Times*, Zeva

Figure 7: Jane wears a vintage '50s skirt layered with a crinoline, Stuart Weitzmann heels and a Dolce and Gabbana bag. Her post does not detail where she wore this outfit, although she describes wearing it often: 'sometimes you need that drama!' (Aldridge, *Sea of Shoes*, 6 May 2016).

Figure 8: Ragini writes that her excited anticipation of her first proper Christmas in years prompted her to '[prance] around with some tinsel in the front yard today afternoon' (Nag Rao, A *Curious Fancy*, 11 December 2014).

discussed her 'personal brand' and was quoted as saying that, in terms of style, she was 'trying to create a new cliché for the next generation to imitate' (Lorentzen 2011). This stands in direct contrast to Gevinson's own reflection on style and blogging, posted in 2009:

> [t]he idea of being a mad eccentric who is constantly slipping into different skins is so appealing to me. I started this blog because I wanted to explore my style. Now I have more of an idea of what it is and will just continue to try and apply it every day.
>
> (Gevinson 2009)

The fluidity of identity inherent in Gevinson's post recalls Rocamora's work on the self becoming on style blogs, as bloggers undertake an ongoing 'identity performance', which, Rocamora argues, is supported on fashion blogs by 'dress's performative quality' (2011: 411). Style blogs become a space for the display of the self in a particular moment, a lived lookbook of personal style always in the process of becoming. The Butlerian idea of a performative self that is constantly constituted through actions is one I will take up in some detail in Chapter Four, as I argue that one's dressed identity, or personal style, is ever becoming through the intimate and everyday process of donning certain clothing, and as a corollary for style bloggers, as they perform that dressed self for their readers through outfit posts. For now, it is worth noting that the intimacy this quotidian process engenders between bloggers and their readers as 'a portrait of [a blogger] emerges' (Rocamora 2011: 412) is subverted, and problematically so, in second wave blogging by the marriage, in blogged content, of 'self and sales pitch' (Banet-Weiser and Sturken, quoted in Luvaas 2013: 57). For example, rather than being comprised of a creative *bricolage* of their own closets, the outfits that second wave bloggers post often conform to the fashionable aesthetic of the season, as styled in their own taste. It is often difficult to discern the provenance of these clothes – whether the blogger purchased them, called them in for their shoot or were gifted them by a label's PR representation – as it is rarely clarified by second wave bloggers, engendering a problematic ambiguity for readers who observe them as clad in a world of fashion that is apparently their oyster.

This is not to characterize second wave bloggers as solely interested in fame or exploring the opportunities for generating income and receiving free product from PR companies. However, prior to this time, even the possibility of blogging with an eye for the opportunities that became increasingly a part of blogging post-2009 was inconceivable. Not only were the characteristics of style blogging in place – outfit posts, a language that blended everyday personal narrative of one's life with thoughts on fashion and style – the genre was now on the map in terms of growing recognition of what style blogs were, what they offered in terms of commercial opportunities for brands and the ways in which bloggers could be engaged to monetize their audience.

If first wave style blogging was characterized by independence, second wave style blogging is characterized by aspiration. As noted by Danielle Meder, there was a 'gold rush' aspect to second wave blogging, in that second wave bloggers 'weren't necessarily as enchanted with the format as a creative medium, than as one that seemed like an easy route to attention [and] cash' (Meder 2013, personal communication). The ways in which second wave blogs differ from first wave blogs are numerous and subtle, and mostly stem from the blogger's desire to be seen as an aspirational figure. It is a shift away from sharing to showing, from an inclusive, collaborative display of individuality to the display of a particular kind of fashionability and prestige.

This shift is also evident in the sites connected with style blogging that began to gain prominence after this time. One of these is Independent Fashion Bloggers (IFB), a site at which style bloggers can create an account to promote their blog to other bloggers as well as read articles on fashion and style blogging written by the IFB team, all of whom have their own blog. Although the articles on IFB range in topic, many share the central theme of offering fashion and style bloggers tips and advice on how to improve their blogs: that is, how to gain more followers, how to professionalize their content and how to develop a more consistent brand.[9] This mentality – that there is a quantifiable list of things a blogger can do to improve their blog – is second wave. It is a perspective that perceives readers as potential 'uniques' (unique visitors), useful not necessarily for their capacity as an invested readership but as means to a monetized end.

Another second wave aspect of the blogosphere was the launch of commercial, invite-only blogging platforms, none of which are currently active. These platforms hosted the blogs of certain selected 'top tier' bloggers – often those with a large number of readers and a certain commercially viable yet still aspirational aesthetic – and acted as their PR representatives to sell advertising space on their blogs and garner them invitations to international fashion weeks and exclusive industry events. Some examples of these were Now Manifest (2011–2015), which hosted top-rated style blogs such as *fashiontoast, Bryanboy* and *Style by Kling* among others, and Australian network Fellt, which was established in 2012 and originally showcased eight blogs, of which six were style blogs (for further discussion of these platforms, see Chapter 3).

What was unmistakable on the blogs of Now Manifest and Fellt was their conformity to the contemporary idea of the fashionable figure: the bloggers hosted were uniformly youthful, slender and conventionally attractive, and they dressed almost exclusively in clothing by designer labels. These bloggers were not representative of the style blogosphere as a whole, but they embodied the characteristics of the model second wave blogger: beautifully dressed and thus both admired by their readers and acknowledged by the mainstream fashion media, enjoying access to industry events such as fashion weeks and parties thrown by fashion labels, receiving gifted product from niche and luxury labels and, ultimately, making a living whilst so doing.

Style blogging has thus undergone a rapid transformation, metamorphosing from a cluster of experimental, independent blogs celebrating individuality and creativity into a blogosphere where bloggers are routinely granted media passes for international fashion weeks, partake in collaborations with fashion labels and lent or gifted hundreds (and in some cases, thousands) of dollars' worth of clothes to shoot for their blog. However, it is important to note that style blogs did not emerge fully-formed in their current iteration, but were the incremental work of many people, blogging about their own interest in fashion and style and discovering, like Danielle Meder, that they weren't the only one out there.

Notes

1   For examples of early news media coverage of fashion blogs, see Zamiatin (2006), Dodes (2006) and Style (2008). There were a multitude of articles published on the attendance and prominent seating of bloggers at the Spring/Summer RTW season of 2009, on media outlets from newspapers (*New York Times*) to fashion magazines (US *InStyle*) to websites (Mediaite). For an overview and a log of hyperlinks to a number of such stories, see Kamer (2009).

2   This is true for members of the fashion media, who compete with one another for access and authority in fashion knowledge. However, for a number of other guests, there are a range of concerns at play beyond seeing and being seen. A fashion buyer, for example, is invited to view the collection presented to gain insight into the designer's vision for that season, to see how the clothes are styled and to get a feel for what they might order in their buying appointment. A public relations (PR) representative, on the other hand, is there to support the label (as their client), ensuring that guests at the show are satisfied and that all runs smoothly. That said, to be present at all indicates that you are a player in the industry of some importance, at least to that showing label.

3   It is important to note here that it is bloggers themselves who label their blogs as fatshion, rather than just calling them style blogs. See Hughes (2011) for blogger Hayley Hughes's personal discussion of this.

4   I write 'traditionally' because at the time of writing, fatshion blogging seems to be in a state of transformation from its political origins to a 'glossier' blogosphere, as has occurred with the style blogosphere at large. For discussion of this, see Faircloth (2013).

5   As of May 2016, Typepad pricing ranged from US$8.95 to $49.95 per month depending on the package selected. This price is all-inclusive, as opposed to blogging from a hosting site, which would require the purchase of a domain name, the payment of a commercial server to host your blog and any other costs incurred in hiring a web designer or learning to code.

6   Unless otherwise attributed, all subsequent quotes from Meder and Fredrickson are taken from the following interviews: Danielle Meder (blogger of *Final Fashion*), in discussion with the author over Skype, June 2012; Julie Fredrickson (blogger of *Almost Girl*), in written communication with the author (e-mail), February 2013.

7   Etsy is an online marketplace where users sell handmade, crafted or vintage goods.

8   'Loli' is a term derived from anime and manga subculture. It refers to something that is young and/or cute, and is specifically linked in anime subculture to the look of pre-teenage girls, also known as 'lolita'.

9   For examples of some such articles, see Jennine Jacob, 10 April 2013a and 29 April 2013b; and Jess Estrada, 28 August 2013.

Chapter 2

Blogging the Bedroom

As I kept *Fashademic*, I often felt I was building or weaving rather than recording or journaling. I would write posts on diverse aspects of my experiences of being a Ph.D. student interested in fashion, which meant that the scope of my blog's content was quite eclectic. The openness of the form allowed me to move between a post musing on the ethics of online shopping, to a discussion of Susan Sontag's *On Photography*, to sharing photographs of myself posing in front of a brick wall 'in which I look surprised for no particular reason but the colours in the bricks somehow do nice things to the colours in my hair' (Findlay, *Fashademic*, 8 March 2012b).

I was building, then, a map of the range and tumble of my thoughts as I wrote them out, off the cuff and with little editing; weaving, as I drew my disparate interests into one cohesive fabric of contemplation and presentation that stretched down the webpage and back through my archive. I wrote about certain aspects of my life but did so through poetic prose or rhapsodized about new designer collections through the haze of my own desire to wear them. Unifying the content that I posted was my own self – what I will argue is an emergent authorial 'I' – so my blog was as much about me, as I performed myself through my posts, as my subject matter.

It is little wonder, then, that during their brief history, there has been a struggle to categorize personal style blogs, both in academia and the fashion media. They are somewhat of a textual anomaly, a hybrid of content about a blogger's life and interests worked into an ongoing narrative, blended with semi-critical content reflecting a blogger's own tastes and opinions. In some ways, blogs' focus on individual perspective and vernacular written content renders them akin to journals, a comparison frequently made in academic literature on this medium (see Scheidt 2006; Hodkinson 2007; Karlsson 2007). Yet, the particularities of style blogs – for example, the way the distinction between aestheticized self and everyday narrative is frequently blurred – require us to find a language to account for the dimensions of the practice not addressed by this comparison.

This chapter will illuminate these dimensions, such as the tension between public and private at work throughout a style blog's content and the tangentially reciprocal nature of the relationship between bloggers and their readers. The relational aspect of blogging intimated here allows for what I think is a more fitting, albeit an initially more strange comparison: that style blogs can be conceived of as bedrooms.

Style blogs as bedrooms

Rebecca Blood wrote that although blogs were originally a site at which people could curate and commentate upon material found on the Internet, they have come to resemble a kind of 'short-form journal' (2000). This is echoed by Rocamora and Bartlett, who define blogs as 'the regular publication – often daily – on the Internet, of short texts recounting various episodes of daily life and the thoughts of an individual in the manner of a personal journal' (2009: 106). Rocamora and Bartlett's definition articulates the similarities between personal blogs and journals: that is, both are comprised of written, chronological and anecdotal recounts of the personal and quotidian experiences of their author.

Aside from the similarities in content and writing style between style blogs and journals, the historical precedent of platforms such as MySpace and LiveJournal may also explain the frequent comparison of journals and personal blogs. These platforms made it possible for users to keep actual online journals of their everyday lives, often recorded in great detail (with photographs as well as text) regardless of the public accessibility inherent in the form itself. Implicit in this practice is a blurring between public and private: the kinds of personal revelatory thoughts, opinions and feelings that were traditionally kept under lock and key are, as Emily Nussbaum relates in her article on LiveJournal, now only 'a Google search away' (2007: 1).

However, despite this provenance, the textual form of journals implies an unrestrained disclosure of information that rarely occurs on style blogs. Rather, bloggers write about fashion and style as it pertains to them, as focused through the lens of their own perspective. Their content is a blend of self and fashion, which literally converges in a blogger's dressed appearance but is also evident in other ways. When significant aspects of bloggers' lives are mentioned, they are often introduced through a relation to fashion. An example of this is evident in Isabel Slone's post about curating a 'meaningful wardrobe', which she introduced by discussing her experiences of depression:

> [i]t is easy to flop around life aimlessly, hoping that things suddenly present themselves to you in a neat, tidy and sensible fashion. But when you've floundered so long that you can barely breathe, instead you must grasp on to all the sense you can, sewing together some meaning out of some fishing line and the utterly random patchwork of jagged edges that comprise your life.

> Depression, at least for me, is like swimming in a wave pool [...] It doesn't always matter what kind of bathing suit you're wearing because it's not going to stop the waves from crashing all around [...] but clothing is your scales, fur, exoskeleton, whatever. Clothing is the first layer of armor you present to the world. What you wear is the version of yourself you want everyone else to see, though there have been more than a few times I could barely muster the energy to put on socks let alone do some colour blocking.
>
> (Slone, *Hipster Musings*, 2011a)

Isabel metaphorically employs fashion a number of ways in this post to illustrate her experience for her readers. There is the initial wordplay of 'fashion' as a manner or mode rather than the style or system of dress, followed by her allusion to the personal labour inherent in her efforts to make sense of her experience through the sewing metaphors she invokes (using fishing line to sew, patchwork of jagged edges). These also demonstrate her struggle to make what feels imperfect and rough cohere in a 'neat, tidy and sensible fashion', another metaphor drawn from cloth.

As she progresses into a more literal discussion of her everyday experiences of depression, Isabel relates her feelings to getting dressed, presumably to move her topic into a realm her readers will themselves be familiar with, as well as one that is linked to the premise of her blog – that it is a personal style blog. She touches here on a foundational concept in fashion theory – that clothing is a visual articulation of one's inner self, making aspects of personal identity visible to the world – while situating her explanation in her personal experience. As such, she tells her readers that fashion cannot stop how she feels ('it doesn't always matter what kind of bathing suit you wear because it's not going to stop the waves from crashing all around'), that it falls short of even its functionality at times when she 'could barely muster the energy to put on socks let alone do some colour blocking' (Slone 2011a).[1]

Evident here is the manner in which a style blog's content differs significantly from a journal: it may be focused on the personal life and perspective of a blogger, but it is reframed and discussed through fashion rather than being written as an unfolding narrative of a blogger's personal life. This is a genre for the exploration and performance of individual style, couched in the private lives of bloggers but explored publicly in a specific way.

While Isabel's blog was a first wave style blog, the practice of sharing personal experience through the lens of one's style is also evident on second wave blogs. In April 2015, Australian blogger Nicole Warne (*Gary Pepper*) announced to her readers that she and her long-time boyfriend (who is also her blog's photographer) were engaged. The post, 'Serendipity', tells the story of his proposal: the couple had been shooting an outfit post shoot on a lake in Tokyo, and as Nicole writes, she heard

> [...] Luke say 'I just want to take one more photo underneath this tree before we head back'. We glided underneath one of the biggest cherry blossom trees on the lake, I hear Luke call my name, I turn around, and he's holding a ring saying the words 'Will you marry me?'
>
> (Warne, *Gary Pepper*, 26 April 2015)

The photographs at the top of the post show Nicole in the boat under the cherry blossom trees, wearing a floaty white dress. In the third of these photographs she is smiling over her shoulder at the camera, allowing us to see her from Luke's perspective, ostensibly moments before he proposed. In this way, even though what we read is a recount, there is a sense for readers of sharing this moment with Nicole and Luke, of being implicated in absentia as they were in the process of shooting an outfit post for this very blog. The centrality of personal style in telling this story – and framing the proposal itself – offers another example of the imbrication of personal storytelling and fashion at work on style blogs.

What we also see in this example is the kind of dynamic co-habitation that occurs in the space between a blogger and their readers. This is a medium in which a reading public is a possibility inherent in the very form. The presence of a readership is invoked as an idea by bloggers in the text of their blogs, as well as less directly in the comment function enabled in most blogs, allowing readers to respond to posts and leave a link to their own blog for subsequent commenters or the original blogger to click. Moreover, the amount of readers a style blog regularly attracts directly affects the kinds of promotional opportunities in which a blogger may be approached to participate.

This is reflected in the content of the articles regularly published by the website Independent Fashion Bloggers (IFB), such as 'Five tips on how to set traffic goals' which advises readers that 'higher traffic on your blog means a greater possibility of making your blog a self-sustaining business' (Burcz 2012). Or, in the words of John Jannuzzi, then-contributing digital editor at *Lucky* magazine and manager of their blogger network Style Collective, 'if you can deliver the impressions, you can play the game' (Bazilian 2012).

In light of the specialized nature of the content on style blogs and the presence of readers, style blogs are better conceptualized as liminal places regularly and temporarily inhabited by bloggers and their readers. These are places that bloggers adorn with images that inspire them and at which they display goods that they covet and/or own. Blogs are inscribed with their very presence, both by the images of themselves that they post and in their writing on their lives as told through the lens of fashion. Moreover, these spaces have a threshold that readers are perpetually invited to cross, engaging with a blogger and temporarily inhabiting a space of their making. For these reasons, style blogs can be likened to bedrooms: privileged and personal spaces for dressing up and hanging out.

Girls, intimacy and virtual bedroom culture

The notion that online spaces can be conceived of as bedrooms is not new. Julian Sefton-Green and David Buckingham first introduced the concept of a 'digital bedroom' in 1998 to describe the physical location of the cyber play of most children: a computer in the only personal space that was theirs, their bedroom. Sandra Weber expands upon this concept, arguing that even when the computer is not located within the actual bedroom of a child, digital space can still be conceptualized as a 'bedroom', in that it is a private space accessed from a computer situated within the familial home (2007: 63).

Jacqueline Reid-Walsh and Claudia Mitchell expanded the concept of digital bedrooms in their own study of girls' websites, arguing that this technology offers girls a means to create 'semiprivate places of creativity and sociality, and to enact a personal, social "virtual bedroom culture'" (2004: 174). They observed that girls would adorn the 'walls' of their websites with the same popular culture artefacts that would be found in their bricks-and-mortar bedrooms, their digital sites thus reflecting the appearance of their material rooms.

It is worth noting here that both the studies of Sefton-Green and Buckingham, and Reid-Walsh and Mitchell were concerned with children, whereas personal style bloggers range widely in age. Yet these studies raise some interesting points that are also applicable here: the significance of the location of the computer within the home, traditionally conceptualized as a place of privacy and leisure, and the ways that this affects the content created as well as the blurring between public and private that is at work in personal blogs and websites. These are ideas that will be taken up throughout this chapter.

Young people's employment of personal places to socialize with peers as well as play with identity and engage with culture was being written about well before the advent of the so-called 'Digital Age'. Even by introducing the term 'virtual bedroom culture', Reid-Walsh and Mitchell are alluding to the first of such studies, McRobbie and Garber's seminal research into girls' subcultures in Britain in 1976. McRobbie and Garber argued that the girls of their study created alternative spaces in which to enact feminine subcultures, due to their exclusion from as well as the perceived risks of entering into the mainstream of male-dominated subcultural lives. The subcultures that McRobbie and Garber focused on operated within girls' homes and those of their friends, and specifically 'within the confines of girls' bedrooms' (2000: 16). They suggested that this emplacement was due to the expansion of leisure industries in the mid-twentieth century, specifically those targeted at teenagers, which gave rise to goods that could be consumed in girls' bedrooms. While these goods (cosmetics, clothing) were intended to be worn outside the home also, 'the rituals of trying on clothes, and experimenting with hair styles and make-up were home-based activities' (16).

McRobbie and Garber also read this specific emplacement of feminine subcultural activity in part as a response to the perceived dangers of the street. Writing specifically about pre-teen girls, they observed that 'girls have access to less freedom than their brothers. Because they are deemed to be more at risk on the streets from attack, assault, or even abduction, parents tend to be more protective of their daughters than they are of their sons' (2000: 23). Girls negotiated these parameters to form a distinctive culture of their own that was 'recognised by and catered to in the girls' weekly comics and magazines' (22), a culture that could be participated in from the safe enclosure of their bedrooms. McRobbie and Garber referred to this as 'the culture of the bedroom', arguing that the bedroom – a 'potentially awkward and anonymous space' – is thus 'transformed into a site of active feminine identity' (24).

This idea is taken up by media studies theorist Siân Lincoln in her ethnography of the private spaces of teenage girls in the late 1990s. For the girls of her study, the bedroom was simultaneously a resting place in which they were 'able to gain privacy from parents and siblings alike', a meeting place between the girls and their peers, and biographical space that '[told] stories of [their] youth cultural interests and, ultimately, cultural identity' (2004: 95–96). For them, as for the girls of McRobbie and Garber's study, the bedroom operated as a locus of rest and respite, although Lincoln is careful to stipulate that the retreat of the girls she was studying was not necessarily spurred by the danger of sexual harassment on the street. Rather, she frames their bedrooms as sites for the construction of personal cultural histories, as girls would prepare for a night out from within their rooms as well as decorate them with tokens indicative of their lived experience and personal taste.

Lincoln intimates that while these rooms also operate as sites of seclusion and recreation, their being such does not derive from a culture of exclusion but from girls' own choice. As their bedrooms were 'often the only space within the home that is personal, personalized and intimate', she argues that the girls she studied would retreat there to freely do and be in ways that they could not in other places (2004: 95). Their rooms offered the possibility of transformable, expressive space within a demarcated place, a function that closely resembles the ways in which style bloggers employ their blogs. Although McRobbie and Garber make a strong case for the emergence of bedroom culture as a practice born from subcultural exclusion and perceived danger, the contemporary iteration of bedroom culture also stems from the possibilities offered by bedrooms that are otherwise unavailable to girls: a personal space that is theirs and theirs only.

Consistent between these two studies is the separation of these girls' bedrooms from the rest of their social-life worlds. Here are personalized, delineated places that offer the possibility of self-expression, identity-play and rest for the girls who inhabit them. Yet the historical protection afforded by a bedroom is a notion that is somewhat inverted when we consider style blogs as the metaphoric bedrooms of the Internet.

Yet it is no great stretch to perceive them as such. As with the bedrooms of the girls of these previous studies, style blogs are personalized spheres of self-performance upon which bloggers congregate, exchange information and ideas with like-minded peers, and shape different identities through their personal style. Style bloggers, too, try on clothes and seek the opinions of others to affirm their choices. They experiment with their appearance and engage with culture (here, specifically a culture of fashion and style) as it interests them, and create 'haven[s] of memorabilia that represent their role in social-life worlds' (Lincoln 2004: 102): that is, as a blogger with an interest in fashion and personal style.

Indeed, as Katherine George observes in her wider discussion about cyberfeminism, fashion blogging allows 'modern women to express themselves in revolutionary ways via a medium that exists within their traditional sphere of comfort and control, the home' (2009: 14). The most apparent reason for style blogging's intimate emplacement within the home seems to be the way in which it developed: as a hobby, an amateur activity. It is unlikely that most early bloggers would have had alternative spaces available to them from which to blog, in keeping with the limited access girls have traditionally had to places to freely inhabit and privately socialize beyond their bedroom (see McRobbie and Garber 2000; Lincoln 2004; Reid-Walsh and Mitchell 2004). Here, the circumstances of writing have in some way dictated the development of elements now characteristic to the genre.

As discussed in the previous chapter, much of the content blogged in first wave style blogging was created out of bloggers' homes: photographs were taken with a personal camera set up on a tripod or shot by a friend or boyfriend of outfits pulled from their personal wardrobes.[2] Domestic locations were conducive to collating such posts more quickly and with less difficulty than travelling to an alternative location, which is no small concern when many bloggers would have been unable to drive and would in all likelihood have had other demands placed on their time (such as school attendance and homework, or the requirements of their job). This is reflected in the experience of Rosalind Jana (*Clothes, Cameras and Coffee*) who told me during our interview that the frequency of her blogging had recently gone down because she was 'just so overworked' and that blogging is a matter of balancing her time: 'it's like I set aside a block of time for it, so I've got my homework, or I've got seeing friends, and I've got "today I need to do a blog post"' (Jana, in conversation with the author, 2011b). She conducts most of her outfit post photo shoots in the countryside surrounding her home in rural England, often having her photographs taken by one of her parents or friends.

Of course, there are other parallels between style blogging and girls' bedroom culture. Just as the girls in the 1970s read fashion magazines like *Jackie* and engaged in 'rituals of trying on clothes and experimenting with hairstyles and make-up' (McRobbie and Garber 2000: 16), so too do style bloggers share editorial spreads from magazines and lookbooks of labels they like and 'try on' clothes in their outfit posts, often asking readers what they think. In a post titled 'Spring Maille', Australian blogger Margaret Zhang asks her readers:

> [h]ow would you wear this baby? When Spring *actually* rolls around, I'm thinking a pair of white leather shorts and white leather cap would be perfect, capiche?
>
> (*Shine by Three*, 2012a, original emphasis)

In a way, it is immaterial how Margaret's readers would wear the lavender knit she is asking about; they do not own it – she does. Her question pushes them to consider the garment, consider Margaret in it and to conceptually style her. Their contributions are given room in the comments section of this post, and yet whether or not she publishes a follow-up incorporating their suggestions into her outfit is Margaret's choice. This is her space; and not only is she showing it to us, she is showing herself through her style, speaking in the tone of a friend sharing her thoughts, interests and the aspects of life that she chooses to divulge.

The intimacy of this exchange is inherent in the mode of address of style bloggers, which is customarily familiar albeit in differing ways according to the personality of individual bloggers. In this instance, Margaret employs hyperbole in her writing ('withholding this knitted lavender brilliance from the world would have been absolutely inconceivable'), before asking her readers how they would style the vest, and signing off with her then-signature '*love* xx' (Zhang 2012a).

Another example is where blogger Leandra Medine advises her readers on how to style their outfits to 'man repel'; that is, 'outfitting oneself in a sartorially offensive mode that may result in repelling members of the opposite sex' (*Man Repeller*, 25 April 2010). In 'Know your onion', she posted tongue-in-cheek step-by-step instructions that directly addressed her readers alongside photographs of her increasingly layered outfit. Accompanying step three, for example, she wrote, '[n]ow it's a lesson in layering and mixing prints. Pair small over big to maintain the subtle curves indigenous to your gender. Sleeve peeks are hip. So are hearts that can see' (Medine, *Man Repeller*, 2012b, see Figure 9). The post had generated 133 comments at the time of writing, all of a uniformly effusive character, thanking Leandra for the post and engaging chattily with different aspects of it.

These posts represent just two examples of the kinds of sociality bloggers instigate on the style blogosphere, and although these two posts are very different in tone and content (in keeping with the individualized content of style blogs) each demonstrates the continuity between style blogs and prior discussions of girls' subcultural activity. Here, the dressed

Figure 9: An image from Leandra Medine's guide to dressing like a 'Fall onion' on *Man Repeller*, 2012b.

appearance of individual bloggers is presented and discussed, both by the bloggers themselves in their posts and by their readers in the comments section, an exchange of the kind that has long been the material of girl-to-girl homosocial exchanges in the 'personal, personalized and intimate' places of their bedrooms (Lincoln 2004: 95).

The desire to connect with people with a similar interest in fashion and style was often brought up in interviews by style bloggers as one of the reasons why they started blogging. This excitement is evident in Danielle Meder's description of how she felt at first discovering blogs.

> I was like 'oh wow, I've been looking for this medium my whole life' because [...] I always feel like I have a lot to say and I have a lot to express visually as well, and I never had the space to do that before. I would try to share the things that interested me with the people that were around me, you know, my classmates at fashion school or my boyfriend at the time and for the most part I found that people don't find the kinds of things I find interesting interesting.
>
> (Meder 2012)

Despite being a student at fashion school in Toronto, it was only through blogging that Danielle found people who shared her particular interests in fashion.

> After a time I started to find some like-minded friends, in the States mostly, who were also interested in fashion from more of a philosophical, theoretical perspective, and for the first time in my life I experienced the kind of affinity you get when you find people who are interested in the same things that you are.
>
> (Meder, in conversation with the author, 2012)

This was an experience echoed by Kayla Telford-Brock, who started her blog, *The F Tangent*, in April 2011.[3] Like Danielle, she described feeling as though there was a lack of people she could talk with about fashion the way she wished to.

> There was really no-one I could spend hours on end talking to about a runway show or about a new collection or about a ridiculous desire to buy an expensive dress that I would probably only get one wear [out] of but that had completely compelled me in a vintage store. I didn't really feel like I had anyone that I could talk to about that kind of thing and so [starting *The F Tangent*] was kind of a way just to go out and see that there were other people who did spend that amount of time thinking about and playing with fashion and style.
>
> (Telford-Brock, in conversation with the author, 2012)

The aspects of fashion that compelled Danielle and Kayla were specific, derived from their personal taste and curiosities, and a desire to explore these in discussion with like-minded people. These are not the kinds of perspectives commonly printed in fashion publications nor would such publications allow for the exercise and development of a personal engagement with fashion history and its convergence with contemporary design (Danielle) or for camaraderie over finding a perfect and perfectly impractical vintage dress (Kayla). Yet these are the kinds of topics that have proliferated on the style blogosphere, as bloggers have written 'stories [of their] cultural interests and [...] cultural identit[ies]' (Lincoln 2004: 96).

Furthermore, doing so can lead to affirmation of one's own interests, as described by Kayla, for whom the most exciting thing about style blogging was 'just to see that there were other people who did spend that kind of time, who didn't feel like it was wasted time', remarking that she felt this 'validated' her choices (Telford-Brock, in conversation with the author, 2012). This is reminiscent of the freedom inherent in the sites of girls' bedrooms as the privileged spaces of style blogs facilitate sociality between bloggers and their readers through a common interest; in this case, fashion and an individual's style. boyd explains this aspect of online interactivity as the outworking of a desire of young people to engage publicly despite their limited access to public space; here online space, like material place, is constituted by sites at which young women write themselves and their community into being (2007: 13–21). Style blogs, then, are best conceptualized as sites that are both public and private, that are intimate and enclosed as well as fluid and social.

Hanging in Tavi's bedroom

One of the first things Tavi shares on this day in February is a photograph of her bedroom floor. This messy portion of her room is not so much inhabited by Tavi as scrawled all over by her, dressed as it is with belongings seemingly cast down by the vortex of her teenage energy. The accompanying prose crowds around the image as if she hardly took a breath whilst writing it:

> I have been a little busy pretending to clean my room but actually listening to the Pixies [...] I cannot see my floor. Except in a couple places, that I have memorized in my head, so I know where to step in case of fire hazard/when I get up in the middle of the night and my lights are out and I can't see anything and I'm on my way to the bathroom when my Spock bobblehead randomly says 'You are being highly illogical' and I freak out.
>
> (Gevinson, *Style Rookie*, 10 February 2010)

I could be quoting from any girl's diary, or penfriend's letter, but despite their personal, informal content, the excerpt above was not taken from a private correspondence between Tavi and myself, but from a post published when Tavi was thirteen years old. And it wasn't just me reading, of course; in October 2010, only eight months after this was published, *The Huffington Post* reported that her blog, *Style Rookie*, was attracting an average of 54,000 daily hits (Epstein 2010). That's 54,000 people who checked back to read about the 'creepy homage' to Bob Dylan Tavi displayed in her room, and the afternoon she spent with Tommy Ton, the fashion photographer behind the hugely influential street style blog *Jak&Jil*, who was flown by *Vogue Paris* to her home in the suburbs of Chicago to shoot her for an upcoming issue (see *Style Rookie*, 10 February 2010).

In this example we are able to witness one of the complex processes that make style blogging a compelling object of analysis: here we experience Tavi as situated within her home, presumably writing this post from the very bedroom that she describes for us. At the same time, her online iteration of self virtually inhabits the space of her blog as she writes herself into view. In this same moment we, her public, metaphorically cross the threshold of her home to inhabit an intimate space with her, as facilitated by her blog, functioning here as her online 'home'. This intimacy works both ways: Tavi is making herself visible to us by recounting the recent events of her life whilst we draw into an intimate proximity to her as we learn more about her through this post – there is her bedroom, and here she is at Paris Fall Couture Week with her father in tow in one photograph and having a tête-à-tête with former head designer of Christian Dior, John Galliano, in another. As readers, we encounter Tavi through this edit of her life written out of her place into her space.

This connection between place and space is one of the primary ways in which style blogs can be considered digital analogues of bedrooms.[4] Here we see Tavi swinging on her backyard swing, sitting on the stone steps of her home and doing the activity that brought her to public attention in the first place, writing her blog on her bed. At the same time, Tavi's bedroom is recreated on-screen as we see photographs of her floor and desk, and read about how she inhabits it, both on her own as she listens to The Pixies and avoids tidying it, and then later, posing for Tommy Ton's camera. This is an intimate trajectory both narrated to and, in some ways, re-enacted in front of her readership. Tavi's room here is the room she sits in as she blogs as well as the room reconstructed in the imagination of her readers as she writes it into being in her post. Yet it is also her blog itself, the 'online home' housing her image and offering her a similar expressive freedom and agency as does her material bedroom located in her family home.

Tavi acknowledges the presence of these readers in her post, demonstrating that it is not only publicly accessible but it is addressed to a public. At the same time, her blog is also private, in that it is about Tavi's own life, and she implicitly reveals that she has withheld some aspects of it from her readership, demonstrated in her revelation that the afternoon on which Tommy Ton visited was 'a couple of months ago' (Gevinson 2010). Mediating this enmeshed dialectic is Tavi's online identity, brought into being through 'writing [her] self through continuous recording of past and present experiences [and…] writing [her] self through interaction with the audience' (Gurak and Antonijevic 2008: 65). Posts such as these demonstrate a blurring between public and private selves that occurs in a space that is both public and private at the same time.

The private in public

Even very recently, the elders could say: 'You know, I have been young and you have never been old.' But today's young people can reply: 'You have never been young in the world I am young in, and you never can be.'

— Margaret Mead, *Culture and Commitment*, 1972

In the early 1970s, anthropologist Margaret Mead published a commentary on the state of modern youth, arguing that prior cultural configurations within which younger generations would learn from their elders could not apply to this group, growing up as they were in a world forever altered by World War II and the cultural shifts that took place in its aftermath. Mead argued that the series of events that took place between 1940 and 1960 'irrevocably altered men's relationships to other men [*sic*] and to the natural world', bringing about 'a drastic, irreversible division between the generations' (1972: 87–88). As such, this generation was growing up in a world foreign to their parents, who were thus rendered unable to speak from experience in advising their children on how to be.

According to Mead, the hope to which each generation clings is that the next will turn out much like themselves 'but balancing this hope there is the fear that the young are being transformed into strangers before our eyes, that teenagers gathered at a street corner are to be feared like the advance guard of an invading army' (1972: 88). Such fears are reflected in the societal attitudes towards the burgeoning youth subcultures that were the subject of numerous studies during the 1960s, 1970s and 1980s, and which are also present in much of the criticism style blogs attract in the mainstream media.

In *Subculture: The Meaning of Style*, Hebdige argues that the suspicion and anxiety surrounding youth subcultures derives from their violation of 'the authorized codes through which the social world is organized and experienced' (2007: 91). This is enacted in the expression of the forbidden and profane through the content and forms by which such subcultures are organized and practised: the consciousness of class expressed through law breaking and transgression of behavioural codes, for example (2007: 91). Interestingly, such anxieties and apparent societal transgressions are absent from McRobbie and Garber's analysis of girls' bedroom culture, published in 1976. The only anxiety discussed in the study is that of the perceived dangers of girls participating in male subcultures, which were usually practised on the street, one of the causes they attributed to girls' subcultures being located within their homes. The space of girls' bedrooms was therefore private, inaccessible space set in opposition to the public space of the street, with its connotations of exposure, potential risk from strangers and opportunities for girls to become involved in transgressive, male-dominated subcultures.

Yet whether the instigating factor for girls' culture being enacted within their bedrooms was due to lack of any other space in which to meet, out of remaining in a safe and perhaps parentally controlled space, or through personal choice, as is the case in Lincoln's study, the binary distinction between private 'safe' and public 'exposed' space/s and place/s is problematized when brought to bear on digital cultures. In the ensuing discussion I will explore the blur between public and private taking place on the space of style blogs and, through a close reading of the kinds of criticism style blogging attracts, examine what kinds of discourses – as published by which kinds of people – are deemed appropriate for public expression.

By way of clarification, by 'public' I mean accessible to many – that is, the information published on style blogs is publicly available. Implicit in the notion of 'public' here is that of *a public*, or readership, and a particular one at that. To borrow the words of Michael Warner, those that comprise a style blog's public are 'a certain kind of person, inhabiting a certain kind of social world, having at their disposal certain media and genres, motivated by a certain normative horizon, and speaking within a certain language ideology' (2002: 10). Of course, the people reading may very well not be a part of the *intended* public of a style blog, who are usually sympathetic readers with a shared interest in the concepts of fashion and personal style. Being publicly accessible means that anyone can access a style blog, which contributes in part to some of the criticism they attract as risky. Public operates in tension to private, the two being realized in their fullest definition in contrast with one another. 'Private' here is taken to mean not publicly accessible. This applies both to the information that may be concealed from a readership as well as the location of an author: girls socializing in the enclosed sites of their bedrooms, as opposed to on public websites, for example.

My definition of public is based in the work of Jürgen Habermas, who argued that the public sphere is one in which 'something approaching public opinion can be formed' (Edgar 2005: 31). The 'public opinion' he refers to here is dialogic, formed through the exchange of ideas in the written word and active debate. It is rational, logical and tied to ideas that affect the general public: philosophy, politics and so on (see Edgar 2005: 27–31). This operates in contrast to the private sphere, also commonly called 'the domestic sphere', the often-feminized realm of individual and social life. This distinction was most emphatically drawn in the eighteenth century, and although it is now commonly accepted in contemporary theoretical literature that the two notions are increasingly indistinct in a contemporary context, the tension between public and private remains. Both concepts are shifting, contested and can have different meanings in different contexts.[5]

On the Internet the distinction between public and private is fluid and over-lapping; indeed, the medium effectively mediates this distinction. Reid-Walsh and Mitchell argue as much in 'Girls' web sites: A virtual room of one's own?', writing that contrary to Foucault's assertion that the binary between public and private space is inviolable, 'the space of the web and the home page may "unsettle" and [...] begin to overturn this opposition' (2004: 180). However, they maintain that there is still a distinction between these two modes of being online, concluding that 'a girl's homepage appears to be a kind of contradictory space – a *private* space that exists in a *public* domain' (2004: 181).

Yet in contrast to the homepages Reid-Walsh and Mitchell theorize, personal style blogs blur even this distinction: to conceive of their spaces as private and not public is to misconstrue the active and participatory role of readers in blogging. Although these pages exist in a public domain, the prevalence of hyperlinks means that their content also acts as an intermediary linking readers to a number of other sites and social media platforms. What we see in this instance is a realization of Brandi Bell's argument that 'blogs are public and private spaces *at the same time*' (2007: 104, emphasis added). Unlike the bedrooms of the girls of previous studies on bedroom culture, the bedroom-spaces of style blogs do not conceal bloggers from the rest of the world as they enact their culture. These online spaces are liminal, rooms without walls, and as such are simultaneously public *and* private.

Style blogs are private, in that they are written out of intimate, material places, comprised of content based on the personal life, opinion and tastes of individual bloggers. Moreover, the manner in which these bloggers communicate with their readers is intimate, informal and discursive, inviting responses and fostering an interpersonal connection. Style bloggers frame what they share of their personal lives through the lens of fashion, thus keeping the majority of their private lives private. Yet at the same time, these blogs are public texts. Bloggers employ technologies that enable readers to comment, to link back to posts on their own blogs and share links on their social media platforms. The practice of hyperlinking also enables a two-way flow of recognition as style bloggers acknowledge the origins of images, video or information that they are posting, while the original sources of the content are able to see who has written about or used their material.[6] This is made possible through statistics tracking websites, which enable users to see what links their readers clicked to land on particular pages, effectively connecting style blogs to a network of other sites.

The tension surrounding style bloggers publishing content about modes of being traditionally restricted to the private sphere has caused them to attract a range of criticism, all of which circulates around the fact that the majority of style bloggers are young and female. This is intriguing as there are a number of active participants in the style blogosphere who are not girls, yet the stereotypical style blogger invoked by such criticism is a girl blogging outfit posts. Perhaps this is because blogging one's personal style is the foundation of the entire practice: this is a discursive space in and through which bloggers explore, play with and perform their sartorial identity. Identity-play is often tied to youth culture, supposedly symptomatic of the process of young people, and especially girls, as they establish a distinct and personal identity in relation to their peers (see Griffiths 1995; Dwyer 1998; Driscoll 2002; Chittenden 2010).

Regardless of the age and gender of style bloggers, the mode of communication on style blogs is invariably consistent: the tone of address from blogger to reader is intimate and friendly, and the content centres on the blogger's person, with a unifying focus on one's sense of style. As we have seen, writing subjectively and creatively about individual experience has traditionally been considered the preserve of the private sphere, feminized in contrast to the masculine rational discourse deemed fit for the public sphere. Thus regardless of one's gender, the prevailing convention of style blogging is to communicate in a hetero-normatively 'feminine' way, evident, for example, on *Bryanboy*, where each post is signed with an enthusiastic virtual kiss – *'Baboosh!'* – from blogger Bryan Grey-Yambao to his readers.

The application of the concept of bedroom culture, traditionally used to describe girls' subcultures, is not intended to marginalize or discount the presence of male bloggers, but rather to account for the intimately personal and public spaces of style blogs. Furthermore, despite the active participation on the style blogosphere of people who are neither teenaged nor female, it is impossible to talk about this practice without acknowledging that this is a sub-genre of fashion blogging dominated by girls and young women.

This itself is a unique development in the history of publics, especially in the consideration of who is permitted to speak in the public sphere, and is one reason that the following discussion will exclusively focus on girl style bloggers. Moreover, the majority of the criticism that style blogs attract is concentrated on the youth and gender of this demographic, so an engagement with it directs me again towards girl style bloggers. Perhaps the fact that style bloggers of alternate genders and ages have not elicited the same criticism further underlines the grounds upon which girl style bloggers are criticized. As such, it is plausible to connect this criticism with the historical circumvention of the visibility and public participation of girls.

'Girls' is a term in perpetual flux. As Driscoll argues, the concepts of 'girlhood' and 'girls' 'are brought into existence in statements and knowledge about girls' (2002: 5). It is not a state of being limited to adolescence, but rather a concept that is applied to females of all ages. I assume Driscoll's definition of girlhood, implied when I refer to 'girl style bloggers', as a term that defines a state of transition of an individual in process to dominant ideas of womanhood (see Driscoll 2002: 6). The bloggers I refer to in the following section range in age from their mid-teens through to their late-twenties, and many have blogged for a number of years.

Risky and narcissistic?

The accessibility of style blogs to the general public has been one of the primary anxieties that have circulated around this practice. In being publicly accessible, style blogs – and, more importantly, style bloggers – are visible and searchable by anyone who knows how to find them. This has been described as alarming and full of potential risks both by journalists commenting on style blogging and online youth cultures in general (see Dewey 2002; Literacy 2.0 2013). In an article published in 2008 by the Associated Press titled 'Young fashion bloggers are [a] worrisome trend for parents', Parry Aftab, creator of an online protection website, is quoted as saying that 'parents have no idea what their kids are doing online [...] Most parents have no idea what a blog is' (Kwan 2008). Style bloggers, on the other hand, are 'in a world where they don't really belong', incognizant of the dangers of making themselves vulnerable by posting personal information online (Kwan 2008).

The article asserts that this presence in a 'world where they don't belong' leaves style bloggers exposed to cyberbullying and predators at an age when they are 'very impressionable' (Kwan 2008). This point is reinforced by the inclusion of an anecdote that occurred after *New York* magazine's blog questioned whether Tavi Gevinson was really the age she claimed to be (at the time, she was 12 years old). Her father, Steve Gevinson, describes what happened after Tavi saw the post and some of the subsequent comments 'dissecting her precocious fashion sense and sophisticated taste in music'.

> She slept in the bed with us that night to get back to sleep [… and the next night] she woke up, and again woke us up, and said – and this is really heartbreaking – 'I just woke up crying and I don't even know why I'm crying'.
>
> (Gevinson, quoted in Kwan 2008)

Although Kwan is careful to quote some bloggers on the positive aspects of blogging as well as acknowledging that some take precautions with their privacy (such as cropping their faces out of photographs), these inclusions are made briefly and placed within the context of the concerns of the adults interviewed for the article. The overall message is that girls are unaware of the risks they take in blogging, a trend that should concern parents.

There is another insinuation at play in the article that is only briefly mentioned, but which speaks to another underlying anxiety about girls' visibility on the blogosphere: '[A]re you posing in a more provocative way? Is it how you want to be remembered when your next boyfriend sees it or your future mother-in-law sees it or your tuition scholarship person's going to review you for Dartmouth?' (Aftab, quoted in Kwan 2008). The reference here, of course, is to the way that girls are seen, as evinced by the use of the word 'provocative'. The implication is that through blogging, girls are making themselves vulnerable to assumptions to be made about their status – moral and sexual – which may have negative ramifications for them in the future both relationally and professionally.

These concerns are worth considering, especially as style blogs are a relatively recent phenomenon and the long-term effects of this sustained and personal mode of self-performance are yet to become apparent. Yet at the same time, such readings subscribe to a kind of moral panic about the visibility of girls in the public sphere, which is consistent with Anita Harris's observation that 'young people's participation in activities with one another, outside adult control, is often trivialised and/or problematised' (2008: 48).

Through their youth and gender, female style bloggers are thus positioned as ignorant of the risks inherent in participating in the public sphere, which is not necessarily the case. Bell writes that 'studies of girls and their blogs have shown that at least some girls are aware of the potential their blogs have for a broad audience of readers, which includes strangers' (2007: 107). This was undoubtedly the case for all of the bloggers I interviewed, who uniformly made mention of their readers and understood that their blogs were publicly searchable. To borrow again from Mead, this is a generation 'at home in [their] time' (1972: 99). They are media-literate and at ease negotiating what content they chose to reveal and what they concealed in the process of writing their blogs.

The skill involved in style blogging

Implicit in the concept of media literacy is the facility with which bloggers create media, as well as a comprehension of a possible readership. This is an aspect of style blogging that is rarely discussed. Style blogs compel bloggers to hone and employ certain skills in order to publish their content. As Harris has argued, literature on the dangers of youth online activity rarely takes into consideration the perspectives of young female participants and tends to overlook 'the forms of literacy involved in being able to control and realise "what you're being" in online spaces' (Gregg and Driscoll, quoted in Harris 2008: 488).

Although the establishment of a blog is relatively easy, the creation of posts can require a blogger to call on an array of skills including, but not limited to, writing, editing and proofreading, outfit styling and photography. Moreover, depending on the approach and desires for the aesthetic and content of their blog, a blogger might learn how to use photo-editing programs, how to make GIFs and video content for their blog, or learn business skills that would aid them in their navigation of business opportunities that might arise through working with PR companies and advertisers.[7]

That this is an important aspect of style bloggers' practice is demonstrated in the popularity of the Independent Fashion Bloggers website, which hosts a forum for bloggers to discuss blogging and regularly publishes online articles for the 'IFB Community'. These articles purport to instruct bloggers on a range of aspects of blogging: everything from using proper grammar, to how to accrue a following on affiliated social media, to providing 'the fashion blogger's guide to editing like a pro' (Jacob 2013c).

The development of these skills is considered valuable by bloggers, as was apparent in a number of interviews I conducted. Rosalind Jana reflected that blogging 'has really helped me sharpen my writing skills [...] because there's no better discipline than writing something on a blog twice a week that you know people are going to see' (Jana, in conversation with the author, 2011b). Rosalind described the way that both the quality of her writing and her interest in writing as an activity developed through keeping her blog. While her earlier posts featured 'an embarrassing sprinkle of smiley faces, and very short amounts of texts and probably grammar errors', blogging led her to discover that she wanted to be a writer (Jana, in conversation with the author, 2011b). Likewise, Kayla Telford-Brock observed that blogging provided her with an opportunity to learn how to use the programs Photoshop and Firework to edit her outfit post photographs and create GIFs (Telford-Brock, in conversation with the author, 2012).

The honing of skills by blogging has translated into broader success for other style bloggers as well: for example, Tavi Gevinson, who famously started *Style Rookie* at the age of 11 years old, went on to found an online magazine for girls called Rookie that generated close to 600,000 unique page views in its first month online (Twohey 2011). What these stories demonstrate is that creating and maintaining a style blog entails work that can lead to the development and improvement of personal resources, the benefits of which extend beyond personal enjoyment. The opportunities to generate income from advertising, to accrue skills for a future career and to build an 'online presence' to facilitate entry into a chosen field are all aspects of blogging spoken to by IFB articles (indicating their relevancy to the IFB Community) and is reflected in the stories of numerous bloggers such as Tavi, who have pursued other opportunities by employing skills honed through style blogging.

Indeed, all of the bloggers I interviewed were aware of the possibility of future employers seeing their blogs, and they were uniformly unperturbed. Isabel Slone (*Hipster Musings*) was approaching the end of her undergraduate degree when I interviewed her in 2012, and so I asked if she was at all concerned about future employers seeing her blog. She replied,

> I think about that all the time […] I think the worst thing they would see is like 'oh this girl takes pictures of herself. She's really into fashion' [laughs] But the fact that I want to be a fashion writer… I think it's good that I have cultivated this online persona and in a lot of ways I think it's helped me because I have received some exposure and I think I would be able to make connections in the writing world […] and get jobs through social media. So it's more of a help if you're on a non-traditional career path. I'm not really worried about what somebody wearing a suit who works in Human Resources is going to say because I'm never going to work for somebody like that, so […].
>
> (Slone, in conversation with the author, 2012)

For Isabel, blogging provides an opportunity for exposure that may benefit her in her chosen career path, a sort of online *curriculum vita*. While some might attribute this confidence to youthful naïveté – after all, despite her then-current intentions, Isabel may indeed one day decide to apply for a job that would involve being interviewed by 'a suit who works in Human Resources' – it also seems unlikely that a potential employer would be deterred from a qualified candidate because they used to keep a style blog. In the meantime, the assumption underlying Isabel's responses is that the 'right' people will understand what she was doing – those who she foresees as her future employers – and that those who do not 'get' style blogging do not concern her.

Negotiating the risk: trolling and online bullying

There are, of course, those who explicitly set out to criticize style bloggers, and who do so by posting on websites established to publicly criticize, or 'troll', style bloggers.[8] For these critics, style bloggers are not stylish so much as overly preoccupied with themselves: narcissists, and absurdly so. One such site was Shamepuff, which, according to its 'about' page, comprised of 'nothing but clucking over the odd attempts at "style" we see around the internet by wannabe fashionistas' and published a series of blogposts criticizing the style, poses and hair of particular bloggers.[9]

This website, written by anonymous bloggers, stood in contrast to the other main site for trolling of this kind, Get Off My Internets (GOMI). GOMI is a network of forums upon which users post, including one titled 'Fashion/Beauty Bloggers' within which threads are listed by the name of a blog or its blogger, indicating the subject of discussion therein. Despite the claims that these websites are harmless ('full of nothing') or that they offer 'constructive criticism' (see Davies 2012), the content published on them is predominantly critiques of style bloggers articulated in a snide, cruel or vitriolic way.

Such sites demonstrate the risk inherent in the public accessibility of information on the Internet; that is, in writing for the public domain, a blogger might become the target of bullying by strangers. Jessica Quirk, who started *What I Wore* in 2008, has been a focus of such attention on both of these sites and believes this is due to the success that her blog generated, making her highly visible. In interview, she described discovering that she was being talked about on these sites by checking her analytics to see who had referred traffic to her site. The discovery evoked the following response:

> I was […] not so happy about it. I went through so many phases of being truly, truly angry to being sort of sympathetic, to think, like, how bad your life must be if your only outlet is to be mean to people you don't know.
>
> (Quirk, in conversation with the author, 2013)

Yet despite being the subject of unfounded rumours about her personal life and criticism of her outfit posts (including photographs of Jessica wearing her bridal gown on her wedding day), she continued blogging. When I asked her why, she replied:

> […] it took a lot of willpower. And that wasn't a process that was just like me sitting down and thinking about it for a night. It was like me crying multiple nights in a row […] talking it out with my husband or with my close friends before I just […] decided not to look at it [any more].
>
> (Quirk 2013)

Jessica rationalizes the behaviour of these commenters as 'children on a playground' (Quirk 2013), and believes that to have a style blog is to be susceptible to the danger of bullying.

> A lot of people believe that the Internet and the real world are the one and the same, but on the Internet people can take things way too far and they can be much more hurtful […] I think it is dangerous.
>
> (Quirk 2013)

The danger, as Jessica defines it, is in allowing your self-worth to be determined by the popularity of your blog or social media presence and, indeed, some style bloggers have allegedly ceased blogging for that very reason. For example, at a blogger breakfast launching swimmable underwear, I had a conversation about online bullying with Marlo

Perry, a fashion and lifestyle blogger who blogged at *A Fatal Attraction to Cuteness*. She told me about the 'Porcelain Blonde', an anonymous Australian fashion blogger who had been the target of online criticism for the expensive clothing and luxurious lifestyle she blogged. Her blog has been deleted and she has disappeared from the blogosphere, a direct result (according to Perry) of the criticism her blog attracted (Marlo Perry, personal communication, 2013).

However, to dismiss the capabilities and work of style bloggers because their practice is perceived as risky is to dismiss their capacity to negotiate such situations and exert agency for themselves. The example discussed above is consistent with the findings of Gregg and Driscoll that young women 'tend to demonstrate significant competencies in regard to risk' (Gregg and Driscoll 2008: 14). For Jessica, this involved recognizing the behaviour as bullying and making a decision to 'stop looking at it, stop even letting it exist in the world' (Quirk 2013).

That many style bloggers have found ways to negotiate and deal with such negative attention is echoed by the experience of Emily Schuman of fashion/lifestyle blog *Cupcakes and Cashmere*, who has also been the subject of criticism on both Shamepuff and GOMI. The following is her reply to a reader's question about how she dealt with 'nasty comments' when she started her blog.

> When I did first start getting nasty comments on my blog I was devastated. I was ready to give up, close my comments section [...] but eventually realized that what you're doing by putting content out on the Internet, you're going to get some feedback. Some of it's going to be positive, some of it is going to be negative, and you kind of have to be okay with it [...] the truth is that not everyone's going to love what I do [and] I have to be okay with it. So when I first started getting negative criticism it took a lot longer to get over it, but now it just, it comes with the territory.
>
> And I also really try to listen to what people say – sometimes those negative comments or nasty things can really have some truth behind them, so I always try to take everything with a grain of salt. But at the end of the day you kind of just have to move on.
>
> (Schuman, *Cupcakes and Cashmere*, 2013b)

The approach of 'taking it with a grain of salt and moving on' is echoed in the experiences of other style bloggers who have attracted negative comments on their own blogs as well as articles written by bloggers on IFB advising others on how to deal with online bullying (see Retherford 2012; Davies 2012; Harrington 2013; Rushford 2013). Rather than being deterred from blogging because of trolling and negative comments, bloggers are finding ways to maturely engage with it. Analyses that characterize such online activity as risky for the young women who participate in it implicitly assert that bloggers are unable to manage the dangers of being so visible. These examples from the style blogosphere demonstrate otherwise.

On their Alexander Wang soapboxes

Another criticism often made of the style blogging is that it is a narcissistic pursuit (see Burvill 2011; Barger 2012; Odell 2013). Such a reading is epitomized in an opinion piece published on the fashion and culture website Always Sometimes Anytime in 2011 in which five writers nominated 'the top five things wrong with fashion blogs':

> [o]utside of school newspapers and ill-conceived zines, I see no reason that teenagers should a) have a platform from which the whole world can read their opinions and b) be taken seriously for said opinions, especially when it comes to fashion. Sure, Tavi is great and an exception to the rule and so precious and on the nose and blah blah blah, but in general teenagers are just awful. Why do we care if they want to dress up as baby prostitutes in Jeffrey Campbell boots? Why are we reading this garbage?
>
> (Cooke et al. 2011)

This sentiment was echoed in a blogpost by the late Franca Sozzani, who was *Vogue Italia's* editor-in-chief. She wrote: 'they don't offer an opinion, only talk about themselves, take their own pictures wearing absurd outfits. What's the point?' (Sozzani 2011).

Clearly expressed in both examples is scepticism about what valid contribution a young blogger could make to a substantive discussion on fashion and a fear that echoes those of previous generations: that 'the young are being transformed into strangers before our eyes' (Mead 1972: 88). The first also offers a particularly sexualized reading of style bloggers: likening them to 'baby prostitutes' ironically underlines the anxiety of the visibility of women on the street that bedroom culture was originally supposed to address.

Narcissistic is the word frequently employed to describe what bloggers do, as opposed to alternatives like 'conceited' or 'vain'. These words carry a similar meaning – excessive pride and extreme admiration for oneself – yet narcissism alone carries pathological connotations. It is not that style bloggers are apparently revelling in their appearance or indulging a high opinion of themselves; 'narcissism' implies a disorder, a psychological delusion. There is also a facile symmetry between outfit posting and the Greek myth of Narcissus. Failing to return the love of Echo, Narcissus was condemned by Nemesis, the goddess of divine retribution, to spend the duration of his days gazing into his reflection in a pool of water. On style blogs, the glassy surface of water is replaced by another mirror-like surface, that of a computer screen.[10] Rocamora argues that the computer screen acts as a mirror through which the female subjects of the photograph (bloggers) both challenge and reproduce their position as 'specular objects' (2011: 410), even as blogs operate as a site for the performance of alternative explorations of femininity. These two aspects of style blogs – as sites to be seen and to see oneself, as well as spaces for exploration of selfhood and identity – are indicative of how style blogging enables bloggers to tell an ongoing narrative of self. However, unlike Narcissus, style bloggers do not stare endlessly at their own image but, by posting photographs, they invite others to.

Jessica Quirk employed the word in relation to herself when describing why she blogs.

> I don't think I could do it just purely for the attention [...] [When I started blogging] I was kind of vain and narcissistic in posting my pictures every day but then when I started getting that positive feedback I was like 'ok it's not [...] just about me'. And then too with the book [a practical illustrated guide to dressing stylishly], I felt like I was just offering something of value and [...] that makes it worth it.
>
> (Quirk, in conversation with the author, 2013)

Jessica's reflection makes two aspects of blogging apparent. First of all, there are other functions to the photographs that she posts, rather than simply personal revelation or self-promotion. On *What I Wore,* her outfit posts form the basis of the styling suggestions she posts for her readers. Although this flourished out of Jessica's self-professed 'like [of] positive attention' (Quirk 2013), her posts represented something else for Jessica's readers, which in turn changed how she viewed – and valued – what she was doing.

At the same time, Jessica's words suggest an underlying sentiment that it was 'not ok' for her blog to be all about herself, and the pleasure she derived from blogging for attention and the affirmation of her skill in dressing, or confirmation of her attractive appearance, was not something of value. Of course, it is impossible to ascertain whether this is an accurate reflection of how she felt when blogging. She may have, as many interviewees do, framed her response in relation to what she thought I wanted to hear (or what she thought she should say.) This is by no means to pass judgement on her, and it is actually a less interesting line of enquiry. Rather, her emphasis reveals the belief that we are not supposed to derive pleasure from how we appear, or from how people appreciate how we look, or, to be more accurate, we are not supposed to say that we do.

Yet the prevalence of social media technologies that allow for the documentation and visual display of the appearance of their users (Instagram, Facebook and blogging platforms that foreground photo-sharing like Flickr, Tumblr and Blogger) as well as the rise of the selfie indicates that our personal appearance does fascinate both ourselves and others, and that style bloggers are not alone in deriving pleasure from creating and sharing images of their appearance.[11]

Indeed, style blogs are not the only kind of blogs characterized as narcissistic. Kris Cohen argues that such criticism is commonly made of personal blogs because bloggers are remarking on the supposedly 'gravely unremarkable': their own lives (2006: 162). Cohen reads this criticism as an implicit assertion that bloggers have not earned the right to speak publicly about their opinions and experiences (2006: 162–63), an argument based on a reading of Michael Warner's seminal work *Publics and Counterpublics.* In this work, Warner interrogates the assumptions underlying publics, writing that 'it is often thought [...] that the public display of private matters is a debased narcissism, a collapse of decorum, expressivity gone amok, the erosion of any distinction between public and private' (2002: 62).

What is exacerbated in the instance of style blogging is that the people behind this 'expressivity gone amok' are young women. Indeed, because of the widespread accessibility of the Internet, the present age may be the first time in history when such a number of young women have had the means to contribute to a public discussion on any topic, presenting their own interests and lives as worthy of consideration. The interrogation of whether or not teenagers should have a platform from which the whole world can read their opinions is reminiscent of a story Warner recounts of social campaigner Frances Wright. Whilst on a speaking tour of the United States in the late 1820s, lecturing against slavery, for birth control and for workers and women's rights, Wright was almost universally criticized. Catharine Beecher, an American advocate for the confinement of women to the domestic sphere, wrote of her:

> [...] who can look without disgust and abhorrence upon such an one [sic] as Fanny Wright, with her great masculine person, her loud voice, her untasteful attire, going about unprotected, and feeling no need of protection, mingling with men in stormy debate, and standing up with bare-faced impudence, to lecture to a public assembly.
>
> (Beecher, quoted in Warner 2002: 22)

Warner marks the masculinization of Wright by Beecher, as if by appearing in public she was negating her very femininity. In conclusion, he states that 'being in public is a privilege that requires filtering or repressing something that is seen as private' (2002: 23).

What is deemed private here is a woman's opinions and her embodied self as the origin of such opinions. At issue for Beecher is the very appearance of a woman in public, apparently transgressing her proper role in society to literally embody what she is not: a man. Interestingly, the contemporary criticism of style bloggers seems to echo Beecher's disgusted rejection: here are the wrong people talking about things they have no right of which to speak, and doing so in public.

In this we see an example of indirect exclusion, which 'prescribe[s] particular ways of interacting in public forums' (Asen 2002: 345). This functions tacitly through what Asen calls 'discursive norms' by compelling participants to contribute via particular ways of speaking using established modes of discourse, effectively negating the perspectives and contributions of previously excluded individuals and groups. In publishing commentary urging style bloggers to 'get off their Alexander Wang soapbox' (Cooke et al. 2011), articles and websites such as Always Sometimes Anytime, Shamepuff and GOMI make a judgement about what kind of people may talk about which topics in the public sphere, and the manner in which they do so. The overriding message of this kind of criticism is that style bloggers should recede from view and be silent.

That doing what they do 'on their own terms' (Harris 2008: 492) has been trivialized and denigrated is consistent with the lack of value traditionally placed on women's and girls' talk and their writing (see Culley 1985; McNeill 2003; Gregg 2006; Bell 2007; Harris 2008). Women's writing is often judged to be insufficiently rigorous or significant, being imbued with too much personal detail which, as Bell argues, has led to a devaluation of women's writing and a lack of popular and academic consideration of the importance of girls and their blogs (2007: 101).

However, as I have here argued, despite the real and perceived risks or apparent narcissism inherent in publicly performing a styled identity, style blogs offer bloggers a space where intimate, exploratory and affirming interactions between girls and their peers can take place in an unprecedented way. The practice of style blogging makes available the possibilities of connecting with others with similar interests, developing particular skills and shaping a particular kind of discussion around a topic that has no alternative public forum. Other possibilities afforded by style blogging, such as the affective qualities and possibilities for self-reflection inherent in outfit posting, will be explored in subsequent chapters. That one of the possible pleasures for bloggers is an opportunity to foster and share a pride in their appearance does not automatically render them narcissists, and to accord that noun with its negative connotations allows cultural commentators to dismiss style blogging without considering the value it has for the people who do it.

Like Anita Harris, I advocate an approach that seeks to consider the inherent value for participants of online youth cultures rather than to pass judgement on them or suggest ways in which they could be involving themselves in more 'conventional participatory practices' (Harris 2008: 492). To read the style blogosphere positively, as a space for the presentation and celebration of everyday experience and personal style, is to begin to map the ways that it is meaningful for its participants. Such a perspective opens up the practice, and recognizes style bloggers as 'young people, and young women in particular [...] participating in their own communities and [...] expressing a desire to occupy public space on their own terms' (Harris 2008: 492) rather than simply dismissing them as conceited girls, riskily exercising their own vanity.

Notes

1 'Colour blocking' was a dominant fashion trend in 2011. It refers to a manner of dressing where a person wears clashing colours in bold block colours: a yellow blouse with purple trousers and red high heels, for example. It was shown by a number of fashion labels at the S/S RTW 2011–12 fashion weeks (namely, Gucci, Marc Jacobs and Lanvin) and subsequently adopted by many style bloggers.

2 I am not aware of any early girl bloggers having their photographs taken by their girlfriends, although there certainly may have been some. In most cases, photographs were taken by a boyfriend or a friend, and this was either acknowledged in the 'About Me' or FAQ on a blog or under each post as an image credit.

3 Some time after our interview, Kayla stopped regularly blogging and made *The F Tangent* private, so that potential readers must log in to their WordPress account (or create one, if they do not already have one) in order to read it.

4 I am indebted to Ian Maxwell who suggested the term 'digital analogue' during a conversation about this chapter.

5   It is beyond the capacity of this research to delve deeply into a discussion of publics beyond their applicability to style blogs, but I will refer the interested reader to the work of Habermas (1989), Asen (2002) and Warner (2002) for more comprehensive explication and application of this theory.

6   For a detailed discussion about hyperlinking on fashion blogs, see Rocamora 2012: 94–96.

7   A GIF (Graphics Interchange Format) is a format for the storage of image files, a technology developed in 1987 that is popularly employed on the Internet in the form of short animations (or animated GIFs).

8   A 'troll' is someone who posts deliberately offensive or inflammatory remarks online about a topic or person in the hopes of provoking them or causing upset.

9   As of July 2013, *Shamepuff* has been deleted, but prior pages are still viewable using Wayback Machine. See http://web.archive.org/web/*/shamepuff.com.

10 Other theorists have explored the correlations between personal blogging, digital photography and mirrors, an argument that, although interesting, is not of central concern here. For those who are interested in reading further on this topic, I recommend the work of Serfaty (2004); Walker (2005); Rocamora (2011).

11 'Selfie' is shorthand for a self-portrait taken using the subject's smartphone.

Chapter 3

Intimacy at a Distance

Most of the people around us belong to our world not directly, as kin or comrades or in any other relation to which we could give a name, but as stranger. How is it that we nevertheless recognize them as members of our world?

– Michael Warner, *Publics and Counterpublics* (2002)

Style bloggers and their readers engage with one another at a remove. This is a different kind of sociality to that realized by the girls of McRobbie and Garber's and Lincoln's studies (2000; 2004) in their bricks-and-mortar bedrooms. The girls of those studies were friends and peers, known to one another and enacting their bedroom culture in the same place, or at the very least in the same temporal moment, as they spoke through the telephone connecting bedroom to bedroom.

On the style blogosphere, bloggers and readers inhabit different places, are often of different ages and nationalities, sometimes speaking different languages, encountering one another not just in different time zones, but at different times of the day, as the continuous present of the Internet makes it possible to 'catch up' with a blogger by reading a post published a number of days, weeks or months earlier. Yet at the same time, bloggers and their readers share an intimacy, albeit an intimacy at a distance. Here, again, the enmeshed dialectic between public and private is at work.

While there is a growing body of research on blog readership, there is very little academic work on style blog readership. If readers are mentioned at all in current work on style blogs, their presence is largely incidental. This presence – or, indeed co-presence with bloggers – will form the basis of this chapter, in which I examine the dynamics at play in style blog writing and reading. These dynamics give rise to a kind of affective and ambiguous relationality between people who are, for the most part, unknown to each other. When blogging, bloggers are aware of a readership, although they often do not precisely know of whom it is constituted. At the same time, as Baumer et al. indicate, 'the position of the blog reader is often an ambiguous one' (2008: 1112). As such, I will argue here that readership on style blogs can best be conceptualized as a kind of intimate acquaintance between bloggers and readers that is enacted in various ways and experienced differently depending on where an individual is situated on the spectrum of engagement with a blog.

In so doing, I will make reference to a number of studies that usefully establish a general framework for identifying the characteristics of blog readership. I will elaborate upon these by exploring the ways that style blog readership is experienced – that is, what it feels like to write for a largely unknown readership and what it is like to be a reader on these intimate, public spaces – which has thus far been largely left unexamined. These two aspects of blogging are two faces of the same coin, and will here be theorized side-by-side, as facilitated by my extended period of participant-observation on and within the style blogosphere.

In drawing on my experiences from both sides of the blogger/reader relationship I argue, first, that bloggers have a partial knowledge of who is reading, and, second, that readers experience a partial belonging to a blog's readership. I elaborate upon these two ideas by nuancing my experience with observations from theorists who have written about blog readership. I then test these two methodological approaches with reference to the perspectives of bloggers I interviewed, as well as readers who participated in my anonymous survey, in order to present a thorough picture of the different modes of writing and reading that occur on the style blogosphere. These explorations have led me to conclude that the relationality that occurs between style bloggers and their readers is most fruitfully conceived of as an intimate public, following the work of Lauren Berlant, here also bearing the traces of feminine sociality and diffuse, partial belonging that Berlant identified in the literary publics she studied whilst developing this term.

A partial knowing

My relationship towards the readers of *Fashademic* was one of partial knowing. When I thought of them, I felt affection, gratitude and vague familiarity: I knew that there were people reading, but I only knew the names of a small handful, those who tweeted, e-mailed or told me in person that they read my blog. Yet even this knowledge was partial: I did not know how often these friends and virtual strangers read or, to a large extent, what they thought of my blog. My experience echoed Lenhart's observation in her ethnography on blogging,

> [...] most bloggers function with a constant awareness of that audience in the back of their minds as they compose entries, add photos and tweak their blog's layout [...] however, for a variety of reasons, it is difficult for a blogger to fully know their audience.
> (2005: 71)

Yet despite this uncertainty, the presence of readers was crucial to me as I blogged. I would think of them as I wrote, and felt that I was actually writing to them, an orientation that influenced what and how I wrote, and how I wrote myself into being on the space of my blog.

Often, when I sat to write a new post, I felt as if I was slipping on a familiar mantle. I would find myself almost unconsciously selecting a particular tone of address, reaching for vernacular and ironic slang to write myself into a genre imbued with the personal. Here was a place for a sharing and shaping of self, for observations on fashion propelled by the personal. Interesting, then, that the Rosie that took shape on *Fashademic* was a particular online iteration of me, distinguishable from my offline selfhood. That is, I was 'myself' and the manner in which I wrote was personal, but it was a particular *kind* of personal.

My 'blogging persona' (Jana 2011b) on *Fashademic* was more 'goofy', and overtly enthusiastic than I feel myself to be when I am offline.[1] I wrote with exaggerated irony and familiar language, and with an unchecked passion for my subject matter. It was a vulnerable mode of being, in that I was writing publicly on subjects about which I cared deeply – my research, my opinions on fashion and style, anecdotes from my personal life – and doing so in a manner that made public my personal investments, not to mention that I was also publishing photographs of myself. At the same time, I trusted my readers and felt a proximity to them. Perhaps the fact that they were obscured by spatio-temporal distance also aided the license I felt; yet I was always aware that I was not writing to myself (as has been found in other studies on bloggers; see Lenhart 2005; Brake 2009). Rather, I felt myself to be writing towards people who were interested, engaged and sympathetic, basing this assumption on the kind of person I imagined would find my blog interesting: someone who had a similar perspective on and interest in fashion, who shared my sense of humour and who was, when I interrogate it, very much like myself.

In this way, my anticipated readership was 'a constitutive element in the process of actualization' (Eco 1979: 4) of my blog, in that their assumed interest shaped the manner in which I wrote 'to them', and the fact that my blog was written to be read. In his foundational work on textual semiotics and readership, Umberto Eco theorizes the influence of a reader in a text's generation, writing of the author's 'generative strategy', directing and shaping their text in order to 'arouse, to forecast and to activate [...] a cooperation from the part of the reader' (4). This strategy seeks to elicit a response from the assumed reader, albeit one that is 'imprecise or undetermined' (7). Eco argues that the author does this by anticipating his [sic] 'model reader': 'to make his text communicative, the author has to assume that the ensemble of codes he relies upon is the same as that shared by his possible reader' (7), thus compelling the author to write in a way that will aid the interpretation of their possible reader.

Eco suggests that an author does this by making three choices: by adopting 'a specific linguistic code', written in 'a certain literary style' and 'of a special specialization', which, he explains, is a direct appeal to a category of addressee or a reference to presupposed knowledge (1979: 7). Such claims could be argued for any text written for a readership, and they certainly apply to style blogs. Style bloggers anticipate a particular kind of audience, one they invite through the language they employ, their familiar writing style, their subject matter, and by projecting a certain kind of invested reader through their mode of familiar direct address.

It is striking that for style bloggers, as with authors (as more generally argued by Eco), this process of selection and direction is apparent in the moment of textual composition. Lenhart noted in her ethnographic study on bloggers and their readers that bloggers do this – that is, imagine their audience – to 'reconcile [the] unknown part with the known part of their audience' (2005: 83). This is echoed by Brake, who observed that:

[...] even when bloggers can construct a mental picture of their readers a divide can emerge between what webloggers know or believe about readers and the way they think about their readership as they write. In practice this suggests that their perception of the communicative space – at least in the moment of production – often tends to be what they would like it to be rather than what [...] they believe it to be.

(2009: 90)

Such reflections on the imaginative act employed by bloggers in the moment of writing can be pushed further through the application of Michael Warner's work on publics and counter-publics.

An imagined public

Building on and critiquing the limits of Jürgen Habermas's work on the public sphere, Warner sets out a comprehensive analysis of the contemporary concept of publics, which he characterizes as 'a kind of fiction that has taken on life' (2002: 8). Warner argues that a public does not exist prior to being addressed as such; rather, it is spoken into being in the moment of address and therefore its composition cannot be known, but must be imagined. He writes that 'in order to address a public, one must forget or ignore the fictional nature of the entity one addresses' (12). As such, 'the available addressees are essentially imaginary, which is not to say unreal' (73), by which he distinguishes between the public invoked by the discourse and the people who actually hear it and recognize themselves as part of that public. In this way, a public is open-ended but, as Warner is careful to explain, shaped by the manner of address: 'each decision of form, style and procedure [in addressing a public] carries hazards and costs in the kind of public it can define' (14, 73).

My reading public was filtered by the way that I wrote, the subjects that I blogged about and that my work was published online. My assumption that like-minded people constituted my public both shaped and was shaped by how I blogged, while also being shaped by the conventions of the sub-genre within which I was blogging. Presumably, my readers were familiar with these conventions also, and so would read my blog within that generic framework.

However, the question of how to acknowledge a readership whose constitution was ambiguous and unbounded was an aspect of blogging I had to learn to negotiate. I often wished to address my readers, to acknowledge their presence to try to diminish the gap between us but, as I knew very little about them, was at a loss as to how to do so. I eventually abandoned the awkward salutation 'fashadellows', settling instead on 'fashion nerds', a choice that equated their presence on the blog with my own, as I often referred to myself as a 'fashion nerd' too. For example, on my blog's 'Title Page' which functioned as an introduction of myself to new readers, I described myself as an 'Australian fashion nerd' and invited these readers to linger by sharing that 'I have strong feelings for red plaid, orange lipstick, anything sheer, navy, or by Dries Van Noten and if you do too you've come to the exact right place'.

I saw this affectionate and direct acknowledgement of a reading public through specific greetings occurring on other blogs too. The most common of these is 'guys', a characteristically youthful choice, egalitarian in its lack of distinction of blogger from readers: if we are 'one of the guys', then so is she, our unprepossessing blog-friend (for example, see Gevinson, *Style Rookie*, 24 July 2011). In some instances, as in my own case, bloggers employ specialized collective nouns to demarcate a specific readership of a specific blog. Variations of this are employed all over the style blogosphere, such as the 'repellows' who read *Man Repeller* (see Medine, *Man Repeller*, 2012a), or the 'loverats' of *Oracle Fox* (see Shadforth, *Oracle Fox*, 25 February 2011). Diminutive handles such as these are direct enough to foster a sense of togetherness and also indistinct enough to allow for the permeable boundaries of blog readership, where 'merely paying attention can be enough to make you a member' (Warner 2002: 71).

Style bloggers' efforts to constitute a collective readership through familiar modes of address is a kind of public imagining, as they interpellate their readers into a particular kind of 'us'. It is a grammatical device that acknowledges the presence of others while at the same time creating an artifice around them and the blogger, implying that not only are we readers known by bloggers (my experience, as detailed in the next section, suggests otherwise) but also that we share equal footing with them: that we are contemporaries, perhaps even friends. However, this linguistic device actually obscures the very real differences between bloggers and readers, emphasizing the shared space of a blog while ignoring the fact that bloggers are the owners and administrators of that space, setting and policing the tone and content of the conversation – that they are, in fact, the subject of most of the content itself – and thus, ultimately, that they wield the most power. By employing familiar modes of address, then, style bloggers make 'stranger relationality normative, reshaping the most intimate dimensions of subjectivity around co-membership with indefinite persons in a context of routine action' (Warner 2002: 76) while also somewhat fictitiously defining this relationality as one of shared, equal intimacy.

Who were my readers?

That 'indefinite persons' were routinely reading my blog was integral to my blogging experience. Yet, whether I called them 'nerds' or not, the fact remained that for the most part, I had scant idea of who was actually reading *Fashademic*. I had a statistics tracker encoded into my blog's HTML so that I could trace user activity, yet this data afforded me only a vague, generic idea of who these readers might be: where people were logging on from (both the country and the specific geographical location within it – 'Marion, Indiana' beside an icon of the American flag, for instance), the IP address of the computer they were using, the keywords they typed and the search engines they used to find my site, the duration of their visit, which posts received the most hits, which images had been downloaded, and how many unique and how many returning visitors I received each day.

The data delivered moments of great excitement: for instance, the day I saw that someone on an IP address registered to Prada in Italy had looked at my blog, or the morning I awoke to find that my pageviews for the previous day had spiked into the thousands overnight because a post of mine had been mentioned on a widely read Australian blog, but these were in the minority. For the most part, my pageviews predictably spiked when I published a new post and plateaued when I had not posted for a while. My average hit count for most of my time blogging on *Fashademic* was around 200 uniques a day: a modest but steady stream of readers, some of whom would regularly return, others who found my blog by looking for something specific and found it by chance. This keyword-search driven traffic led to my most popular post, which was always and inexplicably one I wrote on the style of Charlotte Rampling, which regularly attracted hits from all over the world.

My vague knowledge of who was reading, and from where, was supplemented by the occasional e-mail from someone writing to tell me that they had enjoyed one of my posts, or friends who mentioned a recent post directly to me. This knowledge fed into my perception of my readership, and yet that readership still remained largely imagined as sympathetic and similar to me. When interrogated, this supposition of a likeness with myself also seems predicated on the assumption that if someone was to read my blog, they must have an interest in what I was saying: otherwise, why would they bother?

This assumption was not particular to me: in her study of online diaries, Viviane Serfaty wrote that it is essential, that for diarists to 'communicate their feelings and states of mind [… they must] presuppose the existence of a common ground with others' (2004: 40). Furthermore, my supposition that my readers were sympathetic was echoed by the bloggers on Brake's study who 'perceived their readership as being generally supportive and made up of the kind of people for whom [the bloggers] were intending to write' (2009: 96).

This twofold imagining of the attitude and composition of one's blog readership was reflected in the answers that Scottish blogger Franca Eirich gave to *The Scotsman* newspaper in an interview about her style blog *Oranges and Apples*. In response to being asked how it feels to show her wardrobe to the world, Franca replied that she does not feel like she shows 'the world' her outfits on her blog; rather, she shows them only to 'the part of the world that reads fashion blogs, so these are people that already "get it"' (*The Scotsman* 2009).

Of course, the fact that the Internet is publicly searchable means that potentially anyone could find and read Franca's blog. Her assumption about who is reading, however, is similar to my own: we imagine we are speaking to people who 'get it' and, therefore, who 'get' us. On *Fashademic*, then, I was able to write directly about my chosen subjects – fashion, my research and myself – in a way that was not only appropriate within the conventions of the genre, but also in a way that was implicitly invited by the imagined presence of my readers.

Theirs was a presence I felt despite their absence, perhaps a corollary of the presence my readers would experience of me whilst on *Fashademic*, despite my corporeal absence.

I shaped my words in anticipation of their reading eyes, communicating my thoughts and performing myself in a way that would collapse the distance between us. In writing, I claimed their attention, and, in the moment of so doing, was conscious of how that self would appear to them.

Jessica Quirk of *What I Wore* described a similar consciousness of her readers as she gets dressed each day,

> I also think, like, '[what] have I posted? Have I worn jeans all week? Gotta switch it up. Have I worn too many dresses? Have I worn too much black and white? Or whatever!' I think of it in like the flow of the site.
>
> (Quirk, in conversation with the author, 2013)

For Jessica, even the act of getting dressed is framed by the apprehension of her readers, as she shapes her behaviour towards their anticipated gaze. This is similar to the way in which my own consciousness of my readers led me to perform in certain ways, guided by the knowledge that I was in many ways a stranger to many of them and yet also an acquaintance of sorts. I had knowledge and stories to share, but did not wish my readers to perceive me as arrogant or as thinking too highly of myself, a sentiment mediated by a desire to share myself in certain ways: to show my clothes, to talk about the experience of enjoying them or to write about the ways that my research reframed the ways in which I think about dressing. What I experienced here was described in another instance by Viviane Serfaty: the writer in the moment of composition 'may be said to contain an implicit reader within their very writing process' (2004: 84) – the reader that I imagined to be reconstituted by whoever actually did eventually read my blog.

I was interested to observe in myself a discomfort whenever I met someone who told me they read my blog. Although I was proud of *Fashademic*, if someone unexpectedly told me that they were one of my readers, I often felt as embarrassed and uncertain as I did pleased and encouraged. The blogged bravado that shielded me from the exposure of writing myself into view fell away in the materiality of our live encounter and I experienced a kind of vulnerability.

Here, I was known in some intimate way by someone I did not recognize, even as I felt an affinity with them and gratitude that they had read my writing and (presumably) liked it. Perhaps part of this complex affectivity is particular to my own personality; yet at the same time, the mix of pleasure at meeting someone who has read your blog and slight embarrassment that they have was shared by many other bloggers whom I have interviewed or who have blogged about it. For example, Australian former style blogger Jamie Wdziekonski (*Oh Jamie*) described meeting a fashion editor at a friend's birthday who told him she read his blog – 'I was like "*really?*"' – and he crinkled his nose, laughing, as he told me (Wdziekonski, in conversation with the author, 2012). Recognizing the mix of pride and embarrassment in his response, I asked if he ever felt embarrassed when people tell him they read his blog: 'um yeah, I'm a fairly shy person so whenever a stranger comes up to me in the street and are like, "oh you're *Oh Jamie*" I['m] like [*laughing*] "oh, uh..."" (Wdziekonski, in conversation with the author, 2012).

That moment seemed to represent to Jamie, as I too experienced, the disjunction between our imagined readership and our actual readers. My imagined readership felt challenged by the actual people who told me they were reading, even though the thoughtful and affirming responses of my readers were consistent with those I imagined my audience would have. These moments of interaction were lovely, but also brought home the interaction taking place at a remove on *Fashademic*: however much I imagined them in the moment of writing, actual people did read what I blogged, and were responding to it, considering it, dismissing it, shaping perceptions of me. *Fashademic* may have been my blog, but being its readers, it was also sort of theirs. This sense of meeting at a distance and sharing in something, however ambiguously and diffusely, is what I turn to now, as I consider what it feels like to be a reader of the style blogosphere.

A partial belonging

To read style blogs is to be engaged in a kind of intimacy at a distance. It is a mode of partial knowing about a blogger's personal life and personal style. It is also a mode of partial belonging, as readers become part of a blog's public simply by paying attention (Warner 2002: 88), but they may experience any level of investment from casually reading as entertainment to feeling a kind of friendship with a particular blogger. Claire Allen argues that their 'conversational style' makes the communication of style blogs seem personal, an intimacy emphasized by the reader accessing the post on their personal computer or mobile phone. This not only leads to readers more readily accepting the authority of bloggers, but also allows them to engage at a 'personal and emotional level' by leaving a comment, thus transforming the act of reading into 'an active relationship' between reader and blogger (Allen 2009: 6). Here, she indicates towards the different reception that a blog and a fashion magazine might receive from a reader – blogs must be deemed authentic, popular, and sustainable by readers in order to be 'validated' (2009: 5), as opposed to the supposedly automatic acceptance of a reader of the information presented in a fashion magazine.

Yet, the affective response readers have to bloggers is not as straightforward as this work suggests, and the reciprocity implied by the word 'relationship' bears interrogation. Readers do often experience the kinds of affective responses that are frequently apparent in offline friendships, including affection for and familiarity with a blogger, feeling that they have spent time with a blogger after reading a post, and detailed knowledge about their life and tastes. However, this affective connection is rarely returned in kind by bloggers, although they may also feel an affection and familiarity for their readers. I will now tease out these ideas through a discussion of my own experiences of being a reader of style blogs, which I will contrast to the results of my survey on readership.

I clearly remember the first style blogs that I regularly read, the bloggers' names as casually familiar as those of my friends: Jane, Tavi, Michelle and Marie. I also looked at *fashiontoast* from time to time, but felt that blogger Rumi Neely was too cool for me, with her nonchalant LA aesthetic; more for me the sophisticated, eclectic style of Jane, Tavi's quirky creativity, the metal meets ballerina style of Michelle and whimsical warmth of Marie. Very early on, then, I learned a fundamental aspect of reading style blogs: that readers gravitate towards bloggers who not only have a personal style that attracts or interests them, but also with whom they feel they could possibly be friends.

I became caught up in reading style blogs very quickly. I felt like a curious observer, and that the bloggers whose posts I regularly read were becoming acquaintances. This familiarity accrued gradually, the sedimentary work of daily logging on to 'catch up' (as I thought of it), seeing if any of 'my' bloggers had posted. I remember the keen irritation of seeing a post I had already read populate at the top of the page, indicating that a blogger had not posted since the last time I had checked, and the eager anticipation of sinking into a new post.

Here was an emotional investment of sorts, although the word 'emotion' is perhaps too strong: it was affection, a friendliness that seemed to flow from myself towards those bloggers as, in turn, their words emanated towards me from their blogs. Despite all that I did not know about them, I quickly began to feel a kind of intimate acquaintance with them. This was echoed by a reader who took my survey, who wrote that despite the fact that s/he 'do[esn't]' in fact know them [...] after reading a blog for years [bloggers] begin to seem like friends and reading the blog is like receiving an email' (survey respondent, Findlay 2013). I, too, was aware all the while that I didn't in fact 'know them', that because I never commented there was little chance that they even knew I was reading and that despite my affection for these bloggers, the connection (as I experienced it) was not reciprocal.

'Relatability' versus inspiration

Here is the crux of style blogging readership: style bloggers are aware that people are reading their blog often without a concrete picture of who those people are, writing instead towards an imagined public. At the same time, readers read style blogs with a clear picture of the bloggers, experiencing a degree of familiarity with them whilst at the same time being held at a distance.

This distance is instated by a number of factors: that bloggers and readers frequently inhabit different places, connect at different times and communicate in different languages. Furthermore, bloggers only blog content of their choosing, giving them the liberty to determine how much of their lives they share. Yet with style blogs in particular, and especially in the case of second wave style blogs, the aspirational nature of content can have a distancing effect as well. We see carefully composed photographs of second wave style bloggers in fashionable outfits posing around the world often with little (if any) explanation of what they are doing in Corsica, Paris or Shanghai and how they, as full-time bloggers, can afford their designer outfits and lifestyles. We can make assumptions – that their trip has been subsidized by the companies they blog about whilst away, their clothes gifted, called out or shot for reimbursement – but this ambiguity demonstrates that such instances of style blogging encourages not the understanding of peers, but the admiration of spectators.[2]

This seems to illustrate Khamis and Munt's observation that fashion blogging has not redefined fashion media so much as increased the ways that it reaches consumers. Despite the somewhat romantic view of bloggers writing free from corporate interests, presenting an individual and authentic personal style, the authors argue that some style bloggers 'liaise with the fashion establishment' (2010: 7), the practice thus changing the way that the fashion industry 'do[es] business' without having usurped the power of its existing structure. This exemplifies Jennifer Craik's argument that 'as new media forms have been invented, the fashion industry has been adept at exploiting opportunities to annex its representational possibilities' (Craik, quoted in Khamis and Munt 2010).

Of course, this can have an adverse effect on the way that a reader feels about a blogger, encouraging not admiration but envy, irritation or disinterest. One of the questions posed in my readership survey was 'what is it about style blogs that you regularly read that keeps you coming back?' and it was revealing that some respondents also took the opportunity to articulate what they did not like about such blogs. One wrote:

> [I] don't like blogs that are about high fashion (e.g. [I] find Jane [Aldridge] hugely alienating for that reason). Their style and lives need to be relatable and reflect a budget that doesn't exclude me.
>
> (survey respondent, Findlay 2013)

This response demonstrates the importance – at least to this respondent – of being able to relate not just to a blogger, but also to the life about which they blog. Other respondents answered that they stopped reading certain fashion blogs because they didn't feel they could relate to the women photographed. One commented that 'when a style blogger crosses that realm into megastar I feel like their reliability is sometimes compromised', a sentiment echoed by Kayla Telford-Brock in our interview for this project.

In a conversation prior to our interview, Kayla and I had shared our experiences of sometimes feeling intimidated by the standard of the most successful Australian style bloggers when it came to writing our own, and I asked if she ever wanted her own blog to emulate theirs. She replied that those bloggers are

> [...] very polished [...] but one of the loveliest things about blogs is seeing those mistakes. Seeing [...] that the skirt doesn't always fall right in a photo [...] or sometimes people don't get their eyeliner quite right. Obviously, everyone in putting photos up of themselves online are very careful to present their best self. You're always conscious of that, but it feels sometimes like those blogs aren't perfectly honest and that's entirely their choice and that's entirely up to them and that's fine [...] that's not me.
>
> (Telford-Brock, in conversation with the author, 2012)

These responses demonstrate the importance to readers of 'relatability' to style bloggers: that the blogger is relatable, like someone who, as another respondent observed, 'I could sit down for a coffee with/have a great and interesting conversation with' (survey respondent, Findlay 2013). This phenomenon was also noted by Rocamora and Bartlett who observed that it is the commonplace aspect of style blogging that resonates with readers, an aspect that stands in marked difference to the 'polished images and inoffensive figures of fashion magazines [and…] the hyperreal faces and bodies of the models they feature' (2009: 110). By contrast, then,

> […] bloggers reaffirm the force and desirability of the everyday […] in a culture saturated by celebrity. It is the imperfect aspect of appearance – imperfect because it is human and personal – that is celebrated.
>
> (Rocamora and Bartlett 2009: 110)

Yet as certain bloggers have themselves become celebrities – at least for the regular readers of the style blogosphere who admire and recognize them – the boundary between amateur and professional has blurred to indistinction, giving rise to a second wave of blogs that simultaneously bring us into the world of a blogger and position us outside of it as fans.

Many readers enjoy reading such blogs as inspiration for their own outfits, as well as for entertainment, not put off by the aspirational quality of a blogger's blogged life but rather, viewing it as 'like a magazine for the short of attention-span' (survey respondent, Findlay 2013). In fact, the survey question inviting respondents to consider what it was about style blogs that kept them reading was open-ended, and yet 29.5 per cent used the word 'inspiration' or 'ideas' (in regards to their own dressing) to describe why they read. Another 10.3 per cent responded that they read to see how bloggers were wearing new trends within the framework of their own style. Such a spread in findings demonstrates that people read style blogs for different purposes and to different ends, but that readership is self-selecting, in that if a blog does not resonate with a reader, they will stop reading it.

Bringing us near, holding us apart: A case study of *Shine By Three*

As I have demonstrated, the content of style blogs can have the simultaneous effect of drawing us near and holding us at a distance. Although this is evident on blogs from both first and second wave style blogging, it is more clearly demonstrated in the instance of second wave blogging, due to the aspirational outfits and lifestyle they often display. I will explore the dynamics of this dual pull by examining a particular post from the Australian second wave style blog *Shine By Three*.

Its blogger, Margaret, then-23 years old, wrote an outfit post about celebrating Chinese New Year in New York. Titled 'CHINESE NEW YORK: 恭喜發財' it reads like a photo essay of Margaret's day. In the city to attend New York Fashion Week, she 'lets us in' by writing about her frenetic day: attending fashion shows, shopping in Chinatown and Skyping her family in Sydney. I include an excerpt here to demonstrate her familiar tone, and the detail with which she writes.

> That morning, I baked myself an egg and tomatoes in coconut oil (a far cry from 西紅柿炒雞蛋), spent the day running between shows and Chipotle, shared three serves of Jamaican grilled corn with Michael, Jess and Bridget, and Skyped my dear brother back home, only to fall asleep at the keyboard and wake up with a hilarious collection of screenshots he'd taken the liberty of saving and sharing on Facebook. Such is the life of siblings.
>
> (Zhang 2013a)[3]

Reading the post for the first time, I was struck by the tension that both drew me into the midst of Margaret's day and positioned me on its margin as a spectator. Consider its narrative construction: although Margaret breaks the events of her day down into time brackets (8.30am, 9:00am, 10.30am and so on), detailing her activities therein, her written account stands in contrast to the accompanying photographs. She mentions going to Chinatown at five different times during the day, although all of the photographs are presented as one series, not depicting differing light corresponding to the changing hours, nor is Margaret ever seen carrying the decorations, lucky candy or groceries she describes buying.

I highlight this to draw attention to the discrepancy between what she writes that she actually did and what is visually presented. Although the photographs are shot documentary-style, these discrepancies suggest that they were posed. Rather than simply 'letting us in', though the post partially does this, Margaret is allowing us to observe her, and a particular 'her' that she is performing for us – her clothes are neat, they fall beautifully in motion, and the way she has arranged herself makes the details of her two outfits 'pop' – her arms and hands, for example, are always carefully turned to display the Mulberry Alexa handbag in her casual clasp.

Further, the Mulberry bag itself presents a small mystery. Margaret obliquely writes that 'Mulberry and I teamed up on this red Alexa bag of love' (Zhang 2013a), the name of the brand hyperlinked to the listing of the handbag in their e-shop. As readers, we do not know exactly what 'teamed up' means: Margaret did not design the bag, telling us that it was released not for Chinese New Year but 'technically for Valentine's Day' (Zhang 2013a), but we can surmise from its prominent placement in every outfit photograph that it has been either lent or gifted to Margaret to shoot for her blog. Whether or not it was called out, or if she was paid for this placement, is unclear, although, again, its centrality in the photos and her four mentions of it (two of which are hyperlinked) in the body of her post suggest that it was sponsored. In this way, we are not simply Margaret's readers learning about her day and observing her outfits, we are also potential customers of Mulberry. Such is the uncertain ground that readers of style blogs inhabit, moving between familiarity with a blogger and distance, whether as a result of the limited information made available to them (and the nature of the information itself) or due to their own attitude towards readership.

The spectrum of style blog readership: Relationship or entertainment?

Reading style blogs does not necessarily entail one consistent attitude of reader towards blogger and blog, but rather encompasses a spectrum of reader responses and affiliations. For some, reading is an active investment in a blog, characterized by an affective connection felt towards a blogger and/or a blog, often including some or all of the following behaviours: regular reading of a particular blog, commenting on posts, meeting a blogger offline and following that blogger on their affiliated social network accounts.

Of the 84 respondents of my survey, 44% claimed to read style blogs on a daily basis, with another 35.7% reading them at least once a week. Moreover, 42.9% said that they feel that they have a relationship with the bloggers who kept the blogs they regularly read. Some respondents described a familiarity with a blogger they personally knew before starting to read their blog, or with whom they had developed an offline friendship through having a blog of their own. Yet among those who described a situation in which they did not have a prior relationship with a blogger, coming to know them solely by being a reader, many also described feeling a similar sentiment of familiarity. One respondent described 'a sense of camaraderie when I agree with their point of view or idea [...] this warmth that someone else is on the same page as you', whereas another wrote 'even though it's generally a passive reader/author relationship, I still feel a sense of [connection] and CARE [sic] about them' (survey respondents, Findlay 2013).

At the other end of the spectrum of style blog readership are readers who browse style blogs for inspiration, entertainment or out of curiosity whilst feeling little attachment towards its blogger. 51.2% of my survey respondents said that they did not feel they had a relationship with the blogger who wrote the style blogs they regularly read: 'I'm just an observer', 'they're primarily information outlets for me', 'no relationship other than reader' and, more eloquently, 'not much beyond that of being a specific audience that likes their specific content. I do like the fairly personal/column style writing that bloggers use, but I still don't imagine one could construe that as a relationship beyond that of reader/writer' (survey respondents, Findlay 2013).

The almost even statistical split between readers who felt it was a relationship of sorts and those who did not demonstrates the range of possible reader responses, although the activity of reading style blogs does allow for movement between these two poles. As Baumer et al. have observed, 'blog readers often approach different blogs differently, and may contribute differently in different contexts' (2008: 1117). Thus a reader who is actively invested in one or two blogs may be largely disinterested in a multitude of others, whereas a casual reader of the genre may browse many blogs and feel more interest in one blog without feeling an affective connection with the blogger.

Neither group is more or less legitimate as readers, although interestingly a number of respondents to the survey felt that, because they did not leave comments on the blogs they read, they were less 'part of it' than if they had. When asked if they felt they had a relationship with the bloggers whose blogs they read, many of the respondents who replied in the negative seemed to do so because they saw themselves as 'just an observer' – 'I am an invisible observer', 'my role [is that of] a fan', it's 'generally a passive reader/author relationship'. Many responded that this was because their interaction was limited to reading rather than writing back: 'they write, I read', 'I am the observer and they are the observed [...] I don't comment, though' (survey respondents, Findlay 2013).

Standing in contrast to these were responses from readers who answered that they did interact with bloggers, either through social media or commenting. All of the respondents who engaged in this kind of interactivity felt some kind of interpersonal connection with the bloggers they read, which seems to suggest that the more a reader responds to a blog the more they feel that they are part of an 'active relationship', as Allen has argued (2009: 6). This was certainly affirmed by one of my survey's respondents who wrote that:

> [I feel that I have a relationship with a blogger] when the voice is particularly informal and intimate [...] not that I do in fact know them I suppose. After reading a blog for years they begin to seem like friends [...] it is lovely when they respond personally to comments.
>
> (survey respondent, Findlay 2013)

Other respondents remarked upon the significance of commenting in fostering feelings of a relationship of sorts towards a blogger. One remarked, 'I feel like the more I comment/interact with a blogger, then I really develop a relationship', a sentiment echoed by another respondent:

> [t]here's the sense of a relationship, as you have access to the blogger's personal thoughts and musings. Unless you make the effort to leave a comment, it can be a pretty one-way relationship though.
>
> (survey respondent, Findlay 2013)

Lurkers have feelings too

However, while Allen makes an important point in drawing out the personal, emotive connections fostered by style blogging, her argument that this can be characterized as an 'active relationship' requires some qualification: commenting is not necessary in order for readers to feel that they have a relationship ('active' or otherwise) with a blogger. As Baumer et al. argue, 'connectedness is constituted differently in different contexts; being part of a blog looks different for different readers, and connectedness, even when achieved by different means, is still connectedness' (2008: 1118).

My experience as a reader of style blogs echoed that of the respondent who wrote that although s/he experienced a kind of 'passive' mode of readership, she still feels 'a sense of [connection] and CARE about them' (survey respondent, Findlay 2013). I never left comments on posts even though I read every post on my favourite blogs, and would often click hyperlinks embedded in them to look up featured clothes or media (video clips, songs, fashion films) to complement my understanding of what the blogger was writing about.

A so-called 'lurker' (Preece et al. 2002: 202), I refrained from leaving comments when I started reading blogs. Blanchard notes that even though they may form the 'vast majority' of participants in an online culture, lurkers – the loosely pejorative term for regular readers of blogs who do not leave comments – are generally viewed in a negative light by researchers, as their mode of reading does not 'actively contribute to the virtual community' (2004: 4). Yet, building on her prior work with Markus, Blanchard argues that lurkers themselves often have a 'clear sense of community within the virtual community', although stipulating that this is weaker than that of 'active members', likening them to 'non-commenters' on a blog (2004).

This was certainly true of my experience: like the survey respondent quoted above, I 'CARED' about the bloggers whose posts I read on a daily basis and felt like I was part of their readership. Running in an open-ended narrative as I regularly clicked back to read the most recent posts, the lives of Tavi, Jane, Michelle, Marie and others became, to borrow a phrase from Bachelard, 'with me, in the with-me, with-us' (1994: 188). That is to say that a co-presence seems to arise through this habitual reading, a familiarity of address not just reaching readers at a 'personal and emotional level' as Allen argues (2009: 6), but also prompting a feeling of spending time together, as intimated in my habit of thinking of reading blogs as 'catching up' with bloggers, all without ever leaving a comment.

In fact, as the logics of second wave blogging shifted the genre, when people left comments at all, they tended to be uniformly complimentary in tone and underlined by the hyperlinked URL to the commenter's own blog: an act of enthusiastic self-promotion rather than a thoughtful response to the content of the post. Such comments read like a litany of bright compliments – Love the dress! You look amazing! Perfect as always, and the pictures are stunning!!! – and seem to be a small act of identification: I like your aesthetic, now come look at mine. The majority of readers, however, seem to participate as I did: engaged, interested but not visible. Kate Crawford identifies this as a kind of listening, arguing that lurkers 'directly contribute to the community by acting as a gathered audience: neither agreeing nor disagreeing, but listening (even if distractedly)' (2009: 527). A reader's enjoyment may be more indirectly manifested on the contemporary style blogosphere, measured in likes on a post's corresponding representation on Instagram and Facebook, or in 'pins' on Pinterest. These low-level and diffuse modes of participation – a click, an acknowledgement – are also modes of engagement, the small but significant accretion of approval showing that someone was there and that they liked what they saw.

The co-presence of reading

Reading style blogs can feel like stepping through the threshold of the computer screen to spend time in the world (and the company) of a style blogger, a sense that is contiguous with the spatial inhabitation intimated in the last chapter. In stepping 'through' in this way, the boundary between them as unknown blogger and us as anonymous readers blurs as we engage with their posts as we read. It is an ongoing process of augmenting information previously communicated, enhancing or subtly altering our understanding of a blogger, adding to their narrative of self and advancing our own connection to them. One respondent to the survey admitted as much when they commented that 'after reading some blogs for a while, you begin to feel like you need to "tune-in" to find out what's happening with the blogger' (survey respondent, Findlay 2013), suggesting a sense of being left behind or out-of-date if one's readership lags.

During my prolonged readership of style blogs, I found myself emotionally invested in the lives of the bloggers I regularly read, though in a way that was consistent with my relationship towards them as a reader. That it was one-sided, in that they did not respond to me individually, did not mitigate the relationality I experienced 'between us', because even though I knew the posts were written for a general public, a 'with us', they were written in a manner that suggested that I, too, was familiar. Amanda Lenhart makes a similar observation, writing that 'the audience for a blog is addressed as though they are individuals who make up a larger collective whole' (2005: 97). And so, for example, between feeling like part of Tavi's public and also experiencing an engaged connection towards her as a regular reader, I felt that we had an active relationship.

It is important to clarify here that the reciprocity of this relationship was enacted through the fulfilment of our respective roles within it: Tavi was blogging and I was reading. Moreover, it felt like I was sharing in her success simply by reading along and I missed her company when she slowly ceased blogging on *Style Rookie* to focus on other creative projects. Interestingly, it seems that Tavi felt a similar affectionate connection towards 'us' too, as evident in a post she published on her blog in 2013.

> I do feel an obligation to people who have read my blog for a long time that is not unlike the unspoken understanding you have with your first best friend […] whose insight into whatever you do from now on is shaped by a unique knowledge of all the ties which bind New You to Old You […] In other words, we had a time.
>
> (Gevinson, *Style Rookie*, 3 April 2013)

How to explain this intimacy, especially in light of the distance at which it was experienced? Despite the feeling I described earlier of stepping through the screen, this is not, of course, a literal occurrence. We move closer by reading but read at a remove: reached through our personal computers, tablets or smartphones, we are solitary whilst we are keeping company. We might be reading a post that was written hours before we found it and experience a proximity, an immediacy with the blogger who wrote it, even though she may have scheduled the post's publication and is out doing other things while we are catching up with her on our way home on the other side of the world. Yet in reading we feel that we are co-present, that familiarity is fostering between us, and while this is genuine, it is also mediated by the medium of blogs.

Intimate publics

How can we conceptualize this connection between people on and through style blogs? As mapped so far, it is a complex, tangential, affective, partially imagined, occasionally reciprocal and permeable relationship. Each group – readers and bloggers – attends to the activity of the other, but at a remove of space, place and temporality. This is a remove maintained both by partial knowing and partial belonging and yet at the same time, it can sustain a tangible connection of sorts.

This mediated relationality between style bloggers and their readers is best conceived of as an *intimate public*, after Lauren Berlant's work on the ways that mass media in America made possible communities of intimacy, expression and sentimentality between women. This concept offers us a language to acknowledge the complex and affective mode of reading that occurs on style blogs, while particularly speaking to the central role women and girls play in enacting and participating in the style blogosphere. Conceiving of style blog relationality in this way reframes prior discussions that sought to articulate this reader/blogger dynamic as a kind of virtual community or as a kind of conversation. Rather than play an academic game of splitting conceptual hairs for the sake of cleverness, my efforts to articulate readership on the blogosphere takes place in the midst of the slipperiness of words. That is, words like 'community' and 'conversation' imply dynamics that are simply not widely representative of the modes of readership I have identified on the style blogosphere. I will here tease out these implications before outlining why intimate publics get us closer to the thing itself.

Commingled but not a community

The most common concept employed by digital theorists to describe people engaging in specific practices around shared interests or modes of communicating online is that they are 'virtual communities' (see Chin and Chignell 2006; Wise et al. 2006; Boyd Thomas et al. 2007; Efimova and Hendrick 2005). As Blanchard argues, the term has been used broadly to apply to any kind of computer-mediated communication group (CMC) to the point where it no longer has any real meaning (2004: 1). She reasons that the term 'virtual communities' is employed by theorists ultimately seeking to legitimize the online group as well as explain its significance in the lives of participants, yet she observes that 'not all virtual groups are virtual communities' (1).

Whether or not blogs are virtual communities is the subject of ongoing theoretical debate. A number of theorists have concluded that blogs demonstrate aspects of community but that due to the lack of established interpersonal links, limited interactivity between participants and lack of shared space (or a 'virtual settlement', see Blanchard 2004) they are not communities (Blanchard 2004; Mortensen 2004). However, Chin and Chignell (2006), Ali-Hasan and Adamic (2007) and Efimova and Hendrick (2005) have concluded that the shared interest of participants, the reciprocal linking between bloggers to one another's blogs in their posts and on blogrolls, and the virtual settlement of bloggers in the spaces between personal weblogs all indicate the structure of community.

Complicating any discussion about whether a particular genre or sub-genre of blogs is a community or not is the lack of a single definition of what a virtual community actually is. Despite its somewhat antiquated terminology, most useful is Rheingold's definition of virtual communities as 'social aggregations that emerge from the Net when enough people carry on those public discussions long enough, with sufficient human feeling, to form webs of personal relationships in cyberspace' (Rheingold, quoted in Chin and Chignell 2006: 27). This definition predates the widespread development of the blogosphere, so whether these aggregations are comprised only of bloggers, or include readers also is a moot point. That said, later studies have minimized the input of readers by asserting that many readers are also bloggers, and thereby measuring a person's involvement in the community through their blogroll and citation links (see Ali-Hasan and Adamic 2007). Others have defined blogs as a particular *kind* of community, one with no obvious boundaries and a 'large periphery that is disengaged from the core' (Lampa 2004: 3; see also Efimova and Hendrick 2005).

Whilst these later studies make some useful points about the concept of community and how it might be applied to blogs, the lack of consideration of readers as part of the community is problematic. In a genre where the presence of readers is inherent to the text type of blogs and is desired by bloggers, it does not make sense to apply the notion of community only to bloggers. As I have argued, reading is an active and affective practice in its own right, and as such, should be considered as part of sociality on the style blogosphere. Even though many readers also have blogs, this fact does not necessarily place them in community with the bloggers whose blogs they themselves read. For example, a blogger can list another blog in their blogroll without this being reciprocated, and can leave comments that are never acknowledged by the blogger to whose blog they have been posted, neither of which make either party less a part of the blogosphere.

In order, then, to determine whether 'community' is a useful concept in relation to sociality on style blogs, I will draw primarily on the work of Blanchard, who provides an excellent overview of criteria that can be implemented to test if a virtual group can be deemed a community. She builds on the work of Quentin Jones who argued that researchers must 'differentiate between the technology on which the virtual group exists and the actual virtual community' (Blanchard 2004: 2). According to Jones, a virtual settlement is the grounds within which a virtual community is situated, and it indicates the presence of a virtual community. A virtual settlement exists when there are:

a) a minimal number of b) public interactions c) with a variety of communicators in which d) there is a minimal level of sustained membership over a period of time.

(2004: 2)

Blanchard and Markus (2004) furnish this definition by emphasizing the importance of a psychological sense of community amongst participants in the alleged community, an aspect of virtual community that Jones's model does not emphasize. Blanchard expands further upon this by citing McMillan and Chavis's four characteristics of a sense of community, which elucidate its affective elements. The four characteristics are: feelings of membership (belonging to and identifying with the community); feelings of influence (having influence on and being influenced by others in the community); integration and fulfilment of needs (feeling supported by others whilst supporting them) and shared emotional connection (Blanchard 2004: 2–3).

Applying these criteria to style blogs reveals the way in which they only partially meet the definition of a virtual community. Whilst there are regular 'public interactions' through the conventions of posting and commenting, the output of bloggers and readers is not weighted with equal significance. In selecting the subject matter of their posts, and with all of the content being based in their own appearance, tastes and interests, style bloggers are the primary communicators on their blog. They write the majority of the text that appears on their blog, giving their voice dominance over the opinions of their readers.[4] In this way personal style blogs differ to other CMCs, such as forums or even social media platforms such as Facebook or Twitter, where the post of an initial user might establish a conversation that is subsequently built upon and sustained by the contributions of others.

This aspect of style blogs also counter-indicates the third and fourth of Jones's criteria: whilst there might be a variety of 'communicators' on a style blog, their participation does not necessarily signify a 'sustained membership over a period of time'. As Lampa (2004) and Efimova and Hendrick (2005) have pointed out, weblog communities often do not demonstrate clear boundaries or membership, with many participating from the periphery as lurkers. As the results of my survey indicate, many readers felt a *partial* belonging to a style blog public, feeling affection for or interest in a blogger without necessarily experiencing that as a 'relationship' with them. In this way, the engaged, reciprocal model evoked by McMillan and Chavis's characteristics – of *belonging to* and *identifying with*, of *having influence on* as well as *being influenced by*, and so on – describe a more invested mode of participation than was described by most of the participants of my survey.

The engaged activity of readers and bloggers was, for the most part, more prevalent in first wave style blogging. Bloggers such as Danielle Meder and Jessica Quirk described meeting early in their blogging careers with other bloggers whose blogs they read, and who read their blogs in return. In interview, both described these as instances in which their online friendships deepened. For example, Jessica explained that she used to attend 'meet-ups' with other bloggers, which led to her developing 'a real friendship' with them (Quirk, in conversation with the author, 2013). In fact, when Jessica spoke about the early period of her blogging career, she used the word 'community' to describe the Wardrobe Remix group she joined on Flickr, explaining how she 'got to know people' by commenting on the group and both by keeping her blog and reading those of other people. Yet when I asked her about her use of the word 'community', what it looked like to her in the early days, she said:

> [W]hen I think of community, I think of interpersonal relationships […] unfortunately it's not the same as it used to be because it has become super commercialised and everyone is like 'how do I make a buck? How do I take her spot?'
>
> (Quirk 2013)

Of course bloggers still meet up with and contact one another outside of their blogs. Rosalind Jana, for example, received care packages from two other bloggers with whom she had developed friendships through blogging whilst recovering from surgery in hospital. Moreover, as noted by Ali-Hasan and Adamic, bloggers that are part of the same community – or, who have a reciprocal relationship as readers of one another's blogs and perhaps a relationship also enacted outside their blogs – 'have a tendency to mention one another in blog posts and to communicate with one another through comments' (2007). This is especially evident in the posts of certain bloggers who feature their 'blogfriends' in their posts. While not very common on the blogosphere, when it happens, bloggers usually feature each other due to having worked together or having appeared at the same industry event as each other.

For a brief window in style blogging's history, a number of influential blogs were grouped on specific aggregate websites that coordinated lucrative advertising deals for the bloggers they featured, who were individually invited to join and have their blogs embedded on the website. Condé Nast's version was NowManifest, active between 2012 and early 2015, and it hosted style blogs such as *fashiontoast*, *Style Bubble* and *Bryanboy*. The Australian answer to NowManifest, Fellt, was released by digital publisher Sydney Stockholm in 2012 and featured a hand-picked range of high-profile Australian blogs such as *Shine by Three*, *Gary Pepper*, *Harper and Harley*, *Oracle Fox* and *Zanita*. On both networks, certain bloggers would feature each other: Rumi and Bryan (*fashiontoast* and *Bryanboy*) would post photographs of them lolling together on a couch at a Mulberry party at Coachella, for example, or Sydney-based photographer Zanita would shoot her friend Nicole (*Zanita* and *Gary Pepper*) on a sponsored holiday they took together to Paris. Readers, viewing the images of these blogger hangouts, may surmise that due to being hosted on the same exclusive network, these entrepreneurial bloggers had access to opportunities to consolidate their blogging work and play in a display of genuine friendship.

These friendships were also mutually beneficial, as bloggers linked to each other in their respective posts in a kind of cross-promotion. For example, when Zanita would shoot her blogfriends whose blogs, like hers, were part of the Fellt network, the photographed bloggers would credit Zanita for the shots, which she also would post on *Zanita*. The friendship between these bloggers was also visibly and publicly enacted online in other ways, as they would tweet at one another, take (and subsequently blog) photographs together at industry events and participate in sponsored activities together, such as when Zanita and Margaret Zhang stayed in a private villa in Sri Panwa, Thailand, staging multiple photo shoots that both posted on their respective blogs. Zanita shot Margaret, Margaret shot Zanita, and it was all posted for us to enjoy after the fact (see Whittington, *Zanita*, 2012a, 2012b, 2012c; Zhang, *Shine by Three*, 2012b, 2012c, 2012d).

While these are certainly examples of 'close online relationships naturally progress[ing] to face-to-face interactions' (Ali-Hasan and Adamic 2007: 2), they are not evidence of broader community being enacted on the style blogosphere. Although blogger relationships such as these fulfil McMillan and Chavis's four criteria (membership, influence, integration and fulfilment of needs and shared emotional connection), they are exclusive. As readers, we are spectators rather than participants in these relationships; we are not invited to partake in the activities or conversations being had between the Fellt bloggers, or Rumi (*fashiontoast*) and Bryan (*Bryanboy*), or even Tavi (*Style Rookie*) and 'her wife' Arabelle (*Fashion Pirate*; see Gevinson, *Style Rookie*, 2009d).

For all of these reasons, the concept of 'community' is only partially useful in a consideration of sociality on the style blogosphere. The 'emotionally positive effect' implicit in the term (Blanchard 2004: 2), the possibility of reciprocated communication, and the co-presence of readers and bloggers are all aspects of the concept of virtual community evident in style blogging. Yet at the same time, the only partial applicability of Blanchard's proposed framework demonstrates that this concept inadequately describes the dynamic between style bloggers and their readers.

Conversational, but not a conversation

The relationship between bloggers and readers has also been characterized as a conversation in literature specific to style blogging (see Rocamora and Bartlett 2009). This distinction is based upon the familiar tone with which style bloggers address their readers as well as the comment function on most blogs. This latter aspect is taken as indicative of 'not only the interactive conversational character of communication within the blogosphere, but also the camaraderie many readers feel towards the bloggers they address' (Rocamora and Bartlett 2009: 111).

Camaraderie is certainly present in both the comments left on style blogs as well as in the prevailing attitude of bloggers towards their readers, as is evinced through the tone and familiarity of their address. Yet I hesitate to characterize this mode of communication as a conversation, even if it is conversational and in a basic sense, interactive. This may seem like a fine distinction, but it is an important one: style blogs were sites of engaged conversation in first wave blogging, but the incidence of this has declined across second wave style blogs, resulting in a change in the culture of style blogging.

The word 'conversation' implies reciprocal engagement on a certain topic, whether that be a sustained interaction between two parties or employed in the broader rhetorical sense of an open-ended conversation developing around a certain topic (for example, when newspapers exhort their readers to 'become part of the conversation' by buying a subscription). It is employed by Rocamora and Bartlett to demonstrate the shift in discourse brought about by style blogs, which allow for 'a community of readers' to 'take up the terms of [a blogger's] enquiry and comment' on it (2009: 111). This model operates in contrast to the 'dominant rules' that structure alternative modes of fashion discourse (such as the fashion media), and presents instead the opportunity for readers to engage with and relate to fashion from within the context of their everyday lives (2009: 111–12).

Rocamora and Bartlett make a significant observation here, that fashion blogs mark a shift in which fashion communication became situated within the sphere of a reader's everyday, in contrast – and in addition – to that circulated by the traditional fashion media. However, unlike other sub-genres of fashion blogs that feature more of an even exchange between bloggers and the readers who comment on their posts, the interactivity occurring on style blogs is not adequately described as a conversation. This is mainly due to the ways in which communication is enacted and moderated on them.[5]

While style blogs largely consist of content blogged on the common theme of fashion and personal style, they are singular texts in that what demarcates them from one another is the specificity of their focus on the blogger's personal style and perspective on fashion. If they could be said to implicitly make a shared statement about fashion due to their number and alternative content (such as the individuality of style, or the need for user-driven texts about fashion to reflect its central place in the lives of some), a counter argument could also be made, in that there is little else that unites such blogs beyond participating in this shared sub-genre. Unlike other genres of blogging, such as the Egyptian and Lebanese sociopolitical blogospheres analysed by Sarah Jurkiewicz, for example (see Jurkiewicz 2011), it is difficult to categorize the style blogosphere in terms of a shared sentiment or general thematic focus. Rather, style bloggers focus on their own perspectives: their style, their take on a collection or trend, their own strong feelings about a pair of shoes or deep satisfaction with their new leather leggings.

It might then seem more useful to limit the application of 'conversation' to that which occurs between a blogger and their readers at the level of an individual blog. This figuring is best applied to the kinds of interactions that took place during first wave style blogging, as is evident from the personal histories given by Danielle Meder and Julie Fredrickson in Chapter One. In the early days of fashion blogging, bloggers would have conversations with their readers in the comments section of their blogs. Readers would discuss the content of the post and often the blogger would respond. Readers might expect or hope that bloggers would reciprocate by clicking their hyperlinked name and engaging with the content posted on their own blogs. Occasionally these discursive connections led to bloggers meeting, sending each other packages of clothing and fashion-related material, and referring to one another in their posts ('my wife Belle'). These interactions demonstrate the initially active nature of style blog readership and authorship, which was a mutually enacted conversation that had the possibility of developing into 'a real friendship' (Quirk, in conversation with the author, 2013).

Yet as second wave style blogging has shifted the dynamics of the blogosphere, such engaged commenting practice and cross-posting has diminished. I observed this as a reader and it was also noted by Isabel Slone, who expressed exasperation at the kind of comments her blog was attracting from readers. She said that writing that in the 'olden days [it felt like] people were talking to [me]' whereas at the time of the interview, readers would just post brief, broad compliments – 'NICE SHIRT X' – followed by a link to their own blog (Slone, in conversation with the author, 2012).

Such an experience stands in contrast to Isabel's prior experiences.

I used to feel like other bloggers were my friends and stuff, [because] the comments were so genuine and we would always comment on each other's posts and [...] it was like a relationship that we had. But I don't know [...] now I don't really comment on people's blogs and I don't really know any of the people who comment on my blog because I rarely bother looking at them. I'm just like, 'oh okay, it's there, that's nice'. So, I feel more disconnected I'd say. I started out like being like [a] sort of a web but I guess now I've retreated and I'm more of an island.

(Slone, in conversation with the author, 2012)

Jessica Quirk also noted this shift in communication on style blogs:

[a]t the beginning it was more of an even exchange – like me to you, you to me, like a lot of equal [...] absorbing information and giving it out. And I think now, it's more me giving it out and spreading it and people occasionally coming back to me and responding.

(Quirk, in conversation with the author, 2013)

In second wave style blogging, comments primarily function to express enthusiasm for a post and to attract readers (and in most cases, ideally the blogger whose post the comment was left on) back to the commenter's blog. Whilst this is couched in the traditionally positive tone of communication germane to the style blogosphere, such comments as much signify a desire for 'hits' as it does for engaged readers.

The more hits or uniques their blog receives, the more leverage a blogger has to work with brands and the more income they can generate from advertising revenue, which is predicated on blog traffic. Such an underlying ethos can be summarized by the following advice published on Independent Fashion Bloggers (IFB):

[P]ut yourself in the shoes of a busy, half-crazed publicist trying to stay on top of all the best in emerging blogger talent and help her understand why your blog matters. From blog traffic to social media stats to recent press, build up your reputation and help her pitch your value back to her client by giving her the goods on who you are and why working with you is a win-win.

(Noricks 2013)

IFB was not solely responsible for this change in tenor, but articles such as this demonstrate the prevailing mentality on the contemporary style blogosphere. That is, style blogging is something that can be done 'successfully', and success is measured in particular terms (which seem to resonate with style bloggers based on the affirming and grateful responses such IFB posts commonly attract). That is, to have a large number of followers (both on the blog and on its affiliated social media accounts) and the opportunity to become a professional blogger attracting contracts and advertising revenue and, ultimately, the lifestyle that the most high-profile bloggers seem to live.

The role of readers becomes ambiguous, then, as their presence is not just desirable to be 'part of the conversation' but also is the key to other opportunities for bloggers. This seems to be an outworking of the pervasive neo-liberal logics that increasingly circulate the style blogosphere (and contemporary western society more broadly), in which bloggers are compelled to see themselves as 'tiny corporations' (Graeber, quoted in McNeill and Zuern 2015: xxii), being themselves a kind of capital, their existence reconfigured as an entrepreneurial opportunity. Such a precarious neo-liberal paradigm, McNeill and Zuern argue, 'puts our very selfhood on the defensive, and compels us to privilege our own self-interest over the welfare of others', seeing others as competition for market share (2015: xxii).

In light of this shift in modes of readership and commenting from first to second wave blogging, how important is reciprocity? In her ethnography on blogging and readership, Amanda Lenhart draws on the work of Bakhtin to assert that the lack of reciprocal responses between bloggers and readers does not necessarily mean that they are not in conversation. For Lenhart, blogs conform to Bakhtin's argument about utterances – for 'all conversation that may be responded to' – which assume the presence of an audience to hear them and which operate dialogically with utterances that have come before it (2005: 69). All blogs, then, 'are always in conversation regardless of whether a reader comments or the author is responding to a specific idea from another blog' (2005: 69).

Lenhart, along with other theorists, thus likens the conversational mode of address of weblogs to broadcast (see Nardi et al. 2004; Langellier and Peterson 2004; Lenhart 2005). In their work on storytelling in everyday life, Kristin Langellier and Eric Peterson argue, via the work of Paddy Scannell, that unlike other modes of public address (such as a political speech or theatrical performance), broadcasts 'address the audience in a one-to-one fashion' rather than as one-of-many (2004: 170). Similarly, Lenhart argues, weblogs are written towards individuals as part of a whole – 'a one-to-one relationship, collected as many' (2005: 98) – and, similar to the solo radio listener who must never be addressed as a collective, they often read on their own. Therefore, a blog's reader can feel that a post is written for them, like the reader in my survey who commented that 'reading the blog is like reading an email' (survey

106

respondent, Findlay 2013), even while they know that many other readers already have and will continue to read the same post. However, as Warner argues:

> [W]e might recognize ourselves as addressees, but it is equally important that we remember that the speech was addressed to indefinite others, that in singling us out it does so not on the basis of our concrete identity but by virtue of our participation in the discourse alone and therefore in common with strangers.
>
> (2002: 77–78)

Therefore, while style blogs are *conversational* in the manner of their address to an imagined audience, and while they are written around a specific topic (in this sense, 'joining the conversation' about fashion online), a more useful way to conceptualize the dynamic between bloggers and readers is to think of them as participants in an intimate public.

An intimate public

'How can I call "intimate" a public constituted by strangers who consume common texts and things?' (2008: vii–viii) asks Lauren Berlant in the preface to *The Female Complaint*, her study of the affective and feminized publics invoked by literature aimed at a female readership. This echoes Michael Warner's question that opened this chapter: how is it that we recognize strangers as friends, as somehow sharing in our individual lived experience and proximal to us? Both writers argue that this stranger relationality takes place through publics, an imagined and affective 'us' created and sustained by texts through which readers (or listeners, depending on the text) recognize themselves as being addressed.

Michael Warner argues that publics are ubiquitous in modern life but that often we recognize and participate in them without considering the ways that they structure and constitute social life. In outlining their characteristic features, Warner explains that publics are self-organized, or 'organized by nothing other than discourse itself' (2002: 67), the content and tone of which demarcate the selection of people who will respond to it. What binds this group of strangers together is their orientation towards one another by their mutual apprehension of a text. These people 'are identified primarily through their participation in the discourse and [...] therefore cannot be known in advance' (74), which leads to the mode of address of the public speech being 'both personal and impersonal', or, as Warner evocatively puts it, 'we know that it was addressed not exactly to us but to the stranger we were until the moment we happened to be addressed by it' (76). 'A public is constituted through mere attention', then, as it exists 'by virtue of address', so must be taken up by an addressee (87). Moreover, publics are 'poetic world making', in that a text defines its life-world in its mode of address: its discourse, its subject matter, its position and so on already shaping its 'circulatory fate' that Warner calls 'the realization of that world' (114).

Berlant elaborates upon this definition by defining how it is that certain publics – *The Female Complaint* studied works of popular literature created for a mass market of female readers – speak to certain groups of people, thereby producing particular resonances and effects. She argues that 'publics presume intimacy', and that this intimacy is fostered by an 'expectation that the consumers of [a public sphere's] particular stuff already share a worldview and emotional knowledge that they have derived from a broadly common historical experience' (2008: vii–viii). In other words, it is what we have in common – or what we perceive that we have in common – with other readers and with style bloggers that draws us together and shapes our participation in a kind of distanced, ambiguous togetherness.

The affective element inferred by Berlant's incorporation of 'intimacy' also speaks to the felt proximity of readership evident in this chapter so far. This is consistent with the connotations of positivity and relationality implied by the concepts of style blogs as part of a 'conversation' or 'community': the first by invoking a reciprocal engagement between two or more parties; the second through its vague but 'warmly persuasive' (Williams 1984: 76) invocation of a somewhat united set of relationships. We experience such publics as a place where individual experience assumes aspects of the general, even insofar as what is shared are desires (for example, desire for Jane's amazing YSL cage booties – she loves them and wears them, we think they're cool and long to own them) and interests (in fashion, in the personal style of the blogger, in a space for the discussion and display of clothing and one's appearance in that clothing).

Berlant argues that by expressing a way of living in the world, intimate publics also promise to improve people's experience of social belonging 'partly through participation in the relevant commodity culture, and partly because of its revelations about how people can live' (2008: viii). Her work here gives us a language not only to understand style blogs as creating intimate publics, but also to perceive the differences between affectivity in the publics of both first wave and second wave style blogs. As previously described, for early bloggers and readers, there was a joy in finding and recognizing a network of bloggers writing about fashion in alternative, deeply felt and personal ways. While these blogs were often aesthetically humble, especially in the early years before the widespread adoption of increasingly affordable and easy to use DSLR cameras and photo-editing software, they also made visible ways of conceiving of the intimate relationship between style and identity, between affect and the fashion product that were, up to that point, rarely publically articulated. First wave style blogs thus 'introduced a new type of information into fashion discourse, one nourished by the ordinary experiences and personal viewpoints of their authors' (Rocamora and Bartlett 2009: 108).

The rhetorical and imaginative possibilities offered by first wave blogs created a space for the public sharing of particular kinds of experiences, and for a reimagining of how fashion as a concept could be communicated. This saw bloggers talking about fashion in a way that cohered with their experience of fashion as accessible and enfolded into their everyday experience, their language on their blogs mirroring this by 'privileg[ing] a spontaneous tone grounded in subjectivity and irreverence' (Rocamora and Bartlett 2009:

107). In this way, first wave style blogs spoke to and found a public that 'got it', becoming a space of connection where what was personal resonated with the general, where affective connections between bloggers and readers were fostered and encouraged. By styling themselves into view, and writing about their style in personal and conversational ways, first wave style bloggers thus reimagined 'stranger sociability and its reflexivity' (Warner 2002: 118–19) and did so in contrast to the dominant cultural horizon of the mainstream fashion media. Their mode of sociability abandoned the hierarchical relationship between publication and readership that is common to mainstream fashion publications. Rather than identifying runway trends and translating them into 'key pieces' or looks for their readers, they wrote from within their own perspective: a garment or look was valued because they liked it, not necessarily because it was 'in', and they published under the presumption that their readership would find it interesting rather than necessarily being relevant to their own lives.

Yet despite their aesthetic similarity to the mainstream fashion media, second wave style blogs also create space for imagination, for the revelation of how people can live. I explore this more extensively in the following chapter by outlining the ways that second wave style bloggers perform an aspirational life after the aesthetic of mainstream fashion editorial spreads. Second wave style blogs positively frame participation in consumer culture, providing a space for evaluation of the goods presented, for the dreaming of inhabiting their subject position or acting as inspiration for their readers' own style. These blogs shape a space for the celebration of acquisition, of the new, of the transformative capacities of clothing that can draw us into a different way of being in the world. This is an example of feminized space where commodities such as clothing, shoes and make-up are enjoyed and promoted, presented to us by a blogger for our enjoyment. This illustrates Berlant's argument that 'people marked by femininity' share a common need for a

> [...] conversation that feels intimate, revelatory and a relief even when it is mediated by commodities, even when it is written by strangers who might not be women, and even when its particular stories are about women who seem, on the face of it, vastly different from each other and from any particular reader.
>
> (2008: viii–ix)

On the second wave blogosphere, vastly distinct as it is from first wave blogging, we also see the sharing of the personal as an invitation to reflect on a shared interest in fashion and personal style, to collectively but individually think through personal identity, consumption and beauty. In this way, participating in reading style blogs, as Berlant argues more generally about women's culture, is a 'way of experiencing one's own story as part of something social, even if one's singular relation to that belonging is extremely limited, episodic, ambivalent, rejecting, or mediated by random encounters with relevantly marked texts' (2008: x). I can be ambivalent, then, about a second wave blogger wearing an outfit as shown on the runway even as I am drawn to look at the pictures because I'm interested in how she shot them. I can long for a blogger's Proenza Schouler shoes while wondering if she really bought them or if they were a gift from the label (or from an industry sample sale? A lucky end of season find? *Are they still available?*), and feeling irritated that second wave bloggers rarely disclose how and where they got their clothes, and also thinking she looks really nice. I can stop reading a blog for a couple of years because I'm getting bored of her obsession with a 90s Goth Girl aesthetic but rediscover her (and her blog) at a later date to find her changed in subtle ways but still familiar, still my kind-of friend. The intimate public of the style blogosphere allows for this kind of fluid membership as well as the dynamics of desire, interest, boredom, irritation and pleasure that flicker through the experience of reading style blogs.

Although the style blogosphere is indeed comprised of a dispersed group of mostly strangers united by mutual participation in and engagement with one another through style blogs, this relation of stranger to stranger is imbued with an intimacy that can be fostered through sustained and mediated interaction with others. Not all members of the style blogging public experience a kind of affective connection to the blogger that they read, but many readers do; and furthermore, as I have demonstrated, many style bloggers write with affection towards their readers and experience a relationship of sorts with them. Here we see readers addressed as known persons, drawn into an intimate sociality with bloggers not just through having access to personal content about a blogger's taste, person and (sometimes) life, but also by being invoked as an intimate.

To conceive of a style blog's readership as an intimate public acknowledges the close relationality felt by style bloggers and their readers whilst acknowledging that this is sociality enacted at a distance, peopled by strangers, many of whom will remain anonymous but nevertheless invested members of a blogger's public. In these ways, this concept encapsulates the tangential, permeable, affective and partial modes of sociality particular to the blogosphere, and in this instance, the style blogosphere. Bloggers and readers are aware of one another, have affective responses to the presence and sometimes contributions of the other but often without knowing them in a reciprocal interpersonal way: strangers who, through shared participation, come to constitute a social entity.

Notes

1　Coincidentally, this was also a sentiment echoed by Lenhart, who started blogging seven years before me. She wrote in the preface to her Masters' thesis that her blog was 'a place to be another part of myself: slightly silly, a little morose, "earnestly brainy"' (2005: 2).

2　'Calling out' is an industry term for the stylist's practice of borrowing stock from a fashion label or shop to shoot it for a campaign or editorial spread. The stock is returned after the shoot has taken place.

3　'西紅柿炒雞蛋' translates as 'Xihongshi Chao Jidan', or Chinese scrambled eggs with tomatoes, a traditional and popular Chinese dish.

4   A possible exception to this might be the blog *Atlantic-Pacific*, the content of which consists solely of outfit photographs of blogger Blair Eadie without any accompanying text. However, as all of the imagery is of Blair, and she writes all of the accompanying social media posts for the blog (Twitter, Facebook and so on), it is still her voice and image that is dominant on the blog.

5   There are, of course, other fashion blogs to which this trope applies more fittingly, such as some of the non-style blogs referenced in the article (such as *The Sartorialist* and *Garance Doré*). These bear significant differences to style blogs, and accordingly, their reading public engage in different – and often more discursive – ways. It is outside the scope of this work to analyse these, although Rocamora and Bartlett (2009) provide an excellent overview.

Chapter 4

Performing Fashion's Imaginary

Through clothes we wear our bodies and fabricate ourselves.
— Jennifer Craik, *The Face of Fashion* (1994)

I t is a strange experience to encounter the 'you' of two or three years ago in technicolour intimacy. Keeping a style blog makes such an experience available, easy as it is to scroll backwards through your own archive to re-encounter your younger self in the ever-present tense of the blogged past. When I did this in May 2013, I was startled to find myself feeling that I was observing someone only dimly familiar to me. As I later posted,

> I remember her red hair [...], I remember the proclivity to reach exclusively for black and sharp, finding armour or a veil in the sheer floor-length and the hats and the don't-mess-with-me rings. Those clothes were a material overlay that gave shape to my feelings at the time [... followed by] the colours I burst into as I found my footing assuredly in 2011, and blossomed in brights. How did I get from there to this stage where navy is the colour of choice, often worn top to toe in jumpers, skirts, stockings? With more confidence in my work, more confidence in myself? [...]
>
> I recognise that Rosie, feel affection for her. She is me, but in a different season, and seeing her in those posts gives me a clearer look at her than my memory serves [...] It is both strange and lovely, because I saw the self that grew into the [woman] I feel myself to be today [... it is also odd because] this feeling that I could encounter my own self as a stranger in such a manner – to discover my past self as a 'foreign country', to borrow from L.P. Hartley – this I did not expect.
>
> (Findlay, *Fashademic*, 22 May 2013)[1]

It is tempting to make definitive statements about the intersection of a blogger's personal style and their identity on a style blog. After all, these two equivocal entities have long been invoked in theoretical discussions about the social, semiotic and personal significance of dress, and bloggers themselves often explain (or legitimize) their practice by asserting that their dress is a 'self-expression'.[2] This catch-all phrase kept surfacing throughout my research, both in conversation with bloggers as well as in their posts, and yet it never seemed to accurately describe the mutable, ongoing performance of self through style that I was observing on the style blogosphere.

Figures 10–15: These images show a selection of outfit post photographs that I blogged between 2010–2013. They reveal a number of changes: my hair colour lightening from red to blonde to my natural colour, my mania for hats and sheer floor-length skirt phase, my gradual drift into bright colours and prints. Also evident is my increasing comfort in front of the camera and a number of locations I inhabited during this time: a number of apartments, the University of Sydney campus and the womenswear boutique where I casually worked during my candidature.

The word 'express' derives from the Latin *exprimere*, which translates as 'press out', developing in the Middle Ages to the contemporary English definition of 'expression', as an action or creation manifesting a feeling. In this sense, dress can certainly be deemed as expressive, in making material a feeling, sensibility or desire, yet it is reductive to assert that dress is a kind of self-expression. This implies that dress assumes its significance after the prior constitution of the self, and also suggests the existence of a unified self that can be monologically articulated through clothing. Rather, as the above anecdote of my blogging experience suggests, our dressed identity is as unfixed as our dress itself. Even over the three-and-a-half years during which I kept *Fashademic,* my personal style morphed through many transitions as I sought to dress in ways that materialized how I felt and wished to appear in different periods of my life. Looking back through my archive, it was possible to trace the shift from one iteration of self to another (see Figures 10–15), as I dressed according to how I felt myself to be during that time. In dressing towards my readers, then, I was also dressing into myself.

This was a phenomenon I also observed on other blogs during my prolonged readership of the style blogosphere: over years, bloggers' style would morph, as their influences and tastes changed and as they grew older. Often, this would be gradual: a haircut, a movement away from a signature aesthetic into something new, and sometimes bloggers would comment directly on it. For example, in response to a reader's question asking how she feels her style has evolved since starting her blog *Cupcakes and Cashmere*, Emily Schuman replied,

> I began my blog when I was 24 years old, so as a 30 year old, my style has certainly changed over the years. Not just with the way that I dress now, which I think is a lot more classic and tailored, streamlined, but also it's really my philosophy on how I shop [that has changed…] I think I make smarter investments and I'm a little bit more aware of what looks good on me and what I should avoid.
>
> (Schuman, *Cupcakes and Cashmere*, 2013a)

This chapter will closely engage with the complex interrelation between personal style, image and identity on the space of style blogs. The three are almost inextricable as they flow into one another in a circular way: bloggers dress in outfits that demonstrate their personal style, creating a visual performance of their identity, which is displayed through outfit post images. These three concepts are ambiguous on the style blogosphere, imbricated with a blogger's selfhood in partial, elaborate and shifting ways.

Style blogs are sites for the exploration of subjectivities and the performance of identity, two processes ineluctably bound up with what is presented as a blogger's personal style. The dynamics of feeling and looking, of image and embodiment are intertwined with literally dressing oneself into view. This is a process that both emanates towards a blogger's public and reflexively inwards, as bloggers engage with their selves and their own experiences through dress on their blogs.

The display of personal style on a blog is therefore best understood as performative, in that bloggers' dressed identities are constituted through a series of ongoing performative acts. Style-blogged selves are always in the process of becoming rather than existing *a priori* as revealed through bloggers' outfits. As such, the selves we see on style blogs are selves both coming into being and coming to be understood. These selves are primarily performed through outfit post imagery and reflected upon in the written text of posts. Style bloggers visually align themselves with fashion photography from fashion magazines by mimicking the conventions of that genre, thus tacitly assuming the role of fashion's ideal subject and imbuing their posts with *fashion's imaginary*. Yet while they incorporate the illusory into their posts, style bloggers' identities are not necessarily fictitious. Rather, as I will demonstrate, these performed identities are neither entirely 'real' nor entirely fictive, but somewhere in between. This refiguring of self-representation challenges the anxiety about authenticity that haunts online iterations of self, as conceiving of online selves as mediated and performed allows for some ambiguity, some blurring between how a person might appear in an offline interaction and how they might perform themselves for an anticipated audience.

I will develop this discussion of the performative quality of dress by analysing the ways that such a dynamic between blogger's embodied selves and their clothing is mapped through their posts. Dress makes available an embodied self-knowing, an ongoing negotiation between self-as-perceived and ideal self, consistent with their capacity to make available a platform for the discussion of personal histories and discoveries. It is worth stating here that the concept of dressed identity as I employ it takes as its subject an individual with choice in the selection of what they wear, some economic mobility to access a range of garments with which to create outfits and who subscribes to a post-Enlightenment conception of the individual as autonomous and self-reflexive. However, the attitude towards dress that I describe is not particular to me, but is common on the style blogosphere, evident on blogs written from both the developing and the developed world (for instance, see Luvaas's discussion of Indonesian style blogs, 2013).

Although, as discussed in Chapter One, there are bloggers who negotiate faith-based convictions in regards to their choice of dress, these bloggers display a similar sensibility to style bloggers who do not subscribe to such religious codes. That is, they dress in a style that displays what I have identified as a personal style – their own taste in clothing and the associated personal aesthetic – and is consistent with how they wish to be seen by others.

The performance of self through style

In his seminal volume on everyday performance, *The Presentation of Self in Everyday Life* (1973), sociologist Erving Goffman proposed a theatrical model for analysing face-to-face social interactions, drawing on the material elements of western text-based theatre to draw out the ways in which people foreground some and elide other aspects of themselves to present a particular self to their interlocutor. He employs the term 'performance' to denote

[…] all the activity of an individual which occurs during a period marked by his [*sic*] continuous presence before a particular set of observers and which has some influence on [them].

(1973: 22)

Although style blogging is not a face-to-face mode of interaction, the definition has a striking parallel to this practice: a blogger's performance of self exists in the continuous present before their 'audience' of readers who observe them, a temporally staggered yet nonetheless influential presence.

Style blogs are spaces at which bloggers perform their styled selves for their readers. They dress themselves into view, becoming familiar personages through time. Blogs are always available to be read at the convenience of a reader, who decides when they will look at a blog and for how long, knowing as they do that the blogged self of a blogger is, in a sense, always there. A post, once published, exists in its own continuous present tense unless deleted at a later date.

If we consider bloggers in relation to their readership, we can conceive of them as performers displaying particular aspects of themselves in particular ways towards their readers. Goffman argues that if an 'individual's activity is to become significant to others, he [*sic*] must mobilise his activity so that it will express *during the interaction* what he wishes to convey' (1973: 30, original emphasis). A blogger's performance is created with a consciousness of the subsequent apprehension of their readership, and an understanding that the perception these readers have of the blogger will be predicated on what has been displayed to them. As such, performers tend to conceal any discrepancies that would affect a successful performance. These include (to paraphrase Goffman's categorizations): any profitable activity that is incompatible with the view of their activity a performer hopes to encourage; errors and mistakes, and the concealment of the correction of any errors and mistakes that will betray their initial occurrence; the labour, effort and previous iterations of a final product, which are concealed in the tendency of individuals presenting only the finished product to others; evidence of any 'dirty work' undertaken in order to realize the performance or, 'the discrepancy between appearances and over-all reality' (44); and any sacrifice necessarily made by an individual in order to maintain their embodiment of ideal standard of their role (1973: 43–45). The concealment of such discrepancies is common on the style blogosphere, although the information that is concealed (or not) varies according to individual bloggers and the kind of performance they are enacting. For example, second wave bloggers commonly conceal in their blogging all five areas identified by Goffman, in accordance with the *doxa*, or 'the core values and discourses which a field articulates as its fundamental principles' (Webb et al. 2002: xi), underpinning the practice. Any aspect of creating a post or maintaining a profitable blog that would contradict or threaten the performance of a blogger as effortlessly stylish and successful are obliterated: we do not hear about the length of time it took to style, shoot, edit and upload an outfit post, the sacrifice of other commitments necessary to maintain the blog nor how certain bloggers came to partner with luxury labels like Valentino and Louis Vuitton. In fact, as with Margaret Zhang and 'her' Mulberry Alexa bag, often even the provenance of blogged clothing is undefined, the profitable activity then subsumed into the stylish appearance of the blogger who presumably has access to anything she likes. Of course, it is hardly worth noting that errors and mistakes, if made, are quickly corrected, and the process by which some photographs are selected for uploading and others are not remains opaque to the reader. Arguably, too, the process is invisible to those doing the selecting: the process unfolds 'transparently', as an effect of *habitus*, rather than as an explicit calculation with regard to a self-conscious project of self-production and representation. In this way, the interface of the blog privileges the performance and allows for the concealment of 'the discrepancy between appearances and over-all reality' (Goffman 1973: 44). Therefore, the kind of performance taking place here is not just a performance of self, but a particular kind of self: a stylish one, a successful one, and one imbued with the identity of the individual blogger.

Occasionally second wave bloggers acknowledge some of these aspects – the selection of photographs, errors being corrected – although this is uncommon. When such acknowledgement is made, it is often by bloggers who are already very successful, for whom the alternative narrative does not threaten to overtake the dominant narrative being performed but rather supplements it, instilling their performance with a kind of self-deprecating authenticity. When Margaret intersperses her post on attending Derby Day as a guest of Lexus, for example, with asides that she 'dorkily declared' to Australian television personality Jamie Durie that she grew up watching his programmes and that she accidentally shot renowned photographer Hugh Stewart out of focus, her confessions have the effect of normalizing her presence at the exclusive event. She might be sitting next to Naomi Campbell, looking elegant in every image, but she is still the girl who didn't know that Derby Day has a black-and-white dress code until two days prior to the event (Zhang 2013b). Here, Margaret skilfully blogs a successful, stylish and yet still relatable persona to (and for) her readership. This self-deprecation also counteracts any potential alienation caused by the combination of Margaret's beauty, success and access to prestigious events such as this.

The performances of first wave bloggers are consistent with Goffman's argument in slightly different ways. First wave bloggers are typically more forthright about their profitable activities or their stance against such opportunities, and would not necessarily see a blurry or cropped photograph as being undesirable. Yet both of these choices are consistent with the ethos of this mode of style blogging, which valorizes authenticity, openness and imperfection, a self-conscious alternative to the aforementioned 'polished images and […] hyperreal faces and bodies of the models' of the fashion media (Rocamora and Bartlett 2009: 110).

Declarations such as Susie Lau's, that she likes her outfit 'mistakes' as she's 'not trying to put the best vision of myself out there' (Lau, quoted in Rocamora and Bartlett 2009: 110), or Alison Gary's post about the hard work of blogging (Gary 2013) may dispel the glamour of blogging but at the same time reinforce *what the blogger wishes to convey*: in these instances, this seems to include the impression of trustworthiness and a concern for the fun of style at the behest of gendered expectations of femininity, and a dedication to blogging, respectively.

However, blogged identities such as those of the first and second wave bloggers discussed here are not fake for having been edited, nor unreal for occurring in a digital realm. Rather, they are crafted by bloggers to display themselves, but in a certain way and, as such, they are particular, subjective and partial.

Performative selves on style blogs

In being written through time, blogs inadvertently chart the shifting selfhood of a blogger. So much is evident in my experience of reading my archive, yet it is also evident in the archive of many style bloggers I studied during the course of doing this research. We see Tavi Gevinson grow from a curious, somewhat tentative 11 year old to a 13 year old with an audacity and creativity that shifts again as she moves through her self-confessed 'awkward phase' when she attended the Haute Couture shows in Paris at the age of 15 (Oatman-Stanford 2012). Or we observe as Nicole Warne changes from dressing primarily in her signature outfits of scalloped shorts, long socks, blouses and red lipstick, through her colour-blocked phase, and into her latest shoulder length bob, dressing only in prominent Australian fashion labels and the global luxury labels with whom she now collaborates.

Style blogs, then, become a space for the display of the self in a particular moment, a lived lookbook of personal style always in the process of becoming.[3] The idea of a self 'becoming' stems of course from the work of Judith Butler, whose famous theory of gender as performative is the conceptual basis for this reading of blogged selfhood. In 'Performative acts and gender constitution' (1988), Butler argues that our gendered identity is an aspect of ourselves that constantly comes to be through the 'repetition of stylized acts' (1988: 519), taking shape in the iterative moment of being performed. This is a process informed by societal expectation of gender normativity but one that is also mutable, negotiated by individuals as they transgress or reinterpret gender conventions through their own performative behaviour.

One's identity is thus not prior, innate or fixed, but is a phenomenon that is constituted by a sustained repetition of acts.[4] Likewise, our dressed identity – and indeed our personal style – is ever becoming through the intimate and everyday process of donning certain clothing, and as a corollary, in performing that dressed self for a reading public through outfit posts. Our dressed identity is therefore a *process*, which problematizes the connotations of unidirectional communication implied by the statement that 'dress is a self-expression'.

This is an argument also made by Susan Kaiser, who suggests that 'for some individuals style becomes a critical and creative strategy for negotiating new truths and subjectivities' (2001: 83). She makes this claim within the broader argument that dress marks an ambiguous border between ourselves and our social world as it 'speaks us' visually to those around us, also 'speaking in' as we experience the world and ourselves by experiencing ourselves as dressed. In other words,

[...] we need to begin to understand minding appearances as embodied, nonlinear, integrative, elastic and shifting ways of knowing that become visible because people inevitably appear [...] and interpret their ways of being and becoming in the world accordingly.

(2001: 84)

There is congruence, then, between style blogging as a *performance* of self, and dressed identity as *performative*. Rocamora also makes this connection, arguing, via Lister et al., that personal style blogs are sites of an ongoing performance of self which is constituted through writing (blogging), fashion (clothing worn) and photography 'coming together through [...] the computer screen' (2011: 411, 413–14). For Rocamora, the computer screen operates as a mirror into which women look and evaluate themselves (2011: 416), both a tool of self-representation and a means by which to explore alternative femininities by being both subject and object of the (not necessarily male) gaze. Feminine identity is thus rearticulated, becoming 'by and for women' (2011: 422) as bloggers negotiate their appearance in a manner that fits within and furthers their female identity.

At the same time, the technological capacities of blogs make available horizons of possibility – or 'affordances' (Gibson 1977) – which both implicitly and explicitly constrain the ways in which bloggers perform themselves into view. The medium is not transparent; rather, it shapes and refracts the possibilities of self-representation. As established in the previous chapter, bloggers' presence before their readers is mediated by a number of measures, including the separation of time and place, and the nationality and native tongue of bloggers and/or readers, among others. Bloggers can employ a range of media in their posts, including written text, photography and embedded video as well as hyperlinks to other sites of their choice. Readers see the product of these selections, although it is a communication in which the labour of production is concealed.

What shapes the choices bloggers make, in terms of performing a stylish self, are the logics of the practice: the possibilities they realize are not just constrained by the possibilities and limitations of the technology of blogs, but also by the *habitus* and capital that circulate within and throughout the style blogosphere. These logics are informed by the influence of the conventions of the fashion media on the development of style blogging as a practice, as I will discuss in the next section, as well as the desired outcome of blogging for bloggers. I will take this latter theme up in the next chapter, when I draw on Bourdieu's field theory to examine the underlying structures that organize the style blogosphere.

As well as providing bloggers with a site for creative identity-play, style blogs offer them a location at which to inhabit the role of fashion's ideal. Bloggers achieve this by aligning their imagery with the imagery of fashion magazines by appropriating their conventions as well as tacitly embodying knowledge of style by creating a styled identity upon themselves. This process occurs predominantly through the imagery of outfit posts, a practice I will now explain and examine in detail.

Outfit posts: an overview

Outfit posts have been a key feature of style blogs since they began to populate the fashion blogosphere. They usually consist of a series of photographs in which a blogger poses whilst wearing an outfit they have styled, often but not always followed by a written passage in which the blogger writes about where they wore the outfit or the significance (to them) of the clothes that are pictured. Bloggers often cite the designer or provenance of the garments they are wearing in their images, listing them underneath the photographs, and some provide links to e-stores where similar garments are for sale (see Figure 16).

Originally a catalogue of a blogger's daily garment and accessories, the use of the phrase 'what I wore' or 'today's outfit' in the title or text of these posts customarily alluded to a temporal context. Over time, this quotidian display has transformed into a presentation of a garment styled for the specific purpose of photographing and uploading, thus becoming less diaristic than presentational. It has also become common for bloggers not to mention directly how their choice of garments related to the day on which the photos were taken, leaving it up to the reader to form a narrative around the images. The photography of outfit posts, then, much like fashion photography in general, is 'a record of fashions but it is not

Tried to go to the Yayoi exhibit but the line was super long so I went to Comme des Garçons and played around in my future wardrobe instead. Give me like 6 years and they'll be in my closet. Tayler snapped this photo on the way to CDG, she ordered me into the light. It's nice having someone around who is even more obsessed with lighting than I am! I usually have to art direct everything. Anyway, I'm wearing a vintage coat, Cole Haan shoes and a dress that has been on the blog before. Here are your options if you'd like something similar:

Asos   Asos   Asos   Glamorous   Urban Outfi...

Figure 16: A screenshot from *Fashion Pirate* showing blogger Arabelle posing in her own clothes followed by a number of suggested options for readers who would 'like something similar', *Fashion Pirate*, 17 November 2013.

about fashions. It is about appearances that fascinate' (Sontag, quoted in Angeletti and Oliva 2006: 210); specifically, it is about the appearance of the blogger as styled and inviting our engaged observation.

The 'point' of outfit posting, if a single point can be identified in this complex practice, is to literally dress one's self into view. That is not to say that being seen is the only motivation, but that the practice of style blogging affords bloggers a means with which to express something of who they are (in a controlled environment), to share this with readers and, by so doing, to engage with the conventions of modern fashion; that is, to assert a fashionable and specific presence through performing fashion knowledge on one's embodied self (see Entwistle and Rocamora 2006). In this way, style bloggers' consciously fashioned selves, as presented in outfit posts, are inextricably bound to specific ideas about fashion; the 'who they are' in the context of their particular blog is not only *framed* by style, but *is* their style.

Rocamora touches upon this by arguing that bloggers' documentation of their outfit posts functions as an 'ongoing [...] identity performance' (411) that is inextricably linked with the technological capacities of blogs to reflect an image back to the blogger. Palmgren also takes up the relation between fashion, blogged selfhood and technology stating that we, as a technologized society (of which bloggers constitute a part), employ media as a vehicle for defining both personal and cultural identity (2010: 19–20). She writes that on the style blogs she analysed, 'the blogger is the object of the photograph instead of the clothes, at the same time as the choice of clothes can give a picture of the bloggers [*sic*] identity' (Palmgren 2010: 26).

While this indicates towards an interesting dialectic – that the clothes visually portray a blogger's identity to a reader even as they are obscured by that very embodied identity – Palmgren does not elaborate on the how or why of it, focusing rather on visually analysing a number of blogs to demonstrate the fragmentary ways that bloggers photograph themselves. However, the very complex dialectic that she touches upon bears further elaboration: that it is the garments that bring the blogger into visibility on a style blog even as they, as material objects, are subsumed into the style of the blogger wearing them. In other words, in terms of visual representation, where the blogger ends and where the clothes begin is obscured. There is a continuous flow back and forth between blogger-as-clothed-self and the clothes themselves, between the stylist and the style that they have created on themselves for that post.

The focus of this research, then, is the interanimation between clothing and embodied selfhood so often apparent in outfit posts. The term *interanimation* is employed by anthropologist Keith H. Basso to describe the reciprocal flow of sentiment and perception between a person and the place that they apprehend. For Basso, 'as places animate the ideas and feelings of persons who attend to them, these same ideas and feelings animate the places on which attention has been bestowed' (1996: 55). In a similar way, the clothing someone wears is animated by the style and embodied selfhood of the person within them even as that person is also animated as a result of being dressed in those particular clothes. As such, it is most useful to approach the depiction of clothes and blogger-in-clothes as an articulation of how a blogger wishes to be seen. In an outfit post, a blogger's identity is inextricable from what they wear because the only 'them' an audience can access is the blogger's clothed self as it is rendered visible on the space of the blog.

This manner of visually presenting one's clothing is consistent with the fashion industry's preferred means of communicating knowledge about their product, which has traditionally favoured imagery over text. This primacy of the visual is evident in the way that new collections have always been revealed to consumers through various forms of visual media, from fashion plates of Parisian designs being published in the earliest fashion magazines, to live catwalk presentations, to fashion photography. Any accompanying text often supports the image by giving detail about it, from a description of what is not visible in the image (such as in the early days of *Vogue*) to more contemporary proliferations: a programme for a catwalk show giving a brief context for the inspiration behind the collection and the name of each item, or a fashion magazine's exegesis of a collection or trend, which briefly outlines why it is a key look of the season and how it should be worn.

The aesthetics of outfit posts, although greatly varied, are visually contiguous with the conventions of these more established communications about the fashion product. Rocamora characterizes this (after Bolter and Grusin) as a process of remediation, a 'process whereby both new and old media represent and refashion each other' (2011: 101). As she argues, users of new media (such as bloggers) adopt the conventions of established or traditional media, thereby remediating it. This may involve bloggers reposting material initially published in established fashion media, such as fashion magazines, but also extends to the mimicking of the tropes of fashion media (see Rocamora 2011: 101–04). For example, some bloggers emulate the photographic style of a lookbook by posing against a blank wall in their home or neighbourhood, mimicking the commercial conventions of the industry that would be familiar to them from accessing lookbooks in stores or online. Other bloggers stage photo shoots on location in the style of a fashion editorial. Natural settings such as fields, woods or beaches are popular for these, as are deserted urban landscapes like the middle of the street or a factory lot; as Susie Lau jokes, there's 'nothing like a dose of natural light to show that outfits live beyond the walls' (*Style Bubble*, 19 April 2010).

While the choices a blogger might make in terms of location, garments and accessories, lighting and so on are virtually endless, each outfit post features the same key components: a style blogger, clothed and positioned before our gaze. Of paramount importance on style blogs is being seen, and seen to be stylish. The implicit agreement operating throughout style blogs is that the blogger has an interesting personal style that we as the reader want to see, and which they as the blogger want to share. When style bloggers step in front of the camera, what they are showing us is them-in-their-clothes, an articulation of self literally made material by their clothing.

The relationship between the self, society and fashion has long been of interest to writers from a range of disciplines from sociology to semiology to cultural studies. There is a long tradition of social theory that has sought to explain the significance of clothing in human society, whether it is Veblen reading fashion as an irrational display of wealth (or 'conspicuous consumption') ([1899] 1973), Simmel on the tension between individuals' desires to distinguish themselves from others as well as to conform to societal and class norms (1971), semioticians such as Barthes ([1967] 1990), Lévi-Strauss (1972), Lurie (1981) and Davis (1992) who argue that clothes 'speak' a visual language in varying degrees of ambiguity about the status, values and identity of their wearer, or Hebdige ([1970] 2007) and Clarke (1976) writing about the way that members of British working class subcultures dressed into a particular visual identity as an act of resistance against hegemony and an articulation of their affinity with a particular subculture (punk, teddy boy, mod and so on).[5]

Despite the diversity of their central arguments, these works commonly advance the notion that clothing communicates its wearer's social identities (as wealthy, aspiring, fashionable, punk and so on), or the ways that clothing brings its wearer's interiority into sight. Joanne Finkelstein argues as much when she writes that fashion:

> [...] is a new way of speaking the body, and freeing it from silence [...] It becomes a form of cultural expression, much like writing, which renders the interior exterior. The fashion garment makes the 'inside' the 'right side'.
>
> (1998: 67–68)

Clothes are thus imbued with social codes that are overlaid onto the person wearing them, readable by those who encounter them. The communicative quality of clothing here is unidirectional, emanating from a dressed self towards society. When read this way, fashion and dress can be seen to distinguish groups of people from one another and provide a language by which clothing can be talked about as doing something: not just operating as a material covering but also as a symbolic and communicative overlay. Yet, as Joanne Entwistle has observed, there is also a homogenizing quality to this perspective, the intentions and individual selfhood of the person underneath the clothes obscured by the fixed meanings apparently encoded in their garments (see Entwistle 2000). The prevailing dynamic is of an individual framed in relation to what is external from them: their peers, the expectation of their society and the fashion system of sartorial products that carry signification that people, by donning them, might embody. This is evident in Fred Davis's assertion that dress is 'a kind of visual metaphor for identity' (1992: 25). The way this identity is made visible in outfit posts, however, is more complex than a process of simply externally rendering one's subjectivity. Finkelstein's argument implies that the unclothed body is trapped and silent, which precludes the many kinds of expression made possible by having an embodied self.

An alternative reading of the relationship between a person's embodied self and the clothes that they wear is to see dressing as a temporally contextualized, visual foregrounding of aspects of that person's selfhood: a mutable representation that is as easily shed as donned. This reading derives from Butler's taking up of Merleau-Ponty's proposition that the body is a historical idea gaining its meaning through a concrete and historically mediated expression in the world, and that it is a set of possibilities to be continually realized (1988: 521).

Outfit posts offer a record of this kind of continually realized selfhood in the form of their catalogued visual narrative, in which readers are able to observe and engage with the blogger's changing personal style. The reader shares in a blogger's experiences as they go through phases of dress, rejecting previous incarnations of self, and engaging in an ongoing exploration of how they want to be perceived – and how they want to perceive themselves. The following excerpt from the blog *Style Rookie* illuminates these complexities of dress, identity and affect for its blogger Tavi Gevinson:

> I think that [being creative] is all I really want to do, and have ever wanted to do. The idea of being a mad eccentric who is constantly slipping into different skins is so appealing to me. I started this blog because I wanted to explore my style.
>
> (Gevinson, *Style Rookie*, 2009d)

For Tavi, dressing is an exploration of an aspect of herself – her style – and a moment in which she both defines herself – 'a mad eccentric [capable of] slipping into different skins' – and enjoys her agency, both as she fulfils her desire to be creative and as that fulfilment makes her feel good. The notion of 'different skins' is interesting, too, as it connotes a shifting identity, a realization dependent on the multitude of factors and feelingfulness that shape how a person feels in a day. For style bloggers, this experientiality is somewhat captured and recorded in outfit posts, whether it is a 'what I wore' or an imaginative sartorial fantasy as they publicly perform their own expression of stylishness. This public performance is a central feature of outfit posts; if dress was simply a matter of 'render(ing) the interior exterior', style bloggers could presumably dress however they chose in their private lives and be satisfied. By choosing to upload photographs in the public domain, they move beyond the self-satisfying and temporally expressive capacity of fashion to produce and assert themselves as a stylish presence before a potentially vast and engaged audience.

In photographing themselves, style bloggers are making a claim to have style, and by choosing to upload these photographs in the public domain they assert themselves as someone stylish to be seen. This is not overtly stated; rather, it is implicit in the activity itself. Style bloggers make their image available to an unknown audience, signifying through their command of our attention that the reader should look, that there is something to see.

That is not to say that being seen is style bloggers' only motivation. In response to the question of why she posts pictures of herself online, Grechen Reiter from *Grechen Blogs* wrote that style bloggers

> […] love showing off [their] latest finds & styling abilities – it's all part of who we are. We are not attention-whores, our love of attention is not what defines us, but it does enable us to do what we do. I do it because I want to be an example for the women who find me online, or see me on the street, to be creative, and look outside the mall or magazine dos and donts [*sic*] for inspiration […] I've always written about what I love, and have

been lucky enough to have an audience of women who love the same. It feels only natural to post pictures of myself in that context – how can you really 'know' a person without seeing pictures?

(Reiter, *Grechen Blogs*, 18 May 2011)

This excerpt reveals the creative pleasure inherent in outfit posting for Grechen, as well as its capacity to foster intimacy with her readers. Implicit in this excerpt is the assertion that to see her is to know her; and on a style blog, to see is to see Grechen as clothed, Grechen as seen *through* her clothes, thus 'doing herself' (Butler 1988) as she presents herself to her readers. Judith Butler's performative account of identity as fundamentally dramatic is a useful counterpoint here to Finkelstein's conception of an interior being folded out. Rather, outfit posting allows Grechen to foreground aspects of her selfhood, as well as enabling her to connect with her readers, a mediated and specific kind of performance of self made possible by having a blog.

Moreover, if the self is a set of possibilities to be continually realized, gaining its meaning through its expression in the world, then these online identities can be read as perpetual realizations of a particular aspect of bloggers' selves. I say 'aspect' because the identity at stake on a style blog is not that of the blogger as a complete individual but rather that of the blogger as *stylish*. The way that a blogger chooses to represent herself through her sartorial choices and style speaks of how she sees herself and how she wants others to see her. As such, style blogs are not sites at which the person of the blogger is metaphorically laid bare, but rather a specific frame through which readers see an aspect of their selfhood – bloggers' sense of themselves as it relates to fashion and style – and outfit posts are the technological lenses through which these selves become visible.

Blogging into fashion's imaginary

Somewhat ironically, she is posing on a mantelpiece. The room around her is shadowy, the deep grey of night fallen, and yet her skin glows gold: she is the sun in this hemisphere. It is hard to discern what it is exactly that she is wearing. The mirror behind her reflects the glimpse of a silver boot, and as her body is angled towards the camera, we see the smudge of her cleavage between the glossy black shoulder straps of the garment covering her torso. Hand on her bare thigh, elbow jutting, she has been snapped mid-hair flick. Her dark brown mane with caramel tips is frozen like a wave about to crash down her back. Her face is calm. She gazes at the lens, lips slightly parted.

The series continues with more of the same: her limbs and hair often constituting the focus of each shot, her poses mostly serving to obstruct rather than enhance our perception of the garments she wears. That said, now and then more of the details of her dress are discernible. It is black with a slit over each thigh revealing a sheer underskirt, and a neckline that exposes a matte V of tanned skin between the shoulder straps. Here and there, a glimpse of a fur handbag, a touch of softness in contrast to the studded boots, the dim mirror, and the white marble upon which she poses.

Underneath, she writes that these images were taken 'before a warm night out in Paris', and regular readers would know that this style blogger, Rumi Neely, was there to attend the Spring/Summer RTW 2013 fashion shows. She casually refers to her outfit, in language that reflects the self-supporting logic of Fashion (what Barthes called *la 'raison' de Mode*): 'the car wash dress is gladiator-y without being too literal and the boots just badass in the way that things with nailhead studs tend to be. Easy pieces that go a long way' (Neely 2013). Where these pieces are going with Rumi is a mystery, as is why she is on the mantelpiece in the first place.

Of course, such questions are redundant in a discussion of outfit post imagery. As with fashion photography in general, such photographs 'beckon us into a world of unbridled fantasies by placing fashion and the body in any number of discursive contexts' (Jobling 1999: 2). It doesn't matter why Rumi is on the mantelpiece; what matters is what she is doing whilst there: showing her dressed self to us. Her surrounds are irrelevant beyond functioning to complement this particular iteration of her styled identity.

Outfit posts such as this constitute an ambiguous realm where the disparate entities of fleshly body and illusory imagery intertwine, and where the social functionality of clothing is separated from the freedom of form. Style bloggers thus mimic the conventions of professional fashion photography to situate themselves as the fashionable subject, and do so in a way that aligns them with fashion's dominant aesthetic. That is, of an agent for whom looking stylish (and effortlessly so) is not just a possibility, but is a way of life. For second wave bloggers like Nicole Warne (*Gary Pepper*), her blog literally is her way of life, as the events she publishes about are afforded to her because of her blog's success. The 'Travel' tab on Gary Pepper testifies to this: During September and October 2013, Nicole travelled to Italy, Croatia and Turkey with two other Australian bloggers to write sponsored posts for travel company Contiki, composed a post from Paris where she attended fashion week and flew to China as a guest of department store Lane Crawford, styling an outfit post from their selection of international luxury designers to publicize the opening of their new store in mainland China. Even her holidays are subsidized by the luxury hotels where she stays, who also prominently feature in the background of her posts.

In an essay on fashion photography and Richard Avedon, Susan Sontag writes that

[t]he gestures that create or inspire fashion are defined by camera. It is the photograph that confers celebrity, that makes something fashionable, that perpetuates and comments on the evolving idea – that is, the fantasy – of fashion.

(Sontag, quoted in Angeletti and Oliva 2006: 211)

If it comments on the evolving idea of fashion, the fashion photograph also communicates it, upholds it and perpetuates it. Fashion is a dynamic creative and commercial industry, always seeking and celebrating the new, but one aspect of its shifting countenance always remains the same: the embodiment of fashion's ideal is always found in the fashion image, that depiction of what is most desirable to own and how it is most desirable to appear to be in fashion. This representation is not just a record, but a prompt; in the nineteenth and early twentieth centuries, fashion imagery offered a visual mandate, but in contemporary times, it can be seen as offering a firm suggestion to be taken up by the viewer and incorporated into their dress.

In fashion photography, looking, meaning and feeling are bound up with desire. This can be attributed in part to the origins of fashion photography: it was developed as a genre by the fashion press, namely fashion magazines, in the early twentieth century. Publisher of American *Vogue*, Thomas Condé Nast replaced fashion illustrations with fashion photographs in his magazines because he wanted to satisfy readers who were 'so literally interested in fashion that they wanted to see the mode thoroughly and faithfully reported – rather than rendered as a form of decorative art' (Craik, in Shinkle 2008: 3). This eagerness seems to originate from a number of concurrent desires: from a connoisseur's desire for knowledge of the new; for the aesthetic pleasure of seeing fashions in close detail; to see, perchance to buy; and for the invitation to dream that fashion photographs offer.

Evidently, these dynamics of seeing, meaning and feeling that are inherent in the experience of viewing the fashion photograph – indeed, the simultaneous admiration and identification they invite from the interested reader – have been in place since fashion photography first emerged as a distinct genre. In an essay accompanying an exhibition of 1920s fashion photographs, the Australian National Gallery programme recorded that even in that decade, fashion photographs were '"quite conspicuous constructions" portraying an "unreal", glamorous world designed "to seduce and to captivate the viewer"' (quoted in Craik 1994: 101). Craik extends this sentiment to argue that 'images such as these promise an easy life, for those with the looks and the money – a life whose passing is only marked by the never-ending parade of fabulous new products' (1994: 101). Style bloggers embody this promise by posing out of their everyday, and yet the staged composition as well as the disjunction between the narrative of the shoot and that of their offline life point to the artifice of such posts.

Note that here a familiar premise is at work: the glamorous world of the fashion photograph is predicated on access to means. Moreover, this should not need to be worked for: it should come effortlessly, and if it doesn't, the labour to attain it should be discreetly concealed so as not to disturb the illusion, as neatly summed up by Margaret Thorpe: 'glamour is founded upon an income but real glamour seldom looks at the bill' (Thorpe, quoted, in Postrel 2013: 93). In this way, the glamour of the fashion photograph is not only distant from the reader by virtue of its fantastic aesthetics, but also because of its material and physical unattainability for the majority of readers.

The instance of this unattainable performance of a fashionable life by second wave bloggers has been critiqued in the media, as writers have identified the gap between the goods blogged by bloggers like Jane Aldridge and Leandra Medine and the means of their audience. As writer Kelly Oxford blogged in 2011 about Medine,

The problem? Her fan base is young and they idolize her and Man Repeller dresses young and street and is a mentor to young women […] BUT this target group she's a mentor for cannot afford $900 shoes, or even $350 shoes. These are the price points that she links to, and items she displays on her site. I've read comments from her readers who have gone into major debt buying things that she links for them to buy.

(Oxford, *Eject,* October 2011)

Social media researcher Alice Marwick examines this aspect of blogging in her essay for *The New Inquiry*, arguing that the appearance of authenticity is a crucial 'strategy for establishing a boundary between capitalism and the self' (2013a), otherwise a blogger risks alienating their readers who expect a more representative glimpse into a blogger's life than they would expect, say, from a celebrity. Yet at the same time the unreality of second wave outfit posts forms part of their power: the tension between unattainable lifestyle and fashion products and the 'ordinary' blogger – the blogger who transformed herself into fashion's ideal through her taste (such is the myth of second wave blogging) – drives the genre.

Second wave bloggers exhibit fashion as if it is theirs, appearing to us as models do, dressed in goods for sale. A blogger's presence in the garment, and the conflation of her image with its image, suggests that the right way to wear the garment is to wear it as she does, and the seduction is that to wear it will overlay us with some of her glamour. Here we see realized Craik's claim that '"woman" and "art" are transformed in fashion advertising into the visual and conceptual equivalents of the commodity itself' (1994: 103).

It is worth taking a moment to examine the ambiguity between the real and illusory in outfit posts, as to do so is to see that style bloggers appropriate the visual language of fashion photography as well as its underlying implications to cast themselves as fashion's ideal subject, a subject of knowledge, power and, ultimately, style. This self is neither entirely illusory nor real, but is situated within fashion's imaginary. Although based in style bloggers' offline selfhood, these are selves that take particular shape as bloggers fashion a styled identity and perform it on their blogs. This is a visual performance of self, one that is shaped at the nexus of the fictive and the real, embodied and presented as natural in the imagery of outfit posts.

Fashion's imaginary

Karen de Perthuis describes the synthesis of fashion and the body in fashion imagery as a 'synthetic ideal' in which the two forms merge, where 'artifice, change and imagination coalesce on the body of the model to create a new, previously only imaginable, form' (2005: 409). This occurs through the dissolution of the boundary between self and non-self as the human form is, to employ de Perthuis's language, transubstantiated from 'fleshly, organic substance [… into] the artificial, synthetic substance of the fashion garment' (409). In such images, the garment is of paramount importance, the model transformed from a corporeal figure into one that is synthetic, the fleshly literally enfolded into a new form. This refiguring shapes the body into that which serves to illustrate fashion, a process that de Perthuis ties to the imagination and what she calls 'fashion's imaginary'.

She distinguishes between the concepts of 'imagination' and 'imaginary'. Imagination 'takes place after the constitution of the mind' whereas the imaginary takes place before the mind is fully constituted; it implies an activity, an openness or, as de Perthuis stipulates in relation to fashion, 'it is the realising of a form that announces the idea of a continual becoming' (2005: 421–22). Fashion's imaginary, then, is an ideal, one that continually shifts through reinvention and reinterpretation, and one that is visually brought into being through the fashion photograph.

For de Perthuis, this concept is tied with technological development and non-human appearances, although I read fashion's imaginary as a quality rather than a distinct, homogenous or universally agreed upon aesthetic. As de Perthuis explains, it is form freed from function; and in relation to the photography of outfit posts, we see it at work as life reimagined and re-contextualized within a fashionable world, removed from expense, practicality and the ethical and social implications of making the world into one's backdrop.

The proposition that fashion photography portrays an imaginary that circulates around a model embodying an ideal subjectivity has been put forward by both feminist critics of fashion photography as well as theorists analysing it as a genre.[6] Fashion photography is a genre that 'represents neither the real world nor an aesthetic ideal' (Lehmann 2002: 15), but rather is situated somewhere in between both, presenting a fantasy in each editorial. Lehmann argues that one of the most distinctive features of the fashion photograph is narrative: 'the editorial […] is fashion's characteristic device to invent and construct a story around clothing' (15). Therefore, such series are invitations to consider the garment and to imagine oneself as the subject of the photograph, the 'ritualized gestures and postures [allowing] us to accommodate such unreal realities within our experience and participate in their consumption' (15).

This consumption is a visual as well as a fiscal one: the spectator is tacitly invited to relate to the dressed subject in the fashion photograph, to recognize the model's outfit as being in fashion and indicative of an idealized mode of being. Lehmann argues that such identification is integral to the success of a fashion photograph, 'to draw the spectator into the narrative' of the editorial in order that they be enticed by the products on display (2002: 16), yet at the same time wanting to have what she's wearing. We also want to be her, to look as she does in the garment, to move with ease (as she does) in the fashionable world depicted in the photograph. This creates an evocative and alluring dynamic, and one that is deliberately engineered to appeal.

The illusory qualities of fashion's imaginary might also be usefully addressed through a consideration of Roland Barthes's rhetoric of fashion. Barthes originally applied this idea to his semiotic analysis of fashion writing, although as Paul Jobling demonstrates in his own work, it is equally useful when applied to a consideration of fashion imagery. The rhetoric of fashion is comprised of three systems that Barthes called 'the worldly signified' (*rhétorique du signifié mondain*), the reason of Fashion (*'le 'raison' de Mode*) and the poetics of clothing (*poétique du vêtement*) (see Jobling 1999: 77–79). All three systems explain the logic by which fashion is organized. For example, 'the worldly signified' denotes the inner logic in fashion writing that subsumes the world around fashion as subservient to it. Paul Jobling extends this idea to fashion imagery by making reference to photo shoots in which (predominantly white) models are posed against a backdrop of native inhabitants of a 'foreign country'. He makes reference to a shoot in Sri Lanka, in which the environs and people surrounding the model are rendered less powerful and 'not Fashion[able]' in their different appearance and apparel compared to the models who are the focus of the image (1999: 79).

The poetics of clothing describes the manner in which photographed garments are divested of their functionality and imbued (by virtue of existing as representation of clothing only) with symbolism, equivalent in the image to 'sensation, mood, time and place' (1999: 77). For Jobling, the garment becomes affective, speaking more of seduction than protection (77). In other words, the practicality, comfort and suitability of a garment for the conditions in which the model works is immaterial, as what is of first importance is how the garment looks and how, in concert with the location, model's appearance and photographer's style, the desired image of fashionability is being created and portrayed. This idea is echoed by Lipovetsky, who argues that of central importance in contemporary fashion photography is 'to communicate a message or create an atmosphere or state of mind [... which presents] fictional images expressing a sensibility, a vision of life' (2002: 8).

To briefly return to Rumi on the mantelpiece, we see all three systems at work in her post. The reason of fashion – that a garment means, or is, something because Fashion (or a fashionable blogger) says so – apparent in the casual claim that they are 'easy pieces that go a long way', for example, with the sensual and evocative qualities of the clothing Rumi wears foregrounded over functionality (despite the basic functionality of clothing to conceal nakedness and provide warmth and protection). Moreover, the world surrounding Rumi exists in the photographs to frame her and to position us to see her in a certain way: the stylish blogger in Paris to work – and, in fact, working by creating this very post – but also displaying her leisure, the luxury of her surrounds and of her costume, her youth, playfulness and beauty contrasting to the cool stone and dimly lit room.

The work of all three authors here cited underline the fantasy that circulates in fashion photography. It is not a genre intended simply to display garments in order that they might be sold, as with the photography of catalogues (although the garments photographed by fashion magazines are often for sale), and neither do they purport to accurately or transparently document or represent the lives of the people depicted. Rather, as Michael Carter argued more generally about Art, such photography 'is rather an active transformation of the sensuous materiality of the world' (2000: 60).

Here, then, is fashion's imaginary: what we are presented with in a fashion photograph is fashion's ideal subject dressed in, and indeed formed by, fashion. The garments that are worn, the appearance of the model, and her location in a locale that serves to enhance this portrait of fashionability (be it an 'exotic' locale or a studio backdrop) all constitute the fantasy of fashion. What is depicted is illusion, a 'what is' that exists only within fashion image, but which invites viewers to collective reverie, an association with the imaginary ideal subject and recalibration of the self as a contemporary subject in relation to her.

Within the context of a fashion magazine or fashion advertising, there is an implicit acknowledgement of the artifice of such images. Not only is artifice inherent to the genre, but the labour behind the creation of the illusion is indicated by the customary listing of the names of the individuals involved in realizing the image. Other details that are often given include the label or provenance of the garments and, occasionally, the location of the shoot. Moreover, as consumers increasingly access fashion in online environments, magazines have also started to produce behind-the-scenes photo galleries and videos of their shoots, often uploaded to their websites or published at the front of the book to further involve the reader in the creation of these fashion dreams (see Figure 17).

Figure 17: An image from a gallery titled 'Christine Centenera behind the scenes with Elle Fanning' published on the official website of *Vogue Australia*, depicting the actress's cover shoot in LA for the first print issue of *Miss Vogue*. Christine Centenera is *Vogue Australia*'s Senior Fashion Editor (Centenera 2013).

Although there are many similarities between the conventions of fashion and outfit post photography, in fashion magazines such images are framed as illusory, whereas on style blogs, they are often presented as a seamless representation of the blogger's life. The connection with a blogger's offline everyday is implied by the history of the genre, in which such photographs were couched as recording a blogger's daily outfit and yet the connection between these images and the offline life of the bloggers they depict is deeply ambiguous. This is especially prevalent on second wave style blogs. Despite the assumption that the content of style blogs in some way mirrors the events of bloggers' offline lives, readers are offered few clues to connect each post with the ongoing narrative arc of a blogger's daily activities. The details of where posts were photographed, who photographed them, how the shoot related to the rest of the day in which it took place and, increasingly, whether the clothes portrayed were bought, gifted or loaned are often unclear. What readers are presented with are the images: the figure of a blogger clothed and moving through a landscape without explanation, displayed for the observation and admiration of their readers.

Compounding this ambiguity is the apparent ordinariness of style bloggers. Historically, style bloggers drew on their own resources to create their outfit posts. Their content was shaped by the clothes that were available to them, their personal skills at applying make-up, hairdressing, styling and photo-editing, whether or not they had someone to photograph them, and the places they could access in which to shoot. By not claiming to be professionals, style bloggers appeared to be more relatable: as Marwick has observed, 'we expect the microfamous in social media to be more approachable, more like us, more *authentic* – distinct from the fashion world's fetishization of absurdly expensive consumer goods, coat-hanger bodies, and impractical heels and gowns' (Marwick 2013a, original emphasis).

Yet this expectation is challenged by second wave bloggers. That the perception of relatability can persist in second wave style blogging is attributable to blogging's roots as an intimate, personal medium for the sharing of quotidian stories. Second wave bloggers rarely acknowledge the work behind their outfit posts, the images and opportunities they editorialize presented as naturalized and effortless. Here, their performance of personal shifts into another kind of performance: one of a fashionable life in which they are the very embodiment of glamour.

By assuming the role of the model and replacing her fashion with their own personal style, style bloggers have cast themselves as fashion's ideal subject, fashioning what this looks like in their own image. While they may not be universally recognized as such, in consistently blogging their outfits, style bloggers are tacitly making a claim to have a distinctive or interesting personal style. In this way, they assume the position of the fashionable ideal, even if what they are presenting is their *own* fashionable ideal, appearing before their readers as a figure of interest, admiration or inspiration.[7]

I have emphasized the role of magazines here in circulating the fashionable ideal, though of course this is also visible in advertising campaigns, on the runways of fashion weeks and embodied in the figures of women deemed fashionable by those who claim to know. The fashionable ideal can be stretched further than the ideal appearance promoted as the ideal by those within the fashion industry. It is an ideal that relates directly to clothing: what are the fashionable styles this season? What is the inspiration and lifestyle of the woman who 'gets it', and how does she wear it? There is not one homogenous fashionable ideal each season (even the concept of fashion seasons is ever diminishing); rather, each house or label presents their own interpretation according to their brand's identity and underlying ethos. Alternatively, each fashion magazine will interpret a number of fashionable ideals, a different woman and style presented in each editorial shoot. The unifying factor in all of these ideals is the intimate relation to fashion that she embodies: that she represents what is stylish right now. What underpins her creation is the knowledge of the image-makers behind her – those designing, those dressing, those selecting and styling and photographing – that shape her in a particular way.

As the heroes of their own blogged fashion stories, style bloggers appear before their readers as authorities on style, with the skills and means to realize it in their own dress. Moreover, due to the accessibility of the medium, these bloggers are able to present an alternative ideal if they so desire, ranging from their body shape (such as with fatshion bloggers, who challenge the notion that you must be slim in order to be stylish) to their personal aesthetic, which traditionally has deviated from the trends circulating in the fashion industry. This was and is certainly the case for first wave bloggers, even those whose appearance and personal style echo the aesthetic ideal of the mainstream fashion industry. Such blogs often offer an alternative voice, as their editorial independence ensures that their interpretation of fashion is reflected through the lens of their own aesthetic judgement. On these blogs, the value of a garment, trend or label is innately tied to how a blogger styles it. Thus what is being displayed is not just the product, but the product revalued and resituated within the parameters of a blogger's personal style.

In performing the role of fashion's ideal subject and by doing so in the likeness of fashion editorial imagery, style bloggers align themselves with the conventions of fashion magazines. They perform their style through the display of their dressed embodied selves and in so doing, implicitly authorize their own style, look and body shape. Yet the performance of style and of self on a style blog can communicate inwardly to bloggers as well as emanating visually towards readers. In this way, style blogs offer a space not only for the performance of personal style but also a place for the consideration of the self in relation to style. As I will explore in the final part of this chapter, this consideration can occur both *by* blogging and can also be reflected upon *in* blogging.

Style blogging, then, allows for a public thinking through of the subjective significance of fashion and style. As content is situated within the realm of the personal, it also allows for a public thinking through of self, an exploration of aspects of experience that might not find articulation in other spheres of bloggers' lives. Particularly notable is the way that these two themes converge: this 'thinking through' on a style blog is framed by the lens of a blogger's personal style. Here, style blogs operate as a reflexive space: not just a platform for the performance of a styled self but also of a self in the process of being understood *through* style.

'The best way I knew – through fashion'

On 17 October 2010, 15-year-old Rosalind Jana posted on *Clothes, Cameras and Coffee*, the style blog she has kept since June 2009. At the time, Rosalind posted an average of two or three times a week, yet she described clicking the 'publish post' button in this particular instance as 'nerve-wracking' (Jana, in conversation with the author, 2011b). Even a cursory glance at the post, 'Twisted embrace', reveals why she may have felt this way. At the centre of the post's first image is Rosalind herself; although in this instance, she wears not one of her vintage frocks but a short black dress from a charity shop that she has modified, and she is crouched down, a ball of girl facing away from the lens, so that at the centre of the shot is her back. And her back is precisely where the eye alights.

Her spine is mapped out by a row of silk patches in the shape of vertebrae that are stitched in a sinuous line down the dress. Yet instead of flowing straight and strong down the centre of her back, this spine curves out towards her right side in a gentle parabola. Yet it is not until you scroll down another two images that you see the significance of Rosalind's alteration to her dress. In the third photograph of the post, she stands tall in the sunlight, perpendicular to the even line of the horizon. We can now see that the central section of her back juts out on her right side, traced by the curve of her stitched spine, as if that portion of her body has been firmly pushed out of alignment to mimic a question mark.

Each image in this outfit post is carefully framed so that the warped curve of Rosalind's spine is always the focal point, surrounded by the organic lines of her surrounds. The series of six images has a cumulative effect of normalizing the unusual shape of her back until I notice, on a closer look, that although the central seam of the dress starts between her shoulder-blades, instead of running straight down as such a seam would customarily do, it twists diagonally down her back, ending in a placket over the far side of her left thigh. I became aware at that moment of how the muscle and bone of her back were pulling in two directions, her body demanding more room than the straight tunic was able to give (see Figures 18 and 19).

In the accompanying prose, Rosalind explains what has occurred. At the end of 2009, she discovered that she had scoliosis, a condition in which the spine twists out of alignment due to uneven growth spurts as one side of the body grows faster than the other. What was not a particularly serious condition to begin with worsened as Rosalind kept growing. As her ribs and shoulder blades became further distorted, she began experiencing intense aches and discomfort, and by the time her spine had twisted 80 degrees to the right, she ran the risk of suffering internal damage to her organs if she did not undergo emergency surgical correction. It was this eventuality that led her to write a post about her back and to create what she called the 'scoliodress' (Jana 2010).

This post marked the first time Rosalind had ever made mention of her scoliosis on her blog, and despite the fact that she had regularly uploaded photographs of herself posing in her clothes, there had never appeared to be anything out of the ordinary about her back. In the post itself, she wrote that she had actively tried to 'conceal the more obvious

Figures 18 and 19: Two of the images from Rosalind's post depicting her scoliodress, *Clothes, Cameras and Coffee*, 17 October 2010.

mis-shapes with careful clothing, wide belts, my long hair and good camera angles' (Jana 2010). In a subsequent interview, she elaborated on this, saying that for many months she was 'in denial' about what was happening to her body.

> To some extent, if I had talked about it on my blog then it would have felt much more real to me and at that point I didn't want it to be real […] in some ways [it] was me actually being able to be the Roz who still had a really straight back and just enjoyed fashion and was really enjoying blogging and meeting new people and interacting with them.
>
> (Jana, in conversation with the author, 2011b)

Taking shape on her blog prior to this post, then, was an alternative Rosalind, as attested by her own words written in a personal essay for British *Vogue* two years later: 'I draped and layered myself into an illusion of straightness' (Jana 2013).

Emerging here is a complex performance of self, facilitated both by the presentational possibilities of a blog and the embodied practice of dressing. In dressing into an illusion of straightness, Rosalind employed her clothing and photographs to overwrite her embodied self with a particular dressed self, the kind so often portrayed in mainstream fashion imagery: that of the healthy, slender individual engaging in the world from the threshold of her style. Yet what the scoliodress spoke into being in the space of her blog was an alternative Rosalind, one more closely aligned (as she saw it) with 'the real' by which she meant her offline self (Jana, in conversation with the author, 2011b).

I hesitate to employ the term 'real' to distinguish between what occurs offline and online, that what is online is somehow less real for its occurrence on a digital realm. Rosalind's prior dressed self on her blog, while illusory in that it concealed her scoliosis from her readers, was also real: it was Rosalind herself dressing and photographing herself in particular poses and editing her photos to conceal the shape of her back. This was the Rosalind who her readers were encountering on her blog. It was real in another way as this illusory blogged self enabled Rosalind to distance herself from dealing with her worsening condition. In her article for British *Vogue*, she wrote:

> I was determined to hide it, not only from my friends, peers and increasingly my model agency, but also from myself. I tried to shape it into something separate from me, hidden out of sight […] more than wanting it better, I wanted it swept out of existence, as though it had never happened. I was irritated at any mention of my back, feeling simultaneously responsible for – and completely removed from – my condition.
>
> (Jana 2013)

This is a fascinating realization of Viviane Serfaty's observation that writing diaries online (although 'diaries' is interchangeable with 'blogs' here, in that what Serfaty describes is the presence of the writer's embodied self in the online text, as with style blogs) 'means connecting with embodied experience and inventing an approach of reality in which body surfaces reflect the depths of selfhood, and writing embodies the self' (2004: 121). Here, Rosalind both wrote from her offline embodied self and engaged with her experiences of that self in ways that mediated her discomfort and her desire to inhabit a different kind of self.

Style blogs as performative, reflexive spaces

Evident here is the way that style blogs are a tool in the process of self-knowing and the exploration of possible selves. In fact, these two aspects of style blogging – the explorations of self and of personal style – are often intertwined, due to the manner in which the self is primarily performed through style on these blogs, a process shaped and facilitated by clothing. Style blogs, then, are a locus at which concepts of dress and self, identity and performativity converge. There is an overlap between style blogs and clothing here: both implicated in subjectivity, both operating with simultaneity towards the eyes of those that surround as well as inwards as the subject engages with the doing – the wearing, the blogging – and is constituted as a subject in that moment.

This is reflected in Susan Kaiser's suggestion that the manner in which people dress daily and make sense of their appearances is elastic and integrative, as 'for some individuals style becomes […] a vehicle not only for being, but also for becoming' (2001: 83). Style blogs are a site at which this process of creative discovery both occurs and is discussed. With their writable and visual capacities, they are a space upon which styled identities are shaped and where bloggers are able to reflexively engage with the affective qualities of dress. This affectivity occurs between a wearer's corporeal being and their clothing, a vital aspect of dressing and a fundamentally embodied one that is surprisingly under-theorized in studies on fashion and identity.

To push this idea further, the expressive and identificatory qualities of dress do not just emanate out towards society – they also emanate inwards to the person wearing the clothes, reflexively communicating to them about their identity and being in the world. Perhaps this is discussed on the style blogosphere because it is a space that requires bloggers to articulate and perform themselves towards their readers, leading to a consideration of personal experience. Fashion here facilitates the process of one's identity coming to be known, both for readers and for bloggers themselves.

Also intriguing to consider are the ways in which our dress can be a part of the process of self-knowing, an articulation of what would otherwise be inarticulable. This is a complex, embodied interrelation between an individual's self and the clothes that they wear, a performative process apparent throughout the style blogosphere. An example of this is evident in a post published by Susie Lau in 2007, in which she described that her style was a way of speaking back against her own perceived unattractiveness.

In some ways, I think [my love of fashion] might have helped me escape into a world where I could fool myself into thinking that as long as I clothed myself in beauty […]

what my face looked like might not matter so much [...] I'm deeply passionate and act on whimsy and desire with my style yet probably the one thing holding me back is my ability to be 100% comfortable in my own skin. To illustrate, whilst I have no shame about photographing my outfits in all their various mishapen [*sic*] stages and developments, the camera stays firmly over my face. It's an open invite to view my love of fashion and how I express that in my style but I'm also saying 'Look at the outfit [...]. not the face [...]'.

(Lau, *Style Bubble*, 14 August 2007)

For Susie, like Rosalind, clothing was a means of creating an illusory self to conceal her discomfort with her embodied self. Here we see Susie in dialogue with her clothes, as she dresses with passion and whimsy and yet is 'held back' by her inability to feel comfortable in her own skin. Her eclectic style helps her feel more beautiful while also standing in contrast to what she sees as not beautiful: her face. Clothing here acts as the intermediary between Susie as she feels herself to be and Susie as she wants to be, the tension between these two states played out at the surface of her skin, and reflected back at her from her blog.

Furthermore, as with Rosalind, Susie's blog acts as the space for the articulation – and the thinking through – of this dynamic. These kinds of intimate discussions of personal experience, particularly in regard to clothing and feelings about themselves, is made possible by the writable spaces of blogs, which offer bloggers a means of speaking publicly about their lived experience. Making the scoliodress enabled Rosalind to think through her scoliosis and reconcile herself towards her operation. She later wrote that when she was told that she would have to undergo surgery, 'aside from all the obvious questions – such as, "[h]ow much pain will I be in?" – I wondered how I would introduce the issue on my blog, as it was now unavoidable. In the end, I did it in the best way I knew – through fashion' (Jana 2011a).

The scoliodress literally rendered Rosalind's scoliosis visible, metaphorically turning her embodied self inside out to display her difference. Entwistle's argument that clothing can become like a second skin (2000: 334) is extended by this example, in which the distinction between clothing and embodied self blurs as the dress operates as exoskeleton, rewriting Rosalind's embodied self into fabric while being the means by which she is able to identify and articulate her situation for her readership. Moreover, for Rosalind, this particular moment of dressing – and appearing dressed for her readers (and herself) – was, in her words, 'cathartic', as she 'express[ed] it in a way that felt real for [her]' (Jana, in conversation with the author, 2011b).

Clothing, then, was the interface at which Rosalind could engage with her scoliosis, holding it at a distance before aligning it with her self-perception in a way that she was comfortable with. Here we see dress not just a means of aesthetically performing an identity, but as the means through which that identity is experienced. Dress, then, is implicit in the process of *becoming*, a complex, embodied interrelation between an individual's embodied self, the clothes that they wear and their articulation of narratives of those selves.

This interplay between blogger and style demonstrates that there is a more complex dynamic at work on style blogs and in dressing than simply self-expression. Rather, style blogs make available a space for different discussions about fashion and style, ones that are firmly emplaced within the personal experience of bloggers and, as such, often reflect the process by which they engage with themselves through fashion and style. As I have argued, this process is performative, an ongoing dialogue between fabric and sentient self (or selves) as style bloggers explore ways of being in the world in ways that feel necessary and true to them through the threshold of their dress.

Notes

1   The reference is to L.P. Hartley's novel *The Go-Between*, the first sentence of which reads 'the past is a foreign country: they do things differently there' (1953: 9).

2   Theorists considering the intersection between dress and human identity (ranging from individual to social to gendered to cultural identity) have pursued many different lines of argument. These include Veblen ([1899] 1973); Simmel (1971); Bourdieu (1984); Wilson ([1985] 2013); Evans and Thornton (1989); Craik (1994); DeLong et al. (2005); Entwistle (2015). For examples of bloggers describing their dress as self-expression, see Lau (2013); Peachy (2013); *Tolly Dolly Posh* (2016).

3   A lookbook is a selection of photographs presented together in a folio or booklet to show off a collection or model.

4   Of course, it is worth qualifying that at the same time, we cannot be 'anything' we choose. In the preface to the second edition of *Gender Trouble* (1999), Butler is careful to stipulate that in taking our gender to be an internal essence of ourselves we anticipate and thus produce it through the repetition of bodily acts by which gender is constituted. Yet at the same time, these acts, and the gender that we internalize as 'natural', are informed and enforced by social and moral normativity as well as our location as material beings in a physical world that is, although apprehended through our selves, external to us. As such, we negotiate, navigate, conform to or subvert the societal expectation of our gendered selves against or within external bounds and possibilities.

5   It is beyond the scope of this project to give a comprehensive outline of these ideas, but there are a number of excellent volumes (besides the original texts) that do so, including the introduction to Joanne Entwistle and Elizabeth Wilson's edited volume *Body Dressing* (2001) and Michael Carter's *Fashion Classics from Carlyle to Barthes* (2003).

6   Naomi Wolf's seminal *The Beauty Myth* (1991) is a key example of the kinds of feminist critique fashion photography attracts, as establishing an unattainable model of femininity that is oppressive to women. Such arguments are often taken up in feminist pop-journalism on websites such as Jezebel, Mamamia and Daily Life, which critique fashion photography from a similar, albeit often sensationalized, perspective to Wolf's. For examples of this, see Champ (2013) and Dries (2013).

7   Of course, I assume here that regular readers have a positive perspective on the style bloggers they follow. As demonstrated in the previous chapter, it is common to be unmoved or disinterested in the style of bloggers whose blogs you come across. The likelihood of becoming a regular reader in such a situation is minimal, unless for the purposes of mockery (such as in the case of readers who participate in forums such as GOMI, see Chapter Two).

Chapter 5

Style Bloggers and the Contested Field of Fashion

If fashion is for everyone, is it fashion?

– Suzy Menkes, *New York Times* (2013)

Personal style bloggers occupy a contentious position within the field of fashion media. They have been both celebrated as fashion's new everyday 'style icons' (Bourne 2010), offering a fresh, enthusiastic perspective on a traditionally closed industry, and perceived as unauthorized 'interlopers' (Lau 2012a) whose opinions are baseless, whose enterprise is flawed and expertise is minimal at best. The value of the knowledge about fashion and style that style bloggers offer is itself challenged by this dual representation. Are style blogs 'democratizing fashion' (Widdicombe 2010) by making visible different kinds of style, different dressed bodies claiming to be fashionable? Or is their very output redundant, as designer Christopher Kane suggested when he said 'no-one who wants to read a serious review of a show is going to look at what a 14-year-old thinks' (Milligan 2009)? These two perspectives render style bloggers as a stylish novelty and as a dangerous trend: either the vanguard of or a threat to the professional fashion media.

Both perspectives are evident in the response of Anna Wintour, editor-in-chief of American *Vogue*, when asked for her opinion on fashion bloggers during a public talk on fashion photography at the Pratt Institute.

> We love as much coverage of fashion as possible. We don't care at all where it comes from, and we embrace bloggers and video and social networking, and anyone that's talking about fashion is a good thing. And we now have our own website that incorporates all of that. But I think what's interesting to us with this new phenomenon that 'everyone's a fashion editor, everyone's a fashion writer' is that all of that actually helps *Vogue*, because we have access and the understanding of fashion that, forgive me, but maybe some bloggers and some of the newcomers to this world have a little bit less experience of, but as I said, the more the merrier. We embrace it.
>
> (Wintour, quoted in Moylan 2010)

This response is inherently double edged: *Vogue* 'loves' and 'embraces' 'the newcomers to this world', whose contribution is ostensibly a 'good thing' because it continues to generate a conversation around fashion. This is presumably good because it fortifies fashion as something of interest and value to an increasingly engaged consumer base, whilst also exposing that consumer base to new products and new ways of dressing, all of which will continue to yield profit to the fashion industry. Yet at the same time, there is a patrician undertone to Wintour's words that reinforces the position of her publication in relation to bloggers. With their access, understanding and experience of 'this world', *Vogue* (and presumably its contemporaries in the professional fashion media) has something that bloggers cannot share: they are native to the world of fashion, they don't merely 'talk about' it. What apparently distinguishes these two groups – the professional fashion media and personal style bloggers – is privileged access, understanding and experience. These qualities, and bloggers' apparent lack thereof, constitute the difference between the 'we' and the 'not-we', between the legitimate and the amateur.

This chapter will closely engage with these dual perspectives on the position of style bloggers within the fashion media, both of which are imbricated with wider issues of access, legitimacy and the struggle within the field of fashion media over who gets to say what fashion is and how it should be communicated. I will examine these themes through the lens of Pierre Bourdieu's field theory, arguing that the fashion media can be conceptualized as a field of struggle in which agents (in this discussion, namely fashion bloggers, magazine editors, fashion critics and fashion journalists) compete for the same social, symbolic, cultural and, ultimately, economic capital.

The values and positions that organize the field of fashion media precede the emergence of fashion blogging, and yet style bloggers represent a new challenge in a pre-existing struggle. This challenge is their intrusion into the closed world of the fashion industry – what Bourdieu would describe as a 'field of restricted production' – encompassing both the position they have assumed as the 'everywoman's style icon' (Bourne 2010), intermediaries between fashion producers and their intended market as well as the access and opportunities that have been made available as a result of their creation of their position.

This position was not facilitated by bloggers working their way up through the fashion media and taking up existing positions in that field, but, rather, from the convergence of external factors. This is consistent with Bourdieu's argument that:

> [...] when the newcomers are not disposed to enter the cycle of simple reproduction, based on recognition of the 'old' by the 'young' [...] and recognition of the 'young' by the 'old' [...] but bring with them dispositions and position-takings which clash with the prevailing norms or production and the expectations of the field, they cannot succeed without the help of external changes.
>
> (1993a: 57)

Here, the initial external change was the increased accessibility of the Internet to private citizens and its growing use as a tool for social communication. Party to this development was the emergence of sites (as outlined in Chapter One) that enabled users interested in fashion to circulate opinions and knowledge of fashion amongst themselves as well as develop coverage of it through accessing archives of catwalk photographs and reviews on Style.com.

The change that the Internet wrought for print media in general by enabling users to access information and self-publish was encouraged within the field of fashion by the fashion PR industry. Recognizing the potential of style blogging to shape the perception of brands and build brand recognition amongst an audience with a 'personal' connection to bloggers, PR companies began extending to fashion bloggers (particularly style bloggers) the opportunities that had long been the sole terrain of the professional fashion media.

In fact, the aspects of style blogging that have placed some bloggers in a position where they are perceived as a threat by the professional fashion media – through their access to opportunities and the fashion product, and the ensuing accumulation of symbolic capital (see Rocamora 2013: 12–13) – have largely been brought about by the intervention of the PR industry. Invitations to fashion week and product launch parties are issued to bloggers by a label's PR representation who also handle requests to call out clothing to shoot. If, as increasingly occurs, press releases or garments are sent directly from a designer to a blogger, it is often to achieve a similar effect as orchestrated by their label's PR: to garner publicity for the label and to acknowledge the support (or to encourage future support) from a blogger. An early example of this saw Tavi blog about Rodarte each time the label's designers, Laura and Kate Mulleavy, sent as a gift clothing they had designed (see Gevinson, *Style Rookie* 2009b, 2009c). This was born out of the designers' admiration for Tavi's blog and their burgeoning friendship with her. More recently, Australian blogger Sara Donaldson featured a black dress that was custom-made for her by Australian designers Camilla & Marc. As Donaldson wrote in the post,

[…] offering to make me a dress based on the design of my favourite heels from my recent design collaboration with Tony Bianco (The Ana knot heel), Camilla came up with a one off dress for me to wear to the Australian Elle style awards, which you may have seen feature on episode 4 of Fashion Bloggers. It was actually a match made in heaven as parts of their Autumn Winter 15 collection has a similar look and feel to this dress, so you could take it as a teaser of things to come early next year!

(Donaldson, *Harper and Harley*, 19 November 2014)[1]

Although given as a gift, each mention of the label's name was hyperlinked to their e-boutique, as was the name of the heels the dress was created to match (heels designed by Donaldson in collaboration with Australian shoe label Tony Bianco). The post also covertly advertises Camilla & Marc's upcoming collection: this dress may have been custom-made for Donaldson, but as the blogger herself intimates, it's a 'teaser' for her readers, who may be able to acquire a similar dress themselves when the collection is released.

Opportunities such as these have worked to consecrate certain bloggers within the field, as they accrue capital by working with other agents to strengthen their position. This is crucial within the field of fashion, where to be visible at events such as fashion weeks (and arguably, in other prominent fashion contexts such as appearing in an advertising campaign for a prestigious or successful brand) is to signal one's membership of the field. As Entwistle and Rocamora argue, 'to have a distinct existence [in a field] means not only to exist physically but also socially, "which means *for others*, to be recognised by others, to acquire importance, *visibility*"' (Accardo, quoted in Entwistle and Rocamora 2006: 743, original emphasis).

Certain bloggers have also garnered legitimation through another kind of visibility: being featured in fashion magazines, and thereby consecrated by those publications. I say 'certain bloggers' because those who are invited to attend fashion week, and are offered advertising opportunities such as being the 'face' of a brand or being in a campaign and those who are recognized and thus legitimated by the dominant players in the fashion media, are often drawn from the same group of bloggers. These bloggers universally embody the *habitus* of the field and accord with the *doxa* of the dominant players. In other words, they are the style bloggers who embody the fashionable ideal: young, thin and conventionally attractive, with behaviour that corresponds with the dominant values and discourses circulating within the field.

I will conclude this chapter, then, by surveying the ways in which consecration of some bloggers has not necessarily led to a consecration of the entire style blogosphere, and will closely detail the subsequent hierarchization of style blogging. As a practice, and a sub-field of the fashion media, style blogging has increasingly become structured by the same forces that underpin the overall field of fashion, leading to rupture within the field as (mostly) first wave bloggers criticize the second wave bloggers who have transformed the practice. In this way, a similar struggle for legitimacy and dominance is occurring within the style blogosphere at present as is occurring within the fashion media.

The field of fashion media

French sociologist Pierre Bourdieu developed his theory of artistic and cultural fields throughout a number of works, most notably in *Distinction* (1984), *Sociology in Question* (1993b), *The Rules of Art* (1996) and *The Field of Cultural Production* (1993a). For Bourdieu, field theory is a methodological tool that 'aims to overcome the opposition between objectivism and subjectivism' (Entwistle and Rocamora 2006: 737) by considering both the practices of individuals within sociocultural structures – *fields* – and the structural forces that underpin these practices. For Bourdieu, the concept of a field refers to 'fluid and dynamic, rather than static, entities' (Webb et al. 2002: 22), allowing both for internal shifts and transformations as well as convergence with other fields.

The structure of a field is comprised of the positions of agents within it and the relationships and forces between these agents as they compete for specific kinds of *capital*, or 'skills, knowledge and connections, exchanged within the field to establish and reproduce one's position' (Entwistle and Rocamora 2006: 746). Bourdieu identifies four kinds of capital – social, symbolic, cultural and economic – the specific manifestations of which are particular to the underlying values of each field (with the exception of economic capital, which universally designates financial assets). Symbolic capital refers to an intangible quality, the way that an agent is recognized or perceived by others in their field: for example, their prestige and status as the employee of a respected publication, or reputation as a brand of artisanal quality. Cultural capital is a value associated with the accrual of culturally acknowledged resources, both embodied (tastes, skills, values) and experiential, such as attaining a degree or, as is valued in the field of fashion media, the experience of working up to a dominant position in the field through a long period of immersion in it (whether paid or voluntary) (see McRobbie 1998). Finally, social capital is the value and strength of an agent's social connections and contacts within a given field.

As is evident from the way that capital distinguishes between agents, fields are hierarchical. Moreover, their structure is organized according to two 'fundamental' oppositions: 'the opposition between the sub-field of restricted production and that of large-scale production', and 'the opposition within the sub-field of restricted production between the consecrated avant-garde and the avant-garde', or between the established players and the newcomers who challenge them (Bourdieu 1993a: 53). The first of these could also be construed as the opposition between the artistic (the 'autonomous pole') and the commercial ('heteronomous pole'), in which symbolic and economic value are accorded different weight in the creation and intention of an artistic work.

For example, in the field of fashion, we might consider the difference between luxury or 'high-end' labels and mass-market or 'high-street' labels. The value of luxury fashion is not solely measurable in the monetary cost of the product, but also in the symbolic value circulating that product – the history of Chanel, or the innovation of materials at Balenciaga, for example – that is taken to imbue their products with artistic value. The principles governing production at the autonomous pole are 'imagination, truth and freedom from social and economic influence', and their product is created for those 'in the know', who appreciate and understand the artistry (or history, or social commentary and so on) underpinning its creation (Webb et al. 2002: 160).

The heteronomous pole, on the other hand, is organized around the principle of creating goods for a commercial market. In fashion production, innovations might include creating 'on trend' goods at an accessible price point for a mass market, but they are inextricably linked with generating economic capital. For example, high street labels such as H&M, Zara, Topshop and Sportsgirl create a fashion product 'with the aim of commercial success' (Webb et al. 2002: 159).

However, the relationship between these two poles is best understood as a continuum rather than a binary. Luxury labels also need to generate a profit to stay in business and to cover the expense of producing their product, and as Webb, Schirato and Danaher observe, symbolic capital can often be transformed into economic capital as recognition of the prestige of a label can lead to its desirability on the market (see 2002: 161).

At the same time, labels positioned in closer proximity to the heteronomous pole of fashion production increasingly accrue symbolic capital by blurring the lines between their product and that of the 'high-end' market. For example, Topshop has launched Topshop

Unique, an in-house fashion line marketed as prestigious, priced at a higher price point and shown at London Fashion Week. It has also become commonplace for high fashion designers to create capsule collections for mass retailers such as Target and H&M, raising the symbolic capital of one (by its association with respected designers such as Karl Lagerfeld, Rei Kawakubo and Stella McCartney) and the economic capital of the other, through the license of their brand and the sale of their designs to a mass market.

Bourdieu stipulates that 'there is no other criterion of membership of a field than the objective fact of producing effects within it' (1993a: 42). By being structured by the relations between competing agents employing strategy for accruing capital and maintaining or gaining dominance, fields do not have fixed boundaries, even as agents struggle to define the terms of entry and legitimacy, or, struggle over 'the monopoly of the power to consecrate producers or products' (1993a: 42). In fact, Bourdieu explains that one of the difficulties facing the 'orthodox' agents of the field seeking to conserve it against 'heretical transformation' from newcomers is that in redefining the terms of entry into the field implies 'a form of recognition: adversaries whom one would prefer to destroy by ignoring them cannot be combated without consecrating them' (1993a: 42).

In their work analysing London Fashion Week (LFW) as the material embodiment of the field of fashion, Entwistle and Rocamora (2006) argue that the field of fashion includes 'all the key agents and institutions [including] designers, models, journalists and buyers from stores around the world', all agents that were present at LFW during their fieldwork (2006: 736). Bourdieu and Delsaut also defined the field of fashion, arguing in 'La Couturier et sa Griffe' (1975) that it is 'a field ruled by the competition for the monopoly of specific legitimacy, that is, for the power to constitute and impose the legitimate symbols of distinction in regards to clothing' (Bourdieu and Delsaut, quoted in Rocamora 2016: 236–37).

Within this field are a number of sub-fields that are organized around the same principles and poles as the field of fashion, competing for the 'monopoly of specific legitimacy', but also operating according to specific values generated through the relationships between their own key players. Rocamora defines the field of fashion media as 'a social space made of a range of institutions and agents – magazines, newspapers, journalists, photographers, stylists, makeup artists, and so on – all involved in the definition of its norms and values' (2016: 244). She argues that these values include the definition of what is 'good, tasteful, valuable or innovative fashion' (244), a definition that ultimately depends on the boundaries that a publication will draw around its content; as McRobbie explains, each magazine 'has its "house style", its own image of itself and of its audience or readership' (1998: 161).

This 'house style' often depends on where a publication sits in proximity to the heteronomous or autonomous pole of the field: prestige publications such as *Vogue* and *Harper's Bazaar* construct 'fashion as art and as a luxury consumption for middle-class women' (McRobbie 1998: 162). This perspective is echoed by most professional fashion critics, who are situated closer to the autonomous pole and who also legitimize fashion as art, albeit one grounded in history and sociocultural values (see Martin 1998; Horyn 2004; Graham 2012; Menkes 2013). Other publications that are situated closer to the autonomous pole are niche fashion publications such as *Pop, Dazed, i-D* and *Oyster*, which also present fashion as artistic and subcultural, albeit each with an individual and recognizable aesthetic and often also incorporating brands that are not 'high fashion', such as streetwear labels or the designs of smaller local designers, that resonate with and further the publication's individual brand. Lynge-Jorlén writes that in this way niche fashion magazines 'merge edge and elite, bridging the avant-garde and the establishment' by featuring a blend of popular culture with art and apparel by high fashion labels (2012: 9).

Publications such as *Shop Til You Drop* or *Grazia* are closer to the heteronomous pole, presenting fashion as primarily oriented towards mass-market consumption and fun. While the fashion presented in these publications usually mirrors the trends published in prestige publications, they are characteristically translated through a myriad of cheaper, but still 'on-trend' options for readers. If goods from luxury labels are displayed, they are framed within the same discourse of entertainment: these are goods to be consumed rather than 'art', although they are still characterized as prestigious and therefore desirable.

In this way, the fashion media play a central role in disseminating and framing the fashion product for consumers. Such publications circulate what Bourdieu and Delsaut call 'fashion discourse' (*'le discours de mode'*), which imbues the fashion product with symbolic value. As Rocamora argues, the language used in fashion writing not only *describes* the value of the featured garments, 'they make it' (2016: 238–39). Similarly, the garments, collections or labels that are included are also deemed 'fashionable' by being selected for display in the publication. Accordingly, as fashion critic Robyn Givhan has noted, '[t]he rule of thumb at magazines is that if they don't like something it will be omitted' (Graham 2012). In this way, fashion magazines not only contribute to the discourse of the value of fashion, they define what 'fashionable' is. Moeran sums this up when he writes that fashion magazines

[…] legitimate fashion and the fashion world in cultural terms. They make meaningful connections between things that seem to be essentially independent; they give them social lives by creating an imaginary world about them; they create awareness in participants of the field of fashion in which they work; and they provide historical and aesthetic order in a world whose products, by their very seasonality and potentially chaotic quantity, are likely to go unnoticed. In this way, a fashion magazine helps form a collective concept of what 'fashion' is.

(Moeran 2006: 738)

Fashion critics also circulate fashion discourse by according certain values to a collection, explaining its genesis from a designer's initial inspiration and translating what it means in the context of the fashion industry and the market. This perspective is evident in fashion critic Tim Blanks's consideration of the significance of the reviews he and his peers write.

You know, designers will say, 'I didn't really know what I did till I read what you wrote.' Your perspective in the moment becomes a perspective with the passage of time – no, your perspective in the moment becomes *the* perspective with the passage of time, which I think is fascinating because there is nothing else.

(Blanks, quoted in Schneier 2013: 3, original emphasis)

Finally, the logics around which the field of fashion media are organized are distinct from those of the fashion industry, but are similarly organized around the competition for specific capital. At stake is the power to determine what is fashionable in a way that is recognized by the fashion industry; that is, creatively and calculated in accordance with what the rest of the industry is 'thinking' as a result of having access to the shared knowledge and sensibility of the field (see Entwistle 2009: 13–15). Also at stake is economic capital in attracting and maintaining a wide readership and regular advertisers. McRobbie summarizes these as 'the logics of creative and editorial reputation, circulation figures, competition from rival publications and advertising revenue' (McRobbie 1998: 151).

Having thus mapped out the dynamics of the field of fashion media, I will now analyse the tension between style bloggers and their critics in the fashion media, first situating this debate within the parameters of existing theoretical work on fashion criticism. This will demonstrate the struggle for legitimacy by fashion critics to justify their work, a struggle that was under way before the emergence of style blogging.

The beleaguered art of fashion criticism

A recurring question both in the popular media in relation to style blogs as well as in academic literature on them is whether or not style bloggers are 'citizen journalists' (see Dodes 2006; Widdicombe 2010; Clarke 2011).[2] This question is frequently answered, both by fashion critics and other commentators reporting on fashion, through the assertion that style bloggers do not add anything of substance to critical discourse on fashion and that the opinions they do have are compromised by their increasingly close ties to the labels they enthuse about on their blogs (see Wilson 2009; Graham 2012; Menkes 2013).

Rocamora has contextualized this anxiety over style bloggers within the debate surrounding the challenge digital media has posed to print media, arguing that it can be understood in relation to 'a crisis of the "expert paradigm"' (Rocamora 2011: 100). According to Rocamora this crisis has been brought about by the 'open-ended processes of communication' on digital environments, which are shifting our assumptions and expectations of expertise, effectively displacing fashion journalists' authority 'by the shifting into focus of other voices such as bloggers' (100). She argues that this breakdown of boundaries determining what media work is has been compounded by the prior fact that journalism is itself a field with an 'absence of official credentials, the lack of an established educational trajectory and that of "professional boundaries"' (100).

The permeable boundaries of expertise are exacerbated in the case of fashion criticism, as there is no universally agreed-upon framework of how it should be written or what information is necessary in order to do it well. Richard Martin attributes this lack of framework to the absence of a historical or critical academic discipline of fashion that might provide a critical model in the face of the 'blandishments of cooperation and congratulations' to which a fashion critic (as he alleges) is subject (1998: 57). Those who have formed their own models of critical inquiry on fashion (Martin identifies Colin McDowell and Suzy Menkes) have done so from the merits of their own temperaments and within a tradition that 'is more accustomed to hyperbole and congratulation than to criticism' (58).

Whilst the importance of these traditions in relation to fashion criticism may weigh more in Martin's estimation of what constitutes a good fashion critic, as he is himself an art and fashion historian, the sentiment remains that fashion criticism – indeed, fashion journalism, for Martin also considers former American *Vogue* and *Harper's Bazaar* editors Diana Vreeland, Polly Mellen and Carrie Donovan in his argument – is closely tied to fashion's commerce. Therefore, the critical capacities of fashion critics can be compromised by the close connections they enjoy with the fashion labels they must review (1998: 55–58). Martin observes that 'fashion's commerce may even seem to suppress criticism' (55), the critic placed in the role of facilitator in fashion's 'appeals to the consumer' and their objectivity weakened by 'prime seating' at fashion shows, and the gifts and other privileges given by designers hoping to woo them into favourable reviews (56).

McRobbie also examines the causes of this close connection between fashion producers and media, arguing, like Martin, that the fashion media is more closely affiliated with its subject than are most other journalistic fields (1998: 151). She suggests that this is due to the 'low status of fashion writing within the hierarchical field of print journalism', causing fashion journalists to form closer links with those within the industry with whom they ostensibly have more in common, and that the fashion industry is a 'world which perceives itself to be trivialised and associated with a kind of stupidity' (1998: 151–52).

Moreover, fashion magazines and critics alike are dependent on maintaining good relations with the producers of the fashion they wish to display and review. Fashion magazines draw most of their revenue from advertisers, which results in positive coverage labels that advertise within their pages and simple omission, rather than negative reviews, of those whose collections were unfavourably perceived. So much is evident in the memoir of former editor of *Vogue Australia*, Kirstie Clements, who reflected that:

> […] in magazines we criticise by omission. If we considered that you weren't good enough to be in *Vogue*, then you simply weren't in *Vogue*. An editor-in-chief whose main mission is to create a luxury environment is not expected to point out anything substandard or ordinary. Like Pollyanna, we concentrate only on the wonderful. And don't even think about writing or saying anything remotely negative about an advertiser. Even a potential one. It's a minefield that's best managed with your mouth shut.
>
> (2013: 98–99)

As also intimated in this excerpt, advertisers can influence the content of the magazine by sponsoring 'advertorials', defined by McRobbie as 'lucrative, sponsored advertising features' (1998: 157) in which an advertisement will be shot and designed to look like the other pages in the magazine, so that the products are effortlessly aligned with the brand of the masthead.[3]

In an article titled 'The beleaguered art of fashion criticism', journalist David Graham characterizes the tenor of journalism on fashion as akin to 'cheerleading', writing that fashion magazines 'have always been in passive collusion with the fashion industry. They are notoriously submissive – unwilling to criticize because they are wed inextricably to advertising dollars' (2012). Fashion critics are, famously, similarly dependent on good relations with labels to do their jobs, as an unfavourable review could result in them being blacklisted from attending the recipient's show the following season. Richard Martin discusses this in his essay 'Addressing the dress' (1998), observing that critics have been banned from shows for making 'even mildly negative remarks'. A recent example of this was when Cathy Horyn was banned from attending the Saint Laurent Spring/Summer RTW 2012 show for having said in 2004 that the designs of then-menswear designer Hedi Slimane had been influenced by his rival Raf Simons (see also Chilvers 2012).

All of these factors establish fashion criticism and fashion journalism not as inviolable in terms of their artistic traditions but rather as vulnerable to criticism themselves even as they have traditionally had hegemony over fashion reportage. The question over the value of fashion criticism when its authors are necessarily so dependent on the favour of the subject of their analysis – and, as Martin suggests, potentially susceptible to fashion labels' 'entreaty and charisma' (1998: 55) – undermines a form of writing that is already perceived as feminized and trivial due to its subject matter (McRobbie 1998). It is little wonder, then, that the fashion media has tried to safeguard its tradition: not only perpetuating a set of conventions around how knowledge is gathered and who gets to speak, but also marking within its boundary the right to say what fashion is.

For McRobbie, fashion magazines 'construct style and fashion as insider knowledge' that their staff have access to as participants in the field (1998: 154). The idea of fashion being insider knowledge, relayed by the intermediating fashion media, is perpetuated in the way that fashion knowledge has traditionally been selected and framed – as indeed have the specific set of values that form the basis of the judgement that a look or trend is 'in fashion' – is obscured by the fashion media. As Entwistle argues, 'fashion value is defined through the collective activities and practice of actors inside the market' (2009: 3), making the identification and representation of fashion through media traditionally dependent on access to that market, and in one's position as a translator, an intermediary who 'legitimates fashion and the fashion world in cultural terms' (Moeran 2006: 738).

Style bloggers are not fashion critics

The struggle over access and legitimation of fashion is precisely what is at the heart of the criticism style bloggers have received from fashion critics. Bloggers 'don't have the critical faculties to know what's good and what's not', they 'don't understand the history' (Robert Johnston, associate editor of *GQ* and a fashion director, quoted in *ES* magazine, see Rocamora 2012: 100) and, according to Suzy Menkes (fashion editor for the *International Herald Tribune*):

> [t]here is something ridiculous about the self-aggrandizement of some online arbiters who go against the mantra that I was taught in my earliest days as a fashion journalist: 'It isn't good because you like it; you like it because it's good'.
>
> (Menkes 2013)

This critique is summed up by Robyn Givhan, who has stated that '[a]n awful lot of people not only have an opinion about fashion, they also believe those opinions are worth broadcasting' (2007) and that '[fashion] criticism is not personal opinion' (Graham 2012).

This criticism recalls the second opposition that Bourdieu argues structures the field of cultural production: that between the consecrated avant-garde and the avant-garde, 'the established figures and the newcomers' or between 'cultural orthodoxy and heresy' (1993a: 53). The tension arises when the newcomers, in asserting their difference (in the case of style bloggers, the basis of their opinions, their writing style and medium) endeavour to 'impose new modes of thought and expression, out of key with the prevailing modes of thought and with the *doxa*, and therefore bound to disconcert the orthodox by their "obscurity" and "pointlessness"' (1993a: 58).

So much is evident in the reaction of professional fashion critics to the presence of style bloggers at fashion shows and the style and content of their fashion reportage. Such criticism, as is quoted above, asserts that what style bloggers write is not fashion criticism, which de-legitimizes their contribution to fashion communication and draws into question the appropriateness of their attendance at fashion week.[4]

The first point is accurate: style bloggers are not fashion critics. Moreover, they do not claim to be. During my four years of research and immersion in the style blogosphere, I never once encountered a style blogger identifying what they do as fashion criticism. Even a blogger such as Susie Lau, who does write detailed reviews of the shows she attends and discusses the historical and social significance of a collection – in short, who writes a kind of fashion criticism – has been careful to distinguish what bloggers such as herself do from the work of fashion critics.[5] Rather, she has emphasized the personal, expressive capacities of style blogs as their point of difference: 'instead of wanting [style bloggers] to be critical we need to embrace them as creatives who express points of view by multitasking in photography, styling, illustration, editing and so on' (Lau 2012a). She has also expressed her opinion that the question of whether or not style bloggers are fashion journalists is 'a misguided conception' (2012a); rather, style blogs are 'subjective, expressive' (2012a) rather than objective and analytical.

Fashion critics discrediting the contribution of style bloggers on the basis of their different approach to fashion reportage is a realization of Bourdieu's point that the orthodox criticize the work of newcomers on the basis of 'their "obscurity" and "pointlessness"' (1993a: 58). In fact, such language recalls Franca Sozzani's dismissal of blogging, quoted in Chapter Three: 'they don't offer an opinion, only talk about themselves take their own pictures wearing absurd outfits. What's the point?' (2011).

The content of style blogs celebrates an individual's taste rather than reflecting on the cultural, aesthetic and social implications of a collection or trend, as is the purview of professional fashion critics. This interpretation of what a fashion critic does is drawn from the words of two critics, Robyn Givhan and Suzy Menkes, both of whom have criticized style bloggers by marking a boundary around what they themselves do. For both of these writers, attending shows to see the collections before writing a critical analysis is central to their jobs (see Graham 2012; Menkes 2013), a role that art and fashion historian Richard Martin likens to a 'mediator and facilitator' between a fashion house and their intended market (1998: 56).

This language is mirrored in much of the theoretical writing about the role of the fashion media as communicators. In her discussion of the British fashion industry, McRobbie wrote that 'the fashion media "represents" fashion and in so doing adds its own gloss, its own frame of meaning to the fashion items which serve as its raw material' (1998: 151). The frame of meaning that professional critics ostensibly add is an interpretation of the significance of a collection within the context of a fashion house's history and the sociocultural context within which it was shown. Critics – as well as the rest of the professional fashion media of which they are a part – thus 'work as intermediaries between the industry and the consumer, and impose stability and a narrative that ties past with present to make sense of the plethora of clothing and images that the fashion industry circulates each season' (Moeran 2006: 736).

In fact, Herbert Blumer goes as far as to argue that rather than the result of some inner psychic force, as asserted by Veblen ([1899] 1973) and Flugel (1930), fashion is produced by 'the institutional, social and cultural relations between a number of key players in the industry' (Blumer, quoted in Entwistle 2009: 9). These key players are not just the designers who create the fashion product but also those who mediate between the producers and their market: fashion buyers and journalists. A season's 'look' (or 'looks', as more accurately describes today's fashion marketplace) is the result of the interplay of the choices made by these players, choices that cohere and overlap as a set of identifiable trends as a result of being immersed in the same culture, or the same field, 'and thus seeking out new trends and tastes from the same sources' (Entwistle 2009: 9).

Yet whilst style bloggers' approach to fashion differs greatly from traditional fashion criticism, their position in relation to fashion and to its intended market is identical – that is, they have also assumed the role of intermediaries between fashion producers and their market. However, rather than weaving a linear narrative between a label's history and its current collection, style bloggers impose a different kind of narrative, one that ties a new collection or garment into the story of their own style and tastes.

As intermediaries between fashion producers and potential consumers, style bloggers do more than weave a written narrative around the new. They weave a garment into the visual world of their own style, taking upon themselves the role of stylist and model as well as fashion director and photo editor, and always justifying the inclusion of a garment because they ostensibly like it.[6] Fashion criticism may '[have] to be more than just "I loved it" or "I hated it"' (Givhan, quoted in Graham 2012) but style blogging does not: the subjective and expressive valuation that style bloggers bring to the fashion that they include on their blogs is one of the hallmarks of writing in their genre.

In assuming this role as intermediaries, style bloggers are participating in the struggle for access and legitimacy in their field, their emergence displacing the power relation of the field of fashion media (see Bourdieu 1993a: 32). Bourdieu argues that a field's history 'arises from the struggle between the established figures and the young challengers' whose emergence precipitates the 'slide into the past' of the established players, or

[...] those who have made their mark (*fait date* – 'made an epoch') and who are fighting to persist, and those who cannot make their own mark without pushing into the past those who have an interest in stopping the clock, eternalizing the present state of things.

(60)

This critique emphasizes the different logics, values and discourses – or *doxa* – underpinning fashion criticism and style blogging. In writing that 'it's good because they like it' (to rework Menkes's critique), style bloggers assume the same legitimating power that fashion critics and those working at fashion magazines have long held for themselves (albeit in different capacities according to their position in the field). Ultimately, what is at stake here is a struggle for legitimacy and a struggle for access and the power to decide what is or isn't stylish, what is or isn't a legitimate way to speak about fashion.

The struggle for legitimacy within the style blogosphere

I have not yet addressed in detail the alternative perspective on fashion blogging circulating through the field of fashion media: that style bloggers are a fresh, welcome new voice. This perspective is not frequently commented upon but is evident in the way that the mainstream fashion media (namely, fashion magazines) have incorporated certain bloggers into the fashionable world of their publications.

It is now common to come upon photographs of certain style bloggers in the front pages of fashion magazines, their photographs displayed among those of other 'bright young things' who are displayed as exemplary models of personal style for readers to emulate: models 'off-duty', 'It' girls, actresses and singers of the moment and so on. Moreover, rather than omit bloggers, some publications have indeed 'embraced' them (to invoke Anna Wintour) by creating specific sections on their publication's website to feature their 'edit' of the 'best' blogs. For example, this language is drawn directly from the website of *Vogue*

Australia that displays the page 'Spy Style', which is defined as 'a collective of Australia's best fashion bloggers, as selected by the editors of *Vogue*' (Centenera 2013). These posts are embedded in the website of *Vogue Australia*, rather than taking readers to the blogger's original post. In this way, the work of the featured style bloggers is literally re-oriented within the world of *Vogue*, a move that imbues their work with both symbolic and social capital, while at the same time the magazine assumes the aura of being in touch with a younger demographic.

Of course, as with the rest of Wintour's remark on bloggers, such inclusion comes with an underlying subtext. If bloggers are independent publishers recognized in their own right, why do they need to be edited in order to be presented to readers? This is consistent with McRobbie's reading of fashion magazines: they 'draw their own boundaries around their content' (1998: 154) and, as a corollary, around what is fashionable in their professional opinion. Unsurprisingly, then, the kinds of style bloggers who are selected for inclusion in such publications, and thereby consecrated as legitimate by these dominant agents in the field of fashion media, share the same taste in clothing and wear it on bodies that are young, slim and attractive as is consistent with the dominant fashionable ideal.

These bloggers 'conform to the canons of established fashion media and play by their rules' (Rocamora 2016: 246) by embodying the kind of cultural capital with high currency in the fashion industry. In this way, such bloggers are able to display their 'field membership' (Entwistle and Rocamora 2006: 746) as well as performing their knowledge about fashion through their own online embodiments. Rocamora and Entwistle's observation that 'the field of fashion is one where the appearance of the body is absolutely critical' (746) is here proven. Despite the potential of style blogging to challenge the values of the fashion industry by introducing a different incarnation of fashionability (not only in the instance of fatshion blogs, but also bloggers embodying an alternative femininity or interpretation of fashionability), the bloggers who have qualities that are desirable in the fashion industry are those who are given more opportunity to participate in it. What is important to succeed in the field of fashion, then, is 'the ability to articulate recognized forms of fashion capital and develop an appropriate fashion *habitus* so that one's body looks like it actually belongs' (746).

Not all of the bloggers who have been thus consecrated by the dominant players in the fashion media necessarily embodied all of the desired aspects of the fashionable *habitus*: for every wealthy, Caucasian Chiara Ferragni who has reminisced on her blog about the time she received her first Louis Vuitton bag as a gift from her mother (Ferragni 2012), there is an Asian-Australian Nicole Warne who started her blog wearing reworked second-hand garments that she also sold in her online store. However, what unifies bloggers such as Ferragni and Warne, and their contemporaries who have also been consecrated in different ways by the fashion industry, is their shared youth, slender figures, attractive features and a blogged taste in fashion that is consistent with the prevailing aesthetic promoted by the fashion media: a conventional femininity portrayed through garments made by designers whose work is deemed fashionable.

These bloggers are not only those who have accrued symbolic and social capital in relation to the established players in the field of fashion: they are also those who have become representative of the style blogosphere, quoted in newspaper articles about blogging and held up within the style blogosphere as exemplary of blogging success. On this basis, Rocamora argues that 'hierarchies have not been erased from the fashion blogosphere' and 'fashion blogging can be seen as a subfield of the fashion media [similarly constituted] of newcomers and established players' (2016: 247).

Furthermore, this sub-field is itself a site of struggle. Whilst the bloggers who have been recognized by the dominant players in the field of fashion are also those who are dominant on the style blogosphere, there is also tension at work over who gets to legitimize the practice, a struggle between first wave and second wave bloggers. This has generated impassioned dialogue on the style blogosphere about the legitimacy of second wave bloggers, who have entered the field by emulating the high-profile bloggers such as Rumi Neely or Jane Aldridge, and who first wave bloggers have accused of transforming the field for the worse.

'Selling out' or the state of style blogging

The spread of second wave blogging and its ethos throughout the style blogosphere has given rise to considerable criticism of 'the state of fashion blogging' (Sicardi 2012) by first wave bloggers dismayed at the changes they saw as reshaping the practice. In late 2011 to early 2012, a number of first wave style bloggers published articles, interviews or blogposts decrying the way that style blogging had devolved into a commercial mimicry of the mainstream fashion media (see George 2011; Zou 2012). Among these were a pair of posts published by first wave bloggers Isabel Slone (*Hipster Musings*) and Arabelle Sicardi (*Fashion Pirate*) that operated dialogically as two halves of a critical whole, individually articulating their discomfort with the increasing commercialism and decreasing creativity on the style blogosphere.

Slone's post inspired Sicardi to write her own, with both attracting a strongly affirmative response from readers, who almost universally thanked them for 'saying something'. Significantly, but perhaps not surprisingly, the debate did not appear to be either acknowledged or taken up in any counter-posts by second wave bloggers.

These posts, and their attendant comments, encapsulate both the tone and the main points of criticism made of the contemporary blogosphere by first wave bloggers disillusioned with the commercialism running rampant among style blogging's 'facsimile veneer of personality and intimacy' (blogger Jenny Zhang, quoted in Zou 2012).

In brief, Slone and Sicardi describe feeling 'grossed out' by the contemporary blogosphere. These second wave bloggers are 'glossy' and distanced from readers, and according to both, the blogosphere has been commodified through the widespread uptake of product placement on blogs, and bloggers' desire to be marketable. The quotes that follow are presented one after another here to mimic the style of the blogged conversation taking place in these posts and also, in the manner of Benjamin's convolutes, 'to communicate amongst themselves [...] in a subterranean manner' (Eiland and McLaughlin, 'Translator's foreword' to *The Arcades Project*, 2002: x), conveying the spirit and frustration of these bloggers.

> I'm kind of grossed out by the blogosphere right now and I don't want to be girl-hatey [...] but the thing is, the blogosphere's really commodified right now and it doesn't make me feel good to go through blogs that look the same.
>
> (Arabelle Sicardi, *Fashion Pirate*, 3 February 2012)

> I've been blogging since 2004 and in that time I've seen the general youth orientated blogosphere change so much. Back then, fashion blogs weren't exactly that popular, most blogs were just kids who needed an outlet, like me. We all joined the same forums and had a little community. It was great, that was back when blogging was nerdy, I used to hide the fact that I had a blog from everybody I knew. I was kind of embarrassed by it.
>
> (comment from Magnet, *Fashion Pirate*, 3 February 2012 at 10:54 PM)

> I don't want to be a fashion blogger if that means (once again) being that loser girl with no friends who just doesn't fit in compared to the glossy DSLR photos of girls with sleek hair wearing Céline.[7] I still shop at thrift stores, will never be able to afford Céline and that's totally okay. But I can't compete with that.
>
> (Isabel Slone, *Hipster Musings*, 2011b)

> People can't relate to bloggers that much anymore because who can relate to someone that pays someone to take professional photos for them on a daily basis? While wearing clothes that they don't actually buy themselves and that they requested from a PR agency? That's not personal style; that's like pulling for a photoshoot for a magazine.
>
> (Sicardi, *Fashion Pirate*, 2012)

> It seems like the only substantiative conversation about fashion blogging that ever takes places [*sic*] is how to work with brands! [A]nd how to drive traffic to your site! [A]nd NOT any discussion about how a craft that at it's best is pure and democratizing, but nowadays is adcopy and samey-ness [...] what can be done about this? I can't help but feel completely helpless.
>
> (comment from Meagan, *Fashion Pirate*, 3 February 2012 at 2:11 PM)

> I totally get what you're saying and completely agree!! I still follow a couple of blogs that have perfect photos and perfect hair and perfect clothes all labeled 'c/o somebody or other' and I'm so over it [...] The worst part is that on GOOD blogs, where the girls take their own pics and are unique, I keep seeing this all over the place: 'Ugh you guys, I'm so sorry for the crappy picture quality.' And the pictures are always totally fine and I never

know what they're even talking about. I guess they're seeing all these super high quality blog photos and think that's what you have to have now.

(comment from Lydia on *Fashion Pirate*, 3 February 2012 at 8:24 PM)

I think most fashion bloggers used to be very DIY and they still exist [...] but now fashion blogging has been popularized and the people who are now blogging about fashion are not blogging to be DIY they're blogging to be famous [...] I hate bloggers that just buy designer clothing, wear looks straight from the runway, are tall, skinny, model-like gals (Man Repeller, Fashion Toast, etc.) and constantly talk about how creative they are or how weird they are OR, the worst, talking about other fashion bloggers like they represent the community! The community is so vast and rooted in such grassroots style and thrift-store love that they're so far removed from what the blogging community for fashion used to be.

(comment from Hazel on *Fashion Pirate*, 3 February 2012 at 11:01 PM)

The two identifiable periods of style blogging are seen here to be fundamentally in conflict, at least according to the first wave bloggers who observed the commodification of the blogosphere with dismay. Here, Bourdieu's definition of a field as 'the product and prize of a permanent conflict' (1993a: 34) is apt, as we see the style blogosphere as a cultural field, one constituted by style bloggers as well as other participants who legitimize, disseminate and support the practice. These include websites on style blogging such as IFB, the fashion media who write about and include visuals of style bloggers in their publications, and fashion labels who work with style bloggers (particularly those who have become synonymous with the 'style blogger aesthetic' such as Jeffrey Campbell and e-tailer Nasty Gal).

However, there is some ambiguity about the capital at stake here. It is not simply that first wave bloggers compete for symbolic capital (in this instance, a widely read and recognized blog and the prestige of having an original and admired style) and second wave bloggers for economic capital (such as income generated through advertising and sponsorship deals as well as the receipt of desirable fashion product from labels). For second wave bloggers to achieve economic capital, symbolic capital is also required: it is desirable for them to embody a particular accessible style that will align with companies they wish to work for, and to attract a regular readership.

It is also misleading to think that first wave bloggers do not wish to succeed economically from their blogs. That it was not a value that was underpinning the practice in the beginning seems mostly due to the perception of bloggers that style blogging was a hobby in its early days and, as Jessica Quirk observed, 'nobody had money to pay bloggers' (Quirk, in conversation with the author, 2013). However, as advertisers and brands began to make commercial offers to bloggers on the basis of their traffic and output, a number of first wave bloggers began hosting advertisements in their sidebars and running competitions for their readers to win product from companies the bloggers had 'partnered with' (see Slone 2011b).

As well as the struggle for capital, then, here we see a struggle for legitimacy between these polarized groups of bloggers. Bourdieu's sentiment about the literary field rings true in this instance, as on the style blogosphere, too, 'the fundamental stake […] is the monopoly of literary [or blogging] legitimacy' (1993a: 42). Who gets to define the field? What are the underlying values and discourses that organize style blogging? What has unsettled first wave bloggers is not just the commodification of their practice – the 'chasing' of sponsors, and the depiction of a style that is financially unattainable for many first wave bloggers – but also the oppositional *doxa* underlying these two waves of style blogging, fundamentally restructuring the understanding of what, how and why these bloggers do what they do.

The opposition between these organizing *doxa* is evident in the language of the above quotes, which construe second wave bloggers as 'other', and in a negative light: all of their blogs 'look the same', they 'chase sponsors' (as opposed to the first wave bloggers who were 'nerdy' and 'embarrassed' by their practice, or who do not have the entrepreneurial skill or income to 'compete' in this new arena) and they do not even show personal style on their blogs, 'pulling for a photoshoot' rather than demonstrating an original aesthetic point of view. Therefore, the aspects of style blogging that are valued by first wave bloggers include 'grassroots style and thrift-store love' as opposed to dressing 'trendily' or in designer clothing, blogging in a relatable way in relation to a 'community' as opposed to 'blogging to be famous', and being 'unique' rather than 'perfect'; in short, theirs is an attitude that valorizes an aesthetic of DIY over DSLR.

Furthermore, the appeal of these first wave bloggers to the origins of their practice, rooted as it was in DIY culture, an exploration of personal style and a sense of shared community, undercuts the legitimacy of second wave bloggers, who are characterized by first wave bloggers as oblivious, privileged and opportunistic. This exemplifies Paul Moore's reading of Bourdieu's work, in which he argues established participants in a field 'adopt conservative strategies in order to maintain their privileged position' in order to resist the challenge issued by 'newly arrived competitors' who have, whether intentionally or not, attempted to displace them (2004: 61).

It is especially interesting to note in the quotes above the implicit restructuring of the practice enacted by second wave bloggers: that a certain kind of 'high quality' photography is supposedly expected by readers and self-imposed by second wave bloggers, leading first wave bloggers to apologize when this quality is absent, or the need for entrepreneurial skills, experienced as a lack by Isabel who described herself as 'just a regular person obsessed with fashion'. This is a sentiment echoed by Kat George, a former style blogger who wrote that style blogging was

[…] originally a means of harnessing the awesome power of the Internet and new digital technologies to democratize our perspective of contemporary fashion. By challenging traditional, or 'glossy', notions of beauty and defying the mainstream in order to reshape societal norms and expectations from a citizen viewpoint, blogs across all genres can and have served as powerful social tools.

(George 2011)

Yet rather than continue this tradition of publishing oppositional, supposedly democratic self-representations of beauty, second wave bloggers are seen as perpetuating the beauty standard circulated within the industry, evident in the commenters' references to 'girls with sleek hair wearing Céline' and 'tall, skinny, model-like gals'.

As such, second wave bloggers have not been consecrated by the existing positions in the style blogosphere, but in positions in the field of fashion whose values and discourses are mirrored in the *doxa* of these newcomers. First wave bloggers still occupy a position closer to the autonomous pole of the field, as the avant-garde who wrote from the 'outside'. As explored in Chapter Two, this is realized by bloggers performing a self-determined fashionable self on their blogs in opposition to the homogenous, embodied fashionable ideal, and writing about what they think is stylish: thrifted clothes, niche or emerging labels, certain plus-size clothing labels and so on.

The style blogosphere, then, is as constituted by struggle for legitimacy between agents as is the field of fashion media within which it operates as a sub-field. At stake in both is an ongoing struggle between orthodoxy and heresy, between the established players and the newcomers whose way of writing, opinions and values threaten the hegemony of that which preceded them. As the fashion industry has been 'opened up' by style blogging, so too have the dominant values of the industry challenged and transformed the style blogosphere. Such an analysis of the field of fashion contextualizes the roles and criticisms of those invested in shaping it, or maintaining it to their own advantage. The very permeability of both the field of fashion media and the sub-field of style blogging suggests that any effort to '[eternalise] the present stage of things' (Bourdieu 1993a: 60) is essentially futile.

At the beginning of this chapter, I quoted a rhetorical question posed by Suzy Menkes in her article 'The circus of fashion': 'if fashion is for everyone, is it fashion?' (2013). Is the opinion on fashion of a blogger who decides what to wear by creating a backstory around her outfit – 'today I'm going to dress like a cupcake from the Victorian Era that was friends with Betsey Johnson and suddenly was adopted by Yohji Yamamoto' (Sicardi, quoted on video by SLU Team, 2012) – equal to a sombrely dressed fashion critic, a self-proclaimed 'black crow', albeit one also dressed in Yamamoto (Menkes 2013)? Does a sleek-haired blogger wearing clothes captioned 'c/o somebody or other' have the right to call herself a style blogger? Can a blogger who 'doesn't know the history' offer any insight into the desirability or timeliness of a new collection? In other words, if anyone can do it, what is to prevent the sacred – fashion and, ergo, the words of its oracles – from being overrun by heretics and their profanity?

And the circus rolls on

It is unlikely that style bloggers will ever overrun the field of fashion to such an extent that they challenge the existing power structures that comprise and organize the field, or overturn the dominant *doxa* and *habitus* to completely transform it. As I have argued throughout this book, following Bourdieu, the old always see the new as a threat to the established order, be it young girls writing in public about themselves being perceived as a moral threat, the fashion media criticizing style bloggers' apparent lack of critical perspective and expertise, or first wave bloggers positing that second wave bloggers aren't original, authentic or interesting because they blog according to different values and desired outcomes. I have found these anxieties interesting to interrogate as they lay bare what is at stake in this practice, the way that the 'old' perceive who they are and the value of what they do, and the gap between this and the corresponding values and work of the 'new'.

In many ways, Menkes's question has already been answered. Fashion may have been opened up by the authoritative and amateur voices of style bloggers, making it 'for everyone', but it is still fashion. The field continues to encompass a range of positions and position-takings situated between the autonomous and heteronomous poles. What we see in the case of style blogs is individuals positioning themselves in relation to the field – either taking a position as facilitated by other, more powerful agents within the field, or situating themselves on the margins of the field as blogging (and embodying) an alternative perspective on fashion and style – and in so doing, giving rise to a new kind of fashion communication.

The manner in which the social, playful and performative possibilities made available by personal style blogging are explored and realized by individual bloggers is shaped by their own relationship towards fashion and blogging: why they blog, how they blog and what they seek to embody through their style all shape the content they post. As a corollary, the work of style bloggers is valued differently according to the values and perspective of the reader, giving rise to the tensions both within the field of fashion and within the style blogosphere, as the blogs of different bloggers are alternatively criticized or deemed successful.

What remains is that personal style blogs represent a new iteration of fashion writing, a new mode of performing the self through style and a new way of engaging socially with other people interested in fashion and personal style. This shift is encapsulated in the words of Susie Lau, who reflected that her blog is about the exploration of fashion: 'fashion's not this scary or lofty [thing] […] I want to explore having fun with personal style' (2012b).

Perceiving fashion in this way, as enfolded into the everyday experience of individuals, as a locus of sociality and the playful exploration of selves becoming in a discursive, public way opens up new avenues through which people can engage with it. And yet, at the same time, as this chapter has demonstrated, the field of fashion legitimizes and reifies those who uphold its values and ignore the rest. Meanwhile, style bloggers keep blogging, people keep reading and the circus of fashion rolls on.

Notes

1 In the original blogpost, Sara's mention of the 'Ana knot' heel is hyperlinked to Tony Bianco's webstore.

2 The argument that the Internet made it possible for bloggers to report and commentate on news events with an immediacy and unpartisan perspective, therefore challenging the

conservative structure and speed of the mainstream news media, has been debated since blogs first began attracting attention from the news media. It is outside the capacity of this book to enter into the debate in detail, beyond where it intersects with style bloggers, but I refer interested readers to the works of MacKinnon 2005; Singer 2006; Rettberg 2014.

3   Incidentally, the style blog equivalent of this is a sponsored post.

4   It is worth noting here that all four quotes were direct comments on the presence of style bloggers at fashion weeks.

5   Susie's blog *Style Bubble* is rife with examples of posts that engage with fashion in a similar manner to the work of professional critics. In the same talk that I have quoted, above, Susie said that her blog differs from other style blogs based on her content that includes, but is not limited to, looking at the cultural context of fashion, the history of fashion and spotlighting emerging young designers (2012a). However, for examples of Susie reviewing a collection, see her discussion of Dior Couture under Raf Simons (2012b) or her consideration of the collaboration between British designers Meadham Kirchoff and highstreet retailer Topshop (2013c). For examples of her discussion of the history and culture of fashion, see her posts on *Style Bubble* 2013b and 2013d.

6   This supposition becomes complicated in instances such as when sponsored posts are undisclosed, a point that Marwick raises (2013b) and that I will discuss later in this chapter.

7   'DSLR' is shorthand for 'digital single-lens reflex camera', a professional-grade camera often used by style bloggers (especially those with hopes of becoming/who already are a professional blogger) to take their outfit posts.

Conclusion

Of course, much remains to be said. Even as I write this conclusion, further developments keep advancing and reshaping the mutable style blogosphere. Two weeks ago, a number of American *Vogue* staffers wrote a dispatch on Milan Fashion Week where, among other opinions that discursively consolidated their position as taste-makers, they deemed that the behaviour of fashion bloggers outside shows is 'heralding the death of style', that bloggers are 'pathetic' for 'troll[ing] up and down outside shows, in traffic, risking accidents even, in hopes of being snapped' (*Vogue* 2016). Yet somewhat ironically, some style bloggers do indeed seem to be heeding Creative Digital Director Sally Singer's exhortation to 'find another business' (2016) by doing that very thing.

Take, for example, an e-mail newsletter received from the Business of Fashion only days before the *Vogue* blogpost was published (indeed, *Vogue*'s critique of bloggers was blogged, the irony of which should not escape notice). The subject line read 'The blonde salad ups the ante'. Upon clicking, I was spirited to the BoF website, which repopulated my screen with an image of Chiara Ferragni looking every inch the new media mogul, from her direct gaze to her fashion-professional outfit of cream silk blouse tucked into neat black trousers, 'natural' make-up and simple stacked jewellery. The article announced the redevelopment of Ferragni's personal style blog, to be relaunched as a website in 2017 with an e-shop featuring exclusive products co-produced by *The Blonde Salad* and contemporary designer labels such as Giuseppe Zanotti, Delfina Delettrez and MGSM, 'a selection of vintage pieces Ferragni scouted at flea markets in Los Angeles, London and Berlin, as well as items from her namesake shoe collection, which is currently sold at more than 300 stores worldwide' (Sherman 2016).

Reading on, I learned that the shoe collection, first licensed in 2010 and now fully owned by Ferragni, generates revenue of over $15 million a year. Advertising on her blog is estimated to bring in over $2 million annually, a site which is now authored by an editorial staff including Ferragni's little sister, who not only attracts a younger readership but also opens up new avenues for brand partnership with labels that Ferragni would otherwise not see as a good fit for the blog. In reflecting on this development, Ferragni was quoted as saying, 'when I started back then, I just wanted a personal space […] But for the last three years, we haven't been a blog. We've been a website' (Sherman 2016).

Through this development, *The Blonde Salad* joins the likes of *Man Repeller* and *The Glamourai*, sites that originated as personal style blogs and have since metamorphosed into media brands that actively participate in the professional fashion industry. The creative and commercial concerns of this cultural field have long been indistinguishable in the fashion media, and indeed, have in many instances generated income that has sustained fashion publications and made them profitable, which makes *Vogue*'s critique of bloggers 'playing the game' by 'preening in borrowed clothes' somewhat disingenuous (Phelps quoted in Singer et al. 2016).[7] What marks a new development here is the unprecipitated rise of independent media enterprises run by individuals and predicated on their personal identities, participating in the industry as powerful fashion media-makers, and employing the same logics and practices as the established fashion media to craft a profitable business.

Indeed, from where I type in 2016, style blogs seem to have seamlessly become part of the fashion landscape. Their visibility and influence extends well beyond actual blogs, which now seem to function for many entrepreneurial bloggers as a basis for their business proper: freelance work as photographers, stylists, brand consultants or spokesmodels, or overseeing the production of fashion or accessory lines that cohere with the aesthetic and ethos of their personal brand. Style bloggers have appeared on the cover of mainstream fashion magazines, walked in runway shows, collaborated with luxury labels, department stores, mid-tier fashion labels and cosmetics companies, their faces becoming familiar, and their dressed selves ubiquitous in street style galleries and 'best dressed' lists in magazines that claim to know.

In such an environment, the humble origins of style blogging seem part of the distant past, the practice now just another occurrence in the mediated lives we live in a post-Internet, globalized era. Yet in some ways it is easy to focus on the 'superbloggers' (Pham 2016): through them we can vicariously consume an effortless fashionable life that heretofore was only represented in two dimensions on the glossy page. The success of such bloggers at creating a career out of a practice that did not exist until fairly recently, in addition to their youth and the glamour of their image, compels the eye and threatens to eclipse the rest of the blogosphere.

Yet in mapping the surfaces, the subtle depths and shifting dynamics of the style blogosphere, this book has demonstrated that there is more to style blogging than first meets the eye. It is a practice comprised of a multitude of people who, whether they be blogger or reader, share an interest in fashion and personal style. How this interest is manifested remains diverse and ever subject to transformation. It is a practice that means different things for different people, one that did not emerge in its current iteration, but rather, that has rapidly taken shape through a range of shifting, and sometimes contested, iterations.

In providing a series of close analyses of the different elements of personal style blogging – its emergence, the digital and feminized convergence of space and place it makes available, the particular dynamics of style 'bloggership' and readership, the function of style as a means of visual and reflexive self-making, and its situation within the field of fashion media – this book has told a few of a number of possible narratives of style blogging. There remains much more to be said. And yet the value in finding a language, as articulated through the frame of different conceptual lenses, offers a means by which the complexities and intimacies of this rapidly transforming sub-genre of blogging can be understood.

Throughout this book, an elaborate portrait of the multitudinous style blogosphere has emerged. Here is a digital landscape that has roots in the digital practices that preceded it, as well as the conventions of fashion media, yet which also represents the emergence of something new: the amateur and authoritative publications of 'fashion obsessives' (Dirk Standen in Grede 2011: 32) who resituate the values and the communication of knowledge about fashion within their personal sphere.

Throughout, certain oppositional dynamics have recurred: the tensions between public and private, amateur and professional, individual and corporate and the intimate and the distanced. In some ways, these dynamics form the basis for progress on the style blogosphere, the spur for shifts in how people blog and how their blogs are perceived. At the same time, these dynamics demonstrate that style blogging is complex and multidimensional. I have argued that it is also a pleasurable, meaningful and, for some, profitable endeavour that facilitates connections between people with a mutual fashion interest and allows for the communication of a range of alternative and independent fashion knowledge's. Style blogs also make available a space for a public thinking-through of self through fashion, a performed self, a self becoming, as bloggers tell personal narratives and dress themselves into view towards their readers. They do so in concert with other bloggers doing likewise on the intimate spaces of their own blogs, styling, photographing, editing, writing, uploading and thus collectively bringing into being the 'landscape of sheer life' (Hofmannsthal, quoted in Benjamin 2002: 417) that is the style blogosphere.

Note

1   This point was made by bloggers Susie Bubble, Shea Marie and Bryanboy in their own responses to this blogpost, as published on their respective Twitter and Instagram profiles (see Bobila 2016).

References

Aldridge, Jane (2009a), 'J. Aldridge by Sea of Shoes for Urban Outfitters', *Sea of Shoes*, 23 June, http://www.seaofshoes.com/sea_of_shoes/2009/10/j-aldridge-by-sea-of-shoes-for-urban-outfitters-holiday-collection.html. Accessed 22 March 2014.

——— (2009b), 'More pictures from the Crillon Ball', *Sea of Shoes*, 22 December, http://www.seaofshoes.com/sea_of_shoes/2009/12/more-pictures-from-the-crillon-ball.html. Accessed 22 March 2014.

——— (2016), 'The item of clothing I've worn the longest', *Sea of Shoes*, 6 May, http://www.seaofshoes.com/sea_of_shoes/2016/05/the-item-of-clothing-ive-worn-the-longest.html. Accessed 25 May 2016.

Aleksander, Irina (2010), 'Fashion triumph: Deflecting the male gaze, fashion & style', *New York Times*, 15 December, http://www.nytimes.com/2010/12/16/fashion/16MANREPELLER.html. Accessed 7 December 2016.

Ali-Hasan, Noor F. and Adamic, Lada A. (2007), 'Expressing social relationships on the blog through links and comments', *International Conference on Weblogs and Social Media (ICWSM)*, Boulder, Colorado, 26–28 March.

Allen, Claire (2009), '"Style Surfing": Changing parameters of fashion communications – where have they gone?', *Fashion: Exploring Critical Issues*, conference, Mansfield College, Oxford, 5–7 September.

Angeletti, Norberto and Oliva, Alberto (2006), *In Vogue*, New York: Rizzoli.

Asen, Robert (2002), 'Imagining in the public sphere', *Philosophy and Rhetoric*, 35: 4, pp. 345–67.

Bachelard, Gaston (1994), *The Poetics of Space*, Boston, MA: Beacon Press.

Barger, Jennifer (2012), 'My blog, my self', Express, *The Washington Post*, 24 August, http://www.washingtonpost.com/express/wp/2012/08/24/my-blog-my-self/. Accessed 22 March 2014.

Barthes, Roland (1990), *The Fashion System* (trans. M. Ward and R. Howard), Berkeley and Los Angeles: University of California Press.

Basso, Keith (1996), *Wisdom Sits in Places*, Albuquerque: University of New Mexico Press.

Baumer, Eric, Sueyoshi, Mark and Tomlinson, Bill (2008), 'Exploring the role of the reader in the activity of blogging', *SIGCHI Conference on Human Factors in Computing Systems*, Florence, Italy, 5–10 April.

Bazilian, Emma (2012), 'Fashion's new establishment', Adweek, 10 July, http://www.adweek.com/news/advertising-branding/fashions-new-establishment-141637. Accessed 22 March 2014.

Bell, Brandi (2007), 'Private writing in public spaces: Girls' blogs and shifting boundaries', in S. Weber and S. Dixon (eds), *Growing Up Online: Young People and Digital Technologies*, New York: Palgrave Macmillan, pp. 95–111.

Benjamin, Walter (2002), *The Arcades Project* (eds H. Eiland and K. McLaughlin), Cambridge, MA and London: The Belknap Press of Harvard University.

Berlant, Lauren (2008), *The Female Complaint*, Durham and London: Duke University Press.

Big Think (2011), 'Experts: Scott Schuman', video posted on Big Think, 36: 49, http://bigthink.com/users/scottschuman. Accessed 22 March 2014.

Blanchard, Anita L. (2004), 'Blogs as virtual communities: Identifying a sense of community in the Julie/Julia project', in L. Gurak, S. Antonijevic, L. Johnson, C. Ratliff, and J. Reyman (eds), *Into the Blogosphere*, Minnesota: University of Minnesota.

Blanchard, Anita and Markus, Lynne M. (2004), 'The experienced "sense" of a virtual community: Characteristics and processes', *The Data Base for Advances in Information Systems*, 35: 1, pp. 65–79.

Blood, Rebecca (2011), 'Weblogs: A history and perspective', *Rebecca's Pocket*, 12 July, http://www.rebeccablood.net/essays/weblog_history.html. Accessed 22 March 2014.

Bobila, Maria (2016), 'Susie Bubble and Bryanboy respond to Vogue.com criticism on fashion bloggers [Updated]', *Fashionista*, http://fashionista.com/2016/09/vogue-criticism-bryanboy-susie-bubble. Accessed 14 October 2016.

Bourdieu, Pierre (1984), *Distinction: A Social Critique of the Judgement of Taste*, Cambridge: Harvard University Press.

—— (1993a), *The Field of Cultural Production: Essays on Art and Literature* (ed. R. Johnson), New York: Columbia University Press.

—— (1993b), *Sociology in Question* (trans. R. Nice), London and Thousand Oaks: Sage.

—— (1996), *The Rules of Art: Genesis and Structure of the Literary Field*, Stanford: Stanford University Press.

Bourne, Leah (2010), 'The rise of the style blogger', *Forbes*, 12 February, http://www.forbes.com/2010/02/12/fashion-blogger-clothes-forbes-woman-style-shopping.html. Accessed 22 March 2014.

boyd, danah (2007), 'Why youth (heart) social network sites: The role of networked publics in teenage social life', in D. Buckingham (ed.), *MacArthur Foundation Series on Digital Learning – Youth, Identity and Digital Media Volume*, Cambridge: MIT Press.

Boyd Thomas, Jane, Peters, Cara Okleshen and Tolson, Holly (2007), 'An exploratory investigation of the virtual community MySpace.com', *Journal of Fashion Marketing and Management*, 11: 4, pp. 587–603.

Brady, Mark (2005), 'Blogging: Personal participation in public knowledge-building on the web', Chimera working paper, 2005–02, University of Essex, http://www.ekois.net/wp/wp-content/uploads/2008/08/cwp-2005-02-blogging-in-the-knowledge-society-mb.pdf. Accessed 22 March 2014.

Brake, David R. (2009), '"As if nobody's reading"?: The imagined audience and socio-technical biases in personal blogging practice in the UK', Ph.D. thesis, London School of Economics and Political Science.

Bruns, Axel (2006), 'The practice of news blogging', in A. Bruns and J. Jacobs (eds), *Uses of Blogs*, New York: Peter Lang, pp. 11–22.

Bruns, Axel and Jacobs, Joanne (2006), 'Introduction', in A. Bruns and J. Jacobs (eds), *Uses of Blogs*, New York: Peter Lang, pp. 1–8.

Buck-Morss, Susan (1989), *The Dialectics of Seeing: Walter Benjamin and the Arcades Project*, Cambridge, MA and London: The MIT Press.

Burcz, Chelsea (2012), '5 Tips on how to set traffic goals for yourself', Independent Fashion Bloggers, 24 July, http://heartifb.com/2012/07/24/5-tips-on-how-to-set-traffic-goals-for-yourself/. Accessed 22 March 2014.

Burvill, Lauren (2011), 'The style blog stigma', The Vine, 20 May, http://www.thevine.com.au/fashion/opinions/the-style-blog-stigma/. Accessed 22 March 2014.

Butler, Judith (1988), 'Performative acts and gender constitution', *Theatre Journal*, 40: 4, pp. 519–31.

Carter, Michael (2000), *Imaginary Materials: A Seminar with Michael Carter* (ed. J. MacArthur), Brisbane: IMA Publishing.

—————— (2003), *Fashion Classics from Carlyle to Barthes*, Oxford and New York: Berg.

Caruso, Lauren (2011), 'Why we're not happy about "Vogue" Italia going plus size', Fashionology, 2 June, http://www.ology.com/post/36235/why-we-re-not-happy-about-vogue-italia-going-plus-size. Accessed 22 March 2014.

Centenera, Christine (2013), 'Christine Centenera behind the scenes with Elle Fanning', *Vogue Australia*, 2 September, http://www.vogue.com.au/miss+vogue/news/galleries/christine+centenera+behind+the+scenes+with+elle+fanning,26018. Accessed 22 March 2014.

Champ, Nicky (2013), 'A Victoria's Secret model takes down the fashion industry in just nine minutes', Mamamia, 28 December, http://www.mamamia.com.au/style/cameron-russell-insecurity/. Accessed 22 March 2014.

Chilvers, Simon (2012), 'Hedi Slimane v Cathy Horyn: The story behind a fashion spat', *The Guardian*, 3 October, http://www.theguardian.com/fashion/fashion-blog/2012/oct/03/hedi-slimane-cathy-horyn-fashion-spat. Accessed 22 March 2014.

Chin, Alvin and Chignell, Mark (2006), 'Finding evidence of community from blogging co-citations: A social network analytic approach', *IADIS International Conference on Web Based Communities*, San Sebastián, Spain, 26–28 February.

Chittenden, Tara (2010), 'Digital dressing up: Modelling female teen identity in the discursive spaces of the fashion blogosphere', *Journal of Youth Studies*, 13: 4, pp. 505–20.

Ciarallo, Joe (2008), 'Fashion week: Bloggers welcome?', Media Bistro, 4 September, http://www.mediabistro.com/prnewser/fashion-week-bloggers-welcome_b965. Accessed 22 March 2014.

Clarke, John (1976), 'Style', in S. Hall and T. Jefferson (eds), *Resistance Through Rituals: Youth Subcultures in Post-war Britain*, London: Hutchinson University Library, pp. 175–91.

Clarke, Sarah (2011), 'Citizen bloggers taking the fashion world by storm', Reportage Online, 27 April, http://www.reportageonline.com/2011/04/citizen-bloggers-taking-the-fashion-world-by-storm/. Accessed 22 March 2014.

Clements, Kirstie (2013), *The Vogue Factor*, Carlton, Victoria: Melbourne University Publishing Limited.

Cohen, Kris (2006), 'A welcome for blogs', *Continuum: Journal of Media & Culture Studies*, 20: 2, pp. 161–73.

Connell, Catherine (2013), 'Fashionable resistance: Queer "fa(t)shion" blogging as counterdiscourse', *WSQ: Women's Studies Quarterly*, 41: 1&2, pp. 209–24.

Cooke, Hannah, Miller-Sharma, Emily, Rasmussen, Gemma, Smiley, Alice and Sanders, Courtney (2011), 'The top five things wrong with fashion blogs', *Always Sometimes Anytime*, 12 May, http://www.alwayssometimesanytime.com/new/2011/05/11/opinion-top-five-things-wrong-with-fashion-blogs. Accessed 22 March 2014.

Copping, Nicola (2009), 'Style bloggers take centre stage', *Financial Times*, 13 November, http://www.ft.com/cms/s/2/89f8c07c-cfe0-11de-a36d-00144feabdc0.html#axzz1eJ00zbm7. Accessed 22 March 2014.

Corcoran, Cate T. (2006), 'The blogs that took over the tents', *Women's Wear Daily*, 6 February.

Craik, Jennifer (1994), *The Face of Fashion: Cultural Studies in Fashion*, London and New York: Routledge.

Crawford, Kate (2009), 'Following you: Disciplines of listening in social media', *Continuum: Journal of Media and Cultural Studies*, 23: 4, pp. 525–35.

Culley, M. (1985), *A Day at a Time: The Diary Literature of American Women from 1764 to Present*, New York: The Feminist Press of the City University of New York.

Darling, Lauren (2012), 'Outfit: My second public VBO', *Pocket Rocket Fashion*, 19 November, http://www.pocketrocketfashion.com/outfit-public-vbo/. Accessed 22 March 2014.

Davies, Taylor (2012), 'Guilty pleasure or just guilty? An interview with Get Off My Internets', Independent Fashion Bloggers, 19 April, http://heartifb.com/2012/04/19/guilty-pleasure-or-just-guilty-an-interview-with-get-off-my-internets/. Accessed 22 March 2014.

Davis, Fred (1992), *Fashion, Culture and Identity*, Chicago: University of Chicago Press.

Day, Elizabeth (2013), 'How selfies became a global obsession', *The Guardian*, 14 July, http://www.theguardian.com/technology/2013/jul/14/how-selfies-became-a-global-phenomenon. Accessed 22 March 2014.

Dewey, Lisa (2002), 'Girls online feeling out of bounds', *Camping Magazine*, September/October.

Dodes, Rachel (2006), 'Bloggers get under the tent', *The Wall Street Journal*, 12 September, http://online.wsj.com/public/article/SB115801727410860002-3NtzCOa4qvvjJFhAlAC1llCEhM4_20070911.html?mod=blogsshorter. Accessed 22 March 2014.

Donaldson, Sara (2014), 'The knot', *Harper and Harley*, 19 November, http://harperandharley.com/2014/11/knot/. Accessed 28 February 2016.

Dries, Kate (2013), 'Plenty of women don't remember that models are photoshopped', Jezebel, 26 November, http://jezebel.com/plenty-of-women-dont-remember-that-models-are-photo-sho-1471830454. Accessed 22 March 2014.

Driscoll, Catherine (2002), *Girls: Feminine Adolescence in Popular Culture & Cultural Theory*, New York: Columbia University Press.

Dwyer, Claire (1998), 'Contested identities: Challenging dominant representations of young British Muslim women', in T. Skelton and G. Valentine (eds), *Cool Places: Geographies of Youth Culture*, London and New York: Routledge, pp. 50–65.

Eco, Umberto (1979), *The Role of the Reader*, Bloomington: Indiana University Press.

Edgar, Andrew (2005), *The Philosophy of Habermas*, Chesham: Acumen.

Efimova, Lilia and Hendrick, Stephanie (2005), 'In search for a virtual settlement: An exploration of weblog community boundaries', working paper, *Communities & Technologies Conference*, https://www.academia.edu/3020421/In_search_for_a_virtual_settlement_An_exploration_of_weblog_community_boundaries. Accessed 22 March 2014.

Entwistle, Joanne (2000), 'Fashion and the fleshy body: Dress as embodied practice', *Fashion Theory*, 4: 3, pp. 323–48.

Entwistle, Joanne and Rocamora, Agnès (2006), 'The field of fashion materialized: A study of London fashion week', *Sociology*, 40: 4, pp. 735–51.

Entwistle, Joanne and Wilson, Elizabeth (2001), 'Introduction: Body dressing', in J. Entwistle and E. Wilson (eds), *Body Dressing*, Oxford and New York: Berg, pp. 1–9.

Epstein, Catherine (2010), 'Feminism and the 14-year-old: Tavi Gevinson says do what you want', The Huffington Post, 15 October, http://www.huffingtonpost.com/catherine-epstein/feminism-and-the-14yearol_b_753116.html. Accessed 22 March 2014.

Estrada, Jess (2013), 'What's your 'thing'? 8 examples of defining your blog', Independent Fashion Bloggers, 28 August, http://heartifb.com/2013/08/28/whats-your-thing-8-examples-of-defining-your-blog/. Accessed 22 March 2014.

Evans, Caroline and Thornton, Minna (1989), *Women & Fashion: A New Look*, London: Quartet.

Faircloth, Kelly (2013), 'Fatshion police: How plus-size blogging left its radical roots behind', Betabeat, 6 February, http://betabeat.com/2013/02/fatshion-plus-size-bloggers-amanda-piasecki-marianne-kirby-gabrielle-gregg/. Accessed 22 March 2014.

Ferragni, Chiara (2012), 'Chiara Ferragni in Louis Vuitton official video: Meeting Fabrizio Viti', *The Blonde Salad*, 1 February, http://www.theblondesalad.com/2012/02/chiara-ferragni-in-louis-vuitton-official-video-meeting-fabrizio-viti.html. Accessed 22 March 2014.

Findlay, Rosie (2012a), 'SURVEY', *Fashademic*, 10 January, http://fashademic.blogspot.com.au/2012/01/survey.html. Accessed 22 March 2014.

—— (2012b), 'Outfit post: In defiance of a grey day', *Fashademic*, 8 March, http://fashademic.blogspot.com.au/2012/03/outfit-post-in-defiance-of-grey-day.html. Accessed 22 March 2014.

—— (2013), 'Encountering myself in the past', *Fashademic*, 22 May, http://fashademic.blogspot.com.au/2013/05/encountering-myself-in-past.html. Accessed 22 March 2014.

Finkelstein, Joanne (1998), *After a Fashion*, Melbourne: Melbourne University Press.

Fitzpatrick, Tim (1995), *The Relationship of Oral and Literate Performance Processes in the Commedia dell'Arte: Beyond the Improvisation/Memorisation Divide*, Lewiston: Edwin Mellen Press.

Flugel, J. C. (1930), *The Psychology of Clothes*, London: Hogarth Press.

Fredrickson, Julie (blogger, *Almost Girl*) (2013), Skype interview with author, 19 February.

Garcia, Laia (2009a), 'The new shirt in town', *Geometric Sleep*, 6 April, http://www.geometricsleep.com/2009/04/new-shirt-in-town.html. Accessed 22 March 2014.

—— (2009b), 'Let's get real fashion-y for a minute', *Geometric Sleep*, 13 April, http://www.geometricsleep.com/2009/04/lets-get-real-fashion-y-for-minute.html. Accessed 22 March 2014.

—— (2009c), 'Short and studded', *Geometric Sleep*, 14 April, http://www.geometricsleep.com/2009/04/short-and-studded.html. Accessed 22 March 2014.

Gardner, Jasmine (2009), 'Is this going to be the new route to planet fashion?' *Evening Standard*, 14 September, http://www.standard.co.uk/lifestyle/fashion/is-this-going-to-be-the-new-route-to-planet-fashion-6797723.html. Accessed 22 March 2014.

Gary, Alison (2013), 'The glamorous world of personal style blogging', *Wardrobe Oxygen*, 7 October, http://www.wardrobeoxygen.com/2013/10/the-glamorous-world-of-personal-style.html. Accessed 22 March 2014.

Gauntlett, David (2004), 'Web studies: What's new', in D. Gauntlett and R. Horsley (eds), *Web Studies*, London: Arnold.

Geertz, Clifford (1975), *The Interpretation of Cultures*, London: Hutchinson.

—— (1983), *Local Knowledge: Further Essays in Interpretive Anthropology*, New York: Basic Books.

George, Katherine (2009), 'Democracy and the Internet: How fashion blogging is subordinating the independence of internet discourse and rendering useful subculture a mainstream conundrum', MA thesis, University of Melbourne.

—— (2011), 'The un-democracy of fashion blogging', Thought Catalog, 18 July, http://thoughtcatalog.com/kat-george/2011/07/on-the-un-democracy-of-fashion-blogging/. Accessed 22 March 2014.

Gevinson, Tavi (2009a), 'Write a letter to Eden, moonlight. Please, please, please', *Style Rookie*, 12 January, http://www.thestylerookie.com/2009/01/write-letter-to-eden-moonlight-please.html. Accessed 22 March 2014.

—— (2009b), 'adrewsrtfkuiuyb87r5tfgh', *Style Rookie*, 28 January, http://www.thestylerookie.com/2009/01/adrewsrtfkuiuyb87r5tfgh.html. Accessed 22 March 2014.

—— (2009c), 'AJKFYA4W95843HWTJKEH', *Style Rookie*, 29 April, http://www.thestylerookie.com/2009/04/ajkfya4w95843hwtjkeh.html. Accessed 22 March 2014.

—— (2009d), 'Ramblings, oops', *Style Rookie*, 19 December, http://www.thestylerookie.com/2009/12/ramblings-oops.html. Accessed 22 March 2014.

—— (2010), 'O my god an alpaca', *Style Rookie*, 10 February, http://www.thestylerookie.com/2010/02/oh-my-god-alpaca.html. Accessed 22 March 2014.

—— (2011), 'Hey hey guys look at all my stuff', *Style Rookie*, 24 July, http://www.thestylerookie.com/2011/07/hey-hey-guys-look-at-all-my-stuff.html. Accessed 22 March 2014.

—— (2013), 'Five years', *Style Rookie*, 3 April, http://www.thestylerookie.com/2013/04/five-years.html. Accessed 22 March 2014.

Gibson, James J. (1977), 'The theory of affordances', in R. Shaw and J. Bransford (eds), *Perceiving, Acting, and Knowing: Toward an Ecological Psychology*, Hillsdale: Lawrence Erlbaum, pp. 67–82.

Gilson, Etienne (1963), *Dante and Philosophy*, New York: Torchbooks.

Givhan, Robin (2007), 'Everyone's a fashion critic', *Harper's Bazaar*, 10 August, http://www.harpersbazaar.com/fashion/fashion-articles/fashion-critic-givhan-0907. Accessed 22 March 2014.

Goffman, Erving (1973), *The Presentation of Self in Everyday Life*, Woodstock: The Overlook Press.

Goto, Zoey (2013), 'Susie bubble interview', *ZoeyGoto*, August, http://www.zoeygoto.com/2013/08/susie-bubble-interview/. Accessed 22 August 2013.

Graham, David (2012), 'Fashion week: The beleaguered art of fashion criticism', *The Toronto Star*, 7 March, http://www.thestar.com/life/fashion_style/2012/03/07/fashion_week_the_beleaguered_art_of_fashion_criticism.html. Accessed 22 March 2014.

Grede, Jens (2011), 'The fashion media A-List: Dirk Standen', *Industrie*, 4.

Gregg, Melissa (2006), 'Posting with passion: Blogs and the politics of gender', in A. Bruns and J. Jacobs (eds), *Uses of Blogs*, New York: Peter Lang, pp. 151–60.

Gregg, Melissa and Driscoll, Catherine (2008), 'Broadcast yourself: Moral panic, youth culture and internet studies', in U. M. Rodrigues and B. Smaill (eds), *Youth, Media and Culture in the Asia-Pacific Region*, Cambridge: Cambridge Scholars Publishing, pp. 71–86.

Griffiths, Vivienne (1995), *Adolescent Girls and their Friends: A Feminist Ethnography*, Aldershot, UK: Avebury.

Gupte, Rhea (2014), 'Cosmopolitan March 2014', *Fuss*, 14 March, http://fuss.co.in/cosmopolitan-march-2014/. Accessed 25 May 2016.

Gurak, Laura and Antonijevic, Smiljana (2008), 'The psychology of blogging: You, me and everyone in between', *American Behavioral Scientist*, 52: 1, pp. 60–68.

Gurak, Laura, Antonijevic, Smiljana, Johnson, Laurie, Ratliff, Clancy, and Reyman, Jessica (2004), 'Introduction: Weblogs, rhetoric, community, and culture', in L. Gurak, S. Antonijevic, L. Johnson, C. Ratliff, and J. Reyman (eds), *Into the Blogosphere*, Minnesota: University of Minnesota.

Habermas, Jürgen (1989), *The Structural Transformation of the Public Sphere: An Inquiry into a Category of Bourgeois Society* (trans. T. Burger and F. Lawrence), Cambridge: Polity Press.

Harrington, Cora (2013), 'How to cope with criticism: 5 tips for handling negative remarks', Independent Fashion Bloggers, 16 May, http://heartifb.com/2013/05/16/how-to-cope-with-criticism-5-tips-for-handling-negative-remarks/. Accessed 22 March 2014.

Harris, Anita (2008), 'Young women, late modern politics, and the participatory possibilities of online cultures', *Journal of Youth Studies*, 11: 5, pp. 481–95.

Hebdige, Dick (2007), *Subculture: The Meaning of Style*, London and New York: Routledge.

Hintz-Zambrano, Katie (2010), 'Tavi, a 13-year-old blogger, is the fashion world's latest obsession: Something wrong with this picture?', StyleList, 8 February, http://main.stylelist.com/2010/02/08/tavi-a-13-year-old-blogger-is-the-fashion-worlds-latest-obsession-something-wrong-with-this-picture/. Accessed 22 March 2014.

Hodkinson, Paul (2007), 'Interactive online journals and individualization', *New Media and Society*, 9: 4, pp. 625–50.

Horyn, Cathy (2004), 'Future, take note: Raf Simons was here', *New York Times*, 6 July, http://www.nytimes.com/2004/07/06/nyregion/future-take-note-raf-simons-was-here.html. Accessed 22 March 2014.

Hughes, Hayley (2011), 'Body image and fashion blogging', *Fashion Hayley*, 18 June, http://www.fashionhayley.com/2011/06/body-image-and-fashion-blogging.html. Accessed 22 March 2014.

Jackson, Michael (1996), *Things As They Are: New Directions in Phenomenological Anthropology*, Bloomington: Indiana University Press.

Jacob, Jennine (2008), 'Interview with Susie Bubble', Independent Fashion Bloggers, 23 February, http://heartifb.com/2008/02/22/interview-with-susie-bubble/. Accessed 22 March 2014.

——— (2013a), 'Reality check: 6 Reasons why no one reads your blog', Independent Fashion Bloggers, 10 April, http://heartifb.com/2013/04/10/reality-check-5-reasons-no-one-reads-your-blog/. Accessed 22 March 2014.

—— (2013b), '7 common traits of high quality fashion blogs', Independent Fashion Bloggers, 29 April, http://heartifb.com/2013/04/29/7-common-traits-of-high-quality-fashion-blogs/. Accessed 22 March 2014.

—— (2013c), 'The fashion blogger's guide to editing photos like a pro', Independent Fashion Bloggers, 29 May, http://heartifb.com/2013/05/29/the-fashion-bloggers-guide-to-editing-photos-like-a-pro/. Accessed 22 March 2014.

Jana, Rosalind (2010), 'Twisted embrace – In homage to the late Alexander McQueen', *Clothes, Cameras and Coffee*, 17 October, http://clothescamerasandcoffee.blogspot.com.au/2010/10/twisted-embrace-in-homage-to-late.html. Accessed 22 March 2014.

—— (2011a), 'Blogging against adversity', Independent Fashion Bloggers, 27 April, http://heartifb.com/2011/04/27/blogging-against-adversity/. Accessed 22 March 2014.

—— (2011b), Skype interview with author, 30 September.

—— (2013), 'Twist of fate', *British Vogue*, March.

Jobling, Paul (1999), *Fashion Spreads: Word and Image in Fashion Photography Since 1980*, Oxford and New York: Berg.

Jurkiewicz, Sarah (2011), 'Blogging as counterpublic? The Lebanese and the Egyptian blogosphere in comparison', in N.-C. Schneider and B. Graf (eds), *Social Dynamics 2.0: Researching Change in Times of Media Convergence: Case Studies from the Middle East and Asia*, Berlin: Frank & Timme GmbH, pp. 27–47.

Kaiser, Susan (2001), 'Minding appearances: Style, truth and subjectivity', in J. Entwistle and E. Wilson (eds), *Body Dressing*, Oxford and New York: Berg, pp. 79–102.

Kamer, Foster (2009), 'I hereby declare the fashion bloggers' "front row" status trend piece over', Gawker, 18 September, http://gawker.com/5434670/i-hereby-declare-the-fashion-bloggers-front-row-status-trend-piece-over. Accessed 22 March 2014.

Karlsson, Lena (2007), 'Desperately seeking sameness: The processes and pleasures of identification in women's diary blog reading', *Feminist Media Studies*, 7: 2, pp. 137–53.

Kaye, Barbara K. (2005), 'It's a blog, blog, blog, blog world', *Atlantic Journal of Communication*, 13: 2, pp. 73–95.

Khamis, Susie and Munt, Alex (2010), 'The three Cs of fashion media today: Convergence, creativity & control', *Scan: Journal of Media Arts Culture*, 8: 2, http://www.researchonline.mq.edu.au/vital/access/manager/Repository/mq:11833?exact=sm_type%3A%22Scan+%3A+Journal+Of+Media+Arts+Culture+Collection%22. Accessed 22 March 2014.

King, Joyann (2009), 'Bloggers take over the front row', *InStyle,* 10 September, http://news.instyle.com/2009/09/10/bloggers-take-over-the-front-row-/. Accessed 22 March 2014.

Kinsman, Kat (2012), '"Fatsion" bloggers find beauty in all sizes', CNN, 31 March, http://edition.cnn.com/2012/03/31/living/fatshion-beauty-bloggers/index.html. Accessed 22 March 2014.

Kurutz, Steven (2011), 'Fashion bloggers, posted and represented', Fashion & Style, *New York Times*, 29 September, http://www.nytimes.com/2011/09/29/fashion/fashion-bloggers-get-agents.html?pagewanted=all. Accessed 22 March 2014.

Kwan, Amanda (2008), 'Young fashion bloggers are worrisome trend to parents', *USA Today*, 13 August, http://usatoday30.usatoday.com/tech/webguide/internetlife/2008-08-12-girl-fashion-blogs_N.htm. Accessed 22 March 2014.

Lampa, Graham (2004), 'Imagining the blogosphere: An introduction to the imagined community of instant publishing', in L. Gurak, S. Antonijevic, L. Johnson, C. Ratliff, and J. Reyman (eds), *Into the Blogosphere*, Minnesota: University of Minnesota.

Lau, Susie (2007), 'Look at me, don't look at me', *Style Bubble*, 14 August, http://www.stylebubble.co.uk/style_bubble/2007/08/look-at-me-dont.html. Accessed 22 March 2014.

—— (2010), 'Monday larks', *Style Bubble*, 19 April, http://www.stylebubble.co.uk/style_bubble/2010/04/monday-larks.html. Accessed 22 March 2014.

—— (2012a), 'Portable presents Susie Bubble', Talk given at the Dendy Opera Quays, Sydney, Australia, 3 May.

—— (2012b), 'I feel love', *Style Bubble*, 22 November, http://www.stylebubble.co.uk/style_bubble/2012/11/i-feel-love.html. Accessed 22 March 2014.

—— (2013a), 'Frequently asked questions', *Style Bubble*, 25 September, http://www.stylebubble.co.uk/faq. Accessed 22 March 2014.

—— (2013b), 'Dior x Harrods = J'Adore', *Style Bubble*, 15 March, http://www.stylebubble.co.uk/style_bubble/2013/03/dior-x-harrods-jadore.html. Accessed 22 March 2014.

—— (2013c), 'The cosmology of women for all', *Style Bubble*, 21 November, http://www.stylebubble.co.uk/style_bubble/2013/11/the-cosmology-of-women-for-all.html. Accessed 22 March 2014.

—— (2013d), 'Maison madness', *Style Bubble*, 5 December, http://www.stylebubble.co.uk/style_bubble/2013/12/maison-madness.html. Accessed 22 March 2014.

Lehmann, Ulrich (2002), 'Fashion photography', in U. Lehmann and J. Morgan (eds), *Chic Clicks: Creativity and Commerce in Contemporary Fashion Photography*, Boston: Institute of Contemporary Art.

Lenhart, Amanda B. (2005), 'Unstable texts: An ethnographic look at how bloggers and their audience negotiate self-presentation, authenticity and norm', MA thesis, Georgetown University.

Lévi-Strauss, Claude (1972), *The Savage Mind*, London: Weidenfeld and Nicolson.

Levy, Steven (2002), 'Living in the blog-osphere', *Newsweek*, 26 August, http://www.bolender.com/Dr.%20Ron/SOC1023G%20Social%20Problems/Units/Unit%202%20Technology%20and%20Society/Living%20in%20the%20blogosphere.htm. Accessed 22 March 2014.

Lewis, John Lowell (2013), *The Anthropology of Cultural Performance*, New York: Palgrave Macmillan.

Lewis, Reina (2015), *Muslim Fashion*, Durham and London: Duke University Press.

Lincoln, Siân (2004), 'Teenage girls' "bedroom culture": Codes versus zones', in A. Bennett and K. Kahn-Harris (eds), *After Subculture: Critical Commentaries in Contemporary Youth Culture*, Basingstoke: Palgrave, pp. 94–106.

Lipovetsky, Gilles (c2002), 'More than fashion', in U. Lehmann and J. Morgan (eds), *Chic Clicks: Creativity and Commerce in Contemporary Fashion Photography*, Boston: Institute of Contemporary Art.

Literacy 2.0. (2013), 'A digital gap between kids and parents', 9 June, http://www.literacy20.com/2013/06/digital-gap-widens-between-kids-and-parents/?utm_source=feedly. Accessed 22 March 2014.

Lorentzen, Christian (2011), 'Becoming one of the "relevant"', Fashion & Style, *New York Times*, 7 July, http://www.nytimes.com/2011/07/07/fashion/the-blogger-bebe-zeva-is-featured-in-a-video.html?pagewanted=all. Accessed 22 March 2014.

Lovink, Geert (2008), *Zero Comments: Blogging and Critical Internet Culture*, London: Routledge.

Lurie, Alison (1981), *The Language of Clothes*, London: Heinemann.

Luvaas, Brent (2013), 'Indonesian fashion blogs: On the promotional subject of personal style', *Fashion Theory*, 17: 1, pp. 55–76.

——— (2016), *Street Style: An Ethnography of Fashion Blogging*, London and New York: Bloomsbury.

Lynge-Jorlén, Ane (2012), 'Between frivolity and art: Contemporary niche fashion magazines', *Fashion Theory,* 16: 1, pp. 7–28.

MacKinnon, Rebecca (2005), 'Blogging, journalism and credibility: Battleground and common ground', conference report, Harvard University, Cambridge, MA, 21–22 January.

Manjoo, Farhad (2002), 'Blah, blah, blah and blog', *Wired*, 18 February, http://www.wired.com/culture/lifestyle/news/2002/02/50443. Accessed 22 March 2014.

Marion, Gilles and Nairn, Agnes (2011), '"We makes the shoes, you make the story" teenage girls' experiences of fashion: Bricolage, tactics and narrative identity', *Consumption Markets & Culture*, 14: 1, pp. 29–56.

Martin, Richard (1998), 'Addressing the dress', in M. Berger (ed.), *The Crisis of Criticism*, New York: The New Press.

Marwick, Alice (2013a), 'The other foot', *The New Inquiry*, 12 September, http://thenewinquiry.com/essays/the-other-foot/. Accessed 30 August 2016.

——— (2013b), '"They're really profound women, they're entrepreneurs": Conceptions of authenticity in fashion blogging', unpublished manuscript.

Maxwell, Ian (2002), 'The curse of fandom: Insiders, outsiders and ethnography', in D. Hesmondhalgh and K. Negus (eds), *Popular Music Studies*, London: Arnold, pp. 103–16.

——— (2006), 'Performance studies at the University of Sydney', *The Drama Review,* 50: 1, pp. 33–45.

McNeill, Laurie (2003), 'Teaching an old genre new tricks: The diary on the Internet', *Biography*, 26: 1, pp. 24–48.

McNeill, Laurie and Zuern, John David (2015), 'Online lives 2.0: Introduction', *Biography*, 38: 2, pp. v–xlvi.

McRobbie, Angela (1998), *British Fashion Design: Rag Trade or Image Industry?*, London and New York: Routledge.

McRobbie, Angela and Garber, Jenny (2000), 'Girls and subcultures', in A. McRobbie (ed.), *Feminism and Youth Culture,* Basingstoke: Macmillan, pp. 12–25.

Mead, Margaret (1972), *Culture and Commitment*, London: Panther.

Meder, Danielle (blogger, *Final Fashion*) (2011), 'Both a curiosity and a threat – in defense of teenaged fashion bloggers', *Final Fashion*, 25 July, http://finalfashion.ca/in-defense-of-young-fashion-bloggers-and-bebe-zeva/. Accessed 22 March 2014.

——— (2012), Skype interview with author, 6 June.

Medine, Leandra (2010), 'What is a man repeller?' *Man Repeller*, 25 April, http://www.manrepeller.com/2010/04/what-is-man-repeller.html. Accessed 22 March 2014.

———— (2012a), 'The chronicles of this weekend's Webster event', *Man Repeller*, 16 January, http://www.manrepeller.com/2012/01/chronicle-of-weekends-webster-event.html. Accessed 22 March 2014.

———— (2012b), 'Know your onion', *Man Repeller*, 5 November, http://www.manrepeller.com/2012/11/fall-onion.html. Accessed 22 March 2014.

Menkes, Suzy (2013), 'The circus of fashion', *T magazine*, *New York Times*, 10 February, http://tmagazine.blogs.nytimes.com/2013/02/10/the-circus-of-fashion/?_r=0. Accessed 22 March 2014.

Milligan, Lauren (2009), 'Kane and Able', *British Vogue*, 1 December, http://www.vogue.co.uk/news/2009/12/01/christopher-kane-interview/gallery/434947. Accessed 22 March 2014.

Moeran, Brian (2006), 'More than just a fashion magazine', *Current Sociology*, 54: 5, pp. 725–44.

Moore, Paul (2004), 'Longing to belong: Trained actors' attempts to enter the profession', Ph.D. thesis, University of Sydney.

Mortensen, Torill Elvira (2004), 'Personal publication and public attention', in L. Gurak, S. Antonijevic, L. Johnson, C. Ratliff, and J. Reyman (eds), *Into the Blogosphere*, Minnesota: University of Minnesota.

Moylan, Brian (2010), 'Anna Wintour has some bitchy compliments for fashion bloggers', Gawker, 20 April, http://gawker.com/5520651/anna-wintour-has-some-bitchy-compliments-for-fashion-bloggers. Accessed 22 March 2014.

Nag Rao, Ragini (2010), 'Once more unto the breach', *A Curious Fancy*, 29 May, http://curiousfancy.com/post/641391442/once-more-unto-the-breach. Accessed 22 March 2014.

———— (2014), 'An offering of tinsel', *A Curious Fancy*, 11 December, http://curiousfancy.com/post/104856534131/i-grew-up-having-christmasses-you-know-it-was. Accessed 25 May 2016.

Nardi, Bonnie A., Schiano, Diane J., and Gumbrecht, Michelle (2004), 'Blogging as social activity, or, would you let 900 million people read your diary?', *Computer Supported Cooperative Work and Social Computing Conference (CSCW)*, Chicago, Illinois, 6–10 November.

Neely, Rumi (2009), 'Game girl', *fashiontoast*, 16 January, http://fashiontoast.com/2009/01/game-girl/. Accessed 24 May 2016.

———— (2013), 'Tip toeing on the marble mantle', *fashiontoast*, 7 October, http://www.fashiontoast.com/2013/10/tip-toeing-on-the-marble-mantle.html. Accessed 22 March 2014.

Noricks, Crosby (2013), '3 things to do before contacting a PR agency to send you free stuff', Independent Fashion Bloggers, 5 June, http://heartifb.com/2013/06/05/3-things-to-do-before-contacting-a-pr-agency-to-send-you-free-stuff/. Accessed 22 March 2014.

Nussbaum, Emily (2007), 'Say everything', *New York*, 12 February, http://nymag.com/news/features/27341/. Accessed 22 March 2014.

Oatman-Stanford, Hunter (2012), 'Nostalgia is magic: Tavi Gevinson remixes teen culture', Collectors Weekly, 28 November, http://www.collectorsweekly.com/articles/tavi-gevinson-remixes-teen-culture/. Accessed 22 March 2014.

O'Carroll, Isabelle (2009), 'Fashion blogger t-shirts courtesy of borders and frontiers', Catwalk Queen, 16 April, http://www.catwalkqueen.tv/2009/04/fashion_blogger.html. Accessed 22 March 2014.

Odell, Amy (2013), 'Why the era of personal style blogs must come to an end', Buzzfeed, 13 June, http://www.buzzfeed.com/amyodell/why-the-era-of-personal-style-blogs-must-come-to-an-end. Accessed 22 March 2014.

Oliver, William (2012), *Style Feed: The World's Top Fashion Blogs*, Munich, London and New York: Prestel.

Olsen, Stefanie (2006), 'Google's antisocial downside', CNET News, 13 July, http://news.cnet.com/Googles-antisocial-downside/2100-1038_3-6093532.html. Accessed 22 March 2014.

Oxford, Kelly (2011), 'An open letter/rant about "man repeller" (Google her if you have no clue)', *Eject*, 29 October, http://kellyoxford.tumblr.com/post/12076571348/an-open-letter-rant-about-man-repeller-google-her-if. Accessed 30 August 2016.

Palmgren, Ann-Charlotte (2010), 'Posing my identity: Today's outfit, identity and gender in Swedish blogs', *Observatorio (OBS*), 4: 2, pp. 19–34.

Pappademas, Alex (2012), 'Up from the streets', *GQ*, June, http://www.gq.com/style/profiles/201206/scott-schuman-sartorialist-gq-june-2012-interview?currentPage=5. Accessed 22 March 2014.

Peachy, Amy (2013), 'Fashion: My form of self expression', *Peachy Life, Fashion Inspirations*, 3 January, http://webcache.googleusercontent.com/search?q=cache:fsrS5zDIZlcJ:peachylifefashion.wordpress.com/2013/01/03/fashion-my-form-of-self-expression/+&cd=1&hl=en&ct=clnk&gl=au. Accessed 15 September 2014 (page no longer available).

Pederson, Sarah and Macafee, Caroline (2007), 'Gender differences in British blogging', *Journal of Computer-Mediated Communication*, 12: 4, pp. 1472–1492.

Perseus UK (2003), 'The blogging iceberg: Of 4.12 million weblogs, most little seen and quickly abandoned', 4 October, http://www.perseusuk.co.uk/survey/news/releases/release_blogs.html. Accessed 22 March 2014.

Perthuis, Karen de (2005), 'The synthetic ideal: The fashion model and photographic manipulation', *Fashion Theory*, 9: 4, pp. 407–24.

Pham, Minh-Ha T. (2011), 'Blog ambition: Fashion, feelings, and the political economy of the digital raced body', *Camera Obscura*, 76: 26.1, pp. 1–37.

—— (2013), 'Susie Bubble is a sign of the times: The embodiment of success in the web 2.0 economy', *Feminist Media Studies*, 13: 2, pp. 245–67.

Postrel, Virginia (2013), *The Power of Glamour: Longing and the Art of Visual Persuasion*, New York: Simon and Schuster.

Preece, Jenny, Nonnecke, Blair, and Andrews, Dorine (2004), 'The top five reasons for lurking: Improving community experiences for everyone', *Computers in Human Behavior*, 20: 2, pp. 201–23.

Prensky, Marc (2001), 'Digital natives, digital immigrants', *On the Horizon*, 9: 5, October, pp. 1–6.

Quirk, Jessica (blogger, *What I Wore*) (2013), Skype interview with author, 18 June.

Reid-Walsh, Jacqueline and Mitchell, Claudia (2004), 'Girls' web sites: A virtual "room" of one's own?' in A. Harris (ed.), *All About the Girl: Culture, Power and Identity*, New York and London: Routledge, pp. 173–82.

Reiter, Grechen (2011), 'Why do you post outfit pictures?', *Grechen Blogs*, 18 May, http://www.grechenblogs.com/2011/05/why-do-you-post-outfit-pictures/. Accessed 22 March 2014.

Retherford, Kate (2012), 'Am I too fat?', *All Things Kate*, 13 November, http://www.allthingskate. com/blog/11-13-2012/am-i-too-fat. Accessed 22 March 2014.

Rettberg, Jill Walker (2014), *Blogging*, Cambridge: Polity Press.

Revlon Australia (2013), 'Revlon presents Oracle fox: A photoready life', YouTube, https://www. youtube.com/watch?v=pWc_8SYNZnc. Accessed 30 August 2016.

Rocamora, Agnès (2011), 'Personal fashion blogs: Screens and mirrors in digital self-portraits', *Fashion Theory*, 15: 4, pp. 407–24.

——— (2012), 'Hypertextuality and remediation in the fashion media', *Journalism Practice*, 6: 1, pp. 92–106.

——— (2016), 'Pierre Bourdieu: The field of fashion', in A. Rocamora and A. Smelik (eds), *Thinking Through Fashion: A Guide to Key Theorists*, London: I.B. Tauris, pp. 233–50.

Rocamora, Agnès and Bartlett, Djurdja (2009), 'Fashion blogs: New spaces in fashion discourse', *Sociétés*, 104: 2, pp. 105–14.

Rojas, Peter (2003), 'Now bloggers can hit the road', *Wired*, 20 February, http://www.wired.com/ gadgets/wireless/news/2003/02/57431. Accessed 22 March 2014.

Royal, Tricia (2005), 'Group description', on wardrobe_remix group, Flickr, 17 January, http:// www.flickr.com/groups/wardrobe_remix/rules/. Accessed 22 March 2014.

Rushford, Hilary (2013), 'How to handle online bullying like a lady', Independent Fashion Bloggers, 8 May, http://heartifb.com/2013/05/08/how-to-handle-online-bullying-like-a-lady/. Accessed 22 March 2014.

Schechner, Richard (2002), *Performance Studies: An Introduction*, London and New York: Routledge.

Scheidt, Lois Ann (2006), 'Adolescent diary weblogs and the unseen audience', in D. Buckingham and R. Willett (eds), *Digital Generations: Children, Young People and New Media*, London and New York: Routledge, pp. 193–210.

Schmatolla, Ernest (2013), Blogger profile, 23 September, http://www.blogger.com/profile/ 02772967757760907864. Accessed 22 March 2014.

Schneier, Matthew (2013), 'Turning the tables on Tim', Style.com, 28 May, http://www.style.com/ trendsshopping/stylenotes/052913_Tim_Blanks/. Accessed 22 March 2014.

Schuman, Emily (2013a), 'Ask Emily', *Cupcakes and Cashmere*, 22 August, http://cupcakesand cashmere.com/series-stories/ask-emily-15#feed=/tag/ask-emily. Accessed 26 August 2014.

——— (2013b), 'Ask Emily #7', *Cupcakes and Cashmere*, 20 June, http://cupcakesandcashmere. com/series-stories/ask-emily-7#feed=/tag/ask-emily. Accessed 22 March 2014.

Scotsman, The (2009), 'The online Stepford Wives', 9 November, http://www.scotsman.com/ lifestyle/fashion/the-online-stepford-wives-1-768741. Accessed 22 March 2014.

Scott, Clive (2007), *Street Photography: From Atget to Cartier Bresson*, London and New York: I.B. Tauris.

Serfaty, Viviane (2004), *The Mirror and the Veil: An Overview of American Online Diaries and Blogs*, Amsterdam and New York: Rodopi.

Shachtman, Noah (2002), 'Blogs make the headlines', *Wired*, 23 December, http://www.wired. com/culture/lifestyle/news/2002/12/56978. Accessed 22 March 2014.

Shadforth, Amanda (2011), 'Goodbye New York', *Oracle Fox*, 25 February, http://oraclefox. com/2011/02/25/goodbye-new-york/. Accessed 22 March 2014.

Shamepuff (2013), '{about}', http://web.archive.org/web/20120814131020/http://shamepuff.com/about. Accessed 2 July 2013.

Sherman, Lauren (2016), 'The blonde salad ups the ante', Business of Fashion, 2 September,https://www.businessoffashion.com/articles/intelligence/the-blonde-salad-chiara-ferragni-launches-e-commerce. Accessed 24 September 2016.

Shinkle, Eugenie (2008), 'The line between the wall and the floor: Reality and affect in contemporary fashion photography', in E. Shinkle (ed.), *Fashion As Photograph: Viewing and Reviewing Images of Fashion*, London: I.B. Tauris.

Sicardi, Arabelle (2012), 'The state of fashion blogging', *Fashion Pirate*, 3 February, http://www.fashionpirate.net/2012/02/state-of-fashion-blogging.html. Accessed 22 March 2014.

—— (2013), 'CDG, Chanel, Pat McGrath, Biba', *Fashion Pirate*, 17 November, http://www.fashionpirate.net/2013/11/cdg-chanel-pat-mcgrath-and-biba.html. Accessed 22 March 2014.

Simmel, Georg (1971), *On Individuality and Social Forms*, Chicago: University of Chicago Press.

Singer, Jane B. (2006), 'Journalists and new bloggers: Complements, contradictions, and challenges', in A. Bruns and J. Jacobs (eds), *Uses of Blogs*, New York: Peter Lang, pp. 23–32.

Singer, Sally, Mower, Sarah, Phelps, Nicole and Codinha, Alessandra (2016), 'Ciao, Milano! Vogue.com's editors discuss the week that was', *Vogue*, http://www.vogue.com/13483417/milan-fashion-week-spring-2017-vogue-editors-chat/. Accessed 14 October 2016.

Slone, Isabel (blogger, *Hipster Musings*) (2011a), 'Creating a meaningful wardrobe', *Hipster Musings*, 14 November, http://hipstermusings.blogspot.com.au/2011/11/creating-meaningful-wardrobe.html. Accessed 22 March 2014.

—— (2011b), 'Hello, I love you or why fashion blogging smells like raw fish', *Hipster Musings*, 23 December, http://hipstermusings.blogspot.com.au/2011/12/hello-i-love-you-or-why-fashion.html. Accessed 22 March 2014.

—— (2012), Skype interview with author, 19 January.

SLU Team (2012), 'Arabelle Sicardi for StyleLikeU', StyleLikeU video, 4:23, 19 December, http://stylelikeu.com/profiles-2/closets/arabelle-sicardi/. Accessed 22 March 2014.

Sozzani, Franca (2011), 'Bloggers: A culture phenomenon or an epidemic issue?', Editor's Blog, *Vogue Italia*, 28 January, http://www.vogue.it/en/magazine/editor-s-blog/2011/01/january-28th. Accessed 22 March 2014.

Spiridakis, Elizabeth (2008), 'Post adolescents: Tween bloggers', *T* Magazine, *New York Times*, 13 August, http://www.nytimes.com/2008/08/17/style/tmagazine/17tween.html?_r=0. Accessed 22 March 2014.

Style.com (2012), 'Press center', http://www.style.com/services/presscenter. Accessed 17 April 2012 (page no longer available).

Style, Nova (2008), 'Meet Tavi, the 12-Year-old fashion blogger', The Cut, *New York Magazine*, 22 July, http://nymag.com/daily/fashion/2008/07/meet_tavi_the_12yearold_fashio.html. Accessed 22 March 2014.

Styles, Ruth (2013), '"Fashion magazines are written BY slim women FOR slim women, don't read them if you are fat": Plus-size bloggers bite back as they star in new designer shoot for Evans', MailOnline, 1 May, http://www.dailymail.co.uk/femail/article-2317589/Plus-size-bloggers-hit-skinny-fashion-magazines-star-Clements-Ribeiro-shoot-Evans.html. Accessed 22 March 2014.

Telford-Brock, Kayla (blogger, *The F Tangent*) (2012), Skype interview with author, 11 June.

Tolly Dolly Posh (2016), 'What do you want to know about being yourself and self expression?' *Tolly Dolly Posh*, 29 January, http://tollydollyposhfashion.com/2016/01/being-yourself-self-expression-questions/. Accessed 2 September 2016.

Ton, Tommy (2014), 'Tommy Ton', Style.com, http://www.style.com/trendsshopping/stylenotes/tommyton/. Accessed 22 March 2014.

Twohey, Megan (2011), 'Tavi sees her stylish star grow brighter', *Chicago Tribune News*, 2 October, http://articles.chicagotribune.com/2011-10-02/news/ct-met-tavi-rookie-magazine-20111002_1_tavi-gevinson-stylish-star-oak-park. Accessed 30 August 2016.

Veblen, Thorstein (1973), *The Theory of the Leisure Class*, Boston: Houghton Mifflin.

Walker, Jill (2005), 'Mirrors and shadows: The digital aestheticisation of oneself', *Digital Arts and Culture Conference*, Copenhagen, Denmark, 1–3 December.

Warne, Nicole (2015), 'Serendipity', *Gary Pepper*, 26 April, http://garypeppergirl.com/2015/04/serendipity. Accessed 30 August 2016.

Warner, Michael (2002), *Publics and Counterpublics*, New York: Zone Books.

Wdziekonski, Jamie (blogger, *Oh Jamie*) (2012), Skype interview with author, 24 January.

Webb, Jen, Schirato, Tony, and Danaher, Geoff (2002), *Understanding Bourdieu*, Sydney: Allen and Unwin.

Weber, Sandra with Julia Weber (2007), 'Technology in the everyday lives of "tweens"', in S. Weber and S. Dixon (eds.) *Growing Up Online: Young People and Digital Technologies*, New York and Basingstoke: Palgrave Macmillan.

White, Dave and Winn, Phillip (2009), 'State of the blogosphere 2008', Technorati, 13 October, http://technorati.com/social-media/feature/state-of-the-blogosphere-2008/. Accessed 22 March 2014.

Whittington, Zanita (2012a), 'Dusk', *Zanita*, 2 December, http://zanita.com.au/2012/12/dusk. Accessed 22 March 2014.

—— (2012b), 'Zanita and Margaret take Phuket', *Zanita*, 4 December, http://zanita.com.au/2012/12/zanita-and-margaret-take-phuket. Accessed 22 March 2014.

—— (2012c), 'Equatorial', *Zanita*, 10 December, http://zanita.com.au/2012/12/equatorial. Accessed 22 March 2014.

Widdicombe, Lizzie (2010), 'Tavi says', *The New Yorker*, 20 September.

Williams, Raymond (1984), *Keywords: A Vocabulary of Culture and Society*, (n.p.): Fontana Paperbacks.

Wilson, Elizabeth (2013), *Adorned in Dreams*, London and New York: I.B. Tauris.

Wilson, Eric (2009), 'Bloggers crash fashion's front row', *New York Times*, 24 December, http://www.nytimes.com/2009/12/27/fashion/27BLOGGERS.html. Accessed 22 March 2014.

Wise, Kevin, Hamman, Brian, and Thorson, Kjerstin (2006), 'Moderation, response rate, and message interactivity: Features of online communities and their effects on intent to participate', *Journal of Computer-Mediated Communication*, 12: 1, pp. 24–41.

Wolf, Naomi (1991), *The Beauty Myth: How Images of Beauty are Used Against Women*, London: Vintage.

Zamiatin, Lara (2006), 'Let slip the blogs of wore', *The Sydney Morning Herald*, 27 July, http://www.smh.com.au/news/fashion/let-slip-the-blogs-of-wore/2006/07/26/1153816248787.html?page=fullpage. Accessed 22 March 2014.

Zhang, Margaret (2012a), 'Spring Maille', *Shine by Three*, 30 July, http://shinebythree.com/2012/07/maille-westfield-boohoo-asos-diva/. Accessed 22 March 2014.

—— (2012b), 'Paradise Phuket', *Shine by Three*, 23 November, http://shinebythree.com/2012/11/phuket-sri-panwa-sabo-skirt-gorjana-asos-dark-horse/. Accessed 22 March 2014.

—— (2012c), 'Luxe resident', *Shine by Three*, 2 December, http://shinebythree.com/2012/12/sri-panwa-residence-august-street-zimmermann-gemeli-power-anu-ellery-aelkemi-macgraw/. Accessed 22 March 2014.

—— (2012d), 'Something's quiet', *Shine by Three*, 22 December, http://shinebythree.com/2012/12/sri-panwa-phuket-thailand/. Accessed 22 March 2014.

—— (2013a), 'Chinese New York: 恭喜發財', *Shine by Three*, 12 February, http://shinebythree.com/2013/02/chinese-new-year-nyc-mulberry/. Accessed 22 March 2014.

—— (2013b), 'Derby day', *Shine by Three*, 8 November, http://shinebythree.com/2013/11/lexus-derby-day/. Accessed 22 March 2014.

Zou, Helen (hqzou) (2012), 'Interview with Jenny Zhang', Chictopia, 3 April, http://www.chictopia.com/photo/show/632042-Interview+with+Jenny+Zhang-white-unknown-dress. Accessed 22 March 2014.

Zucker, Sara (2009), 'Fashion bloggers, where they belong: In the front row', Mediaite, 29 September, http://www.mediaite.com/online/fashion-bloggers-where-they-belong-in-the-front-row/. Accessed 22 March 2014.

Index